NEIL
YOUNG

To Kath, for your patience, support and good humour during the writing of this book (and for sharing Neil's love of full moons and ginger cats).

NEIL YOUNG

ALBUM BY ALBUM

CHRIS WHITE

WHITE OWL

AN IMPRINT OF PEN & SWORD BOOKS LTD.
YORKSHIRE – PHILADELPHIA

First published in Great Britain in 2024 by
PEN AND SWORD WHITE OWL
An imprint of
Pen & Sword Books Ltd
Yorkshire – Philadelphia

ISBN 978 1 39906 818 5

Typeset in Times New Roman 10/13 by
SJmagic DESIGN SERVICES, India.
Printed and bound in the UK by CPI Group (UK) Ltd, Croydon, CR0 4YY.

Pen & Sword Books Limited incorporates the imprints of Atlas, Archaeology,
Aviation, Discovery, Family History, Fiction, History, Maritime, Military,
Military Classics, Politics, Select, Transport, True Crime, Air World,
Frontline Publishing, Leo Cooper, Remember When, Seaforth Publishing,
The Praetorian Press, Wharncliffe Local History, Wharncliffe Transport,
Wharncliffe True Crime, White Owl and After the Battle.

For a complete list of Pen & Sword titles please contact

PEN & SWORD BOOKS LIMITED
George House, Units 12 & 13, Beevor Street, Off Pontefract Road,
Barnsley, South Yorkshire, S71 1HN, England
E-mail: enquiries@pen-and-sword.co.uk
Website: www.pen-and-sword.co.uk

or
PEN AND SWORD BOOKS
1950 Lawrence Rd, Havertown, PA 19083, USA
E-mail: uspen-and-sword@casematepublishers.com
Website: www.penandswordbooks.com

Contents

Contents

Introduction

🎧   🎧   🎧

There is no other musician like Neil Young. For almost 60 years, he has been a constant, unwavering presence in popular culture, from his early years as an integral member of Buffalo Springfield and Crosby, Stills, Nash and Young (CSN&Y), to the indefatigable septuagenarian of the 2020s, still rocking hard and with plenty to say at a time when most of his contemporaries have long since either left the stage or settled for cosy, artistically moribund semi-retirement. A few weeks before I began this book, Young was in the headlines again, accusing the leading podcaster Joe Rogan of promoting COVID-19 misinformation and demanding that the music streaming giant Spotify - who reportedly paid $100m (£75m) for rights to The Joe Rogan Experience podcast in 2020 - remove either his music or Rogan's show from their platform.

Neil didn't win that particular battle - as I write, his albums remain absent from Spotify - but he won the respect of millions for his stand and showed once again that he is unswervingly true to himself, fearlessly taking the path he feels is right irrespective of what anyone else thinks. This single-minded approach hasn't endeared him to everyone - take, for example, his infamous falling out with Geffen Records, who sued him in 1983 for making albums "musically uncharacteristic of Neil Young's previous recordings" following the critical and commercial disasters of 1982's *Trans* and 1983's *Everybody's Rockin'*. But what it does make him is endlessly, unfailingly interesting as an artist.

The popular perception of Neil Young is that he is something of a musical schizophrenic - either the acoustic country-folk troubadour of *Harvest* and *Harvest Moon*, or the snarling, earth-shudderingly loud guitar-wielding frontman of his Crazy Horse albums. Like many fans of Young, I first came to him through one of these two routes - in my case, when I first listened to the near-perfection of his 1970 classic *After The Gold Rush*, which generally sits very much in the gentler camp. Yet categorising Young's work so neatly feels reductive when you consider the sheer variety of different musical styles he's explored over his long career - whether that be synth-rock on *Trans*, pure unadulterated country on 1985's *Old Ways*, orchestra and big band on 2014's *Storytone*, grunge on the 1995 Pearl Jam collaboration *Mirror Ball*, or sparse, improvised instrumentals on 1996's *Dead Man* soundtrack. Plus of course, Young's never been averse to wearing both his acoustic and electric hats on the same record, most famously on the two contrasting sides of 1979's towering *Rust Never Sleeps*.

It is this sheer versatility, and the sense of not knowing what's going to come next, that makes Young truly unique. Not every stylistic experiment is a success, sure, and there are times when you wish he'd just stop messing around and give us another 'The Needle and the Damage Done' or 'Cortez The Killer'. And if you were feeling particularly harsh, then there's an argument there are few Neil Young songs that pass the 'average man in the street' recognition test, in the way that 'Let's Dance' and 'Starman' do for Bowie, or 'Mr Tambourine Man' and 'Knockin' On Heaven's Door' for Dylan. But make no mistake, in terms of being a consistently bold, innovative creative force, from the 1960s to the 2020s, then Young is hard to beat. In the words of the man himself, when asked by the writer Paul Zollo in 1991 about the song writing process: "That's all I do. It's my main thing. Writing and playing music. There's nothing else I really care about as much. Songwriting is my life."[1]

1 Paul Zollo, Songwriters on Songwriting (1991), p.356.

My approach to the content in this book

🎧   🎧   🎧

The aim of this book is - as the title suggests - to provide a comprehensive overview of Neil Young's entire recording career as a solo artist, with a parallel narrative running throughout which tells the story of Young's life and how it influenced his music. The content has been written chronologically, starting with 1968's eponymous debut album and running right through to 2023's *Before and After*, and is split into several sections, each focusing on a series of albums from Young's back catalogue and providing timelines charting the key events of his life and career.

The fact the back catalogue in question is one of the deepest in the history of popular music meant the decisions on which albums to include were far from straightforward. Unlike some artists, who often have breaks of many years between records, Young has always been incredibly prolific, with only one gap between studio albums of more than two years in a solo career of more than half a century (the four-year hiatus between 1996's *Broken Arrow* and 2000's *Silver and Gold*). In addition to this formidable output, I also had to consider the extensive range of live albums, soundtracks, and archive material that Young has released, a seemingly inexhaustible supply of music that shows no sign of slowing down even as the man himself enters his late seventies.

One key choice I made from the beginning was that my book would focus purely on works where Young is indisputably the principal artist. So, that automatically discounted his records as part of Buffalo Springfield and Crosby, Stills, Nash and Young, as well as his later collaboration with Stephen Stills as the Stills-Young Band on 1976's *Long May You Run*. Of course, one of the quintessential elements of Young's music ever since 1969's *Everybody Knows This Is Nowhere* has been his frequent collaborations with Crazy Horse, and it would be simply sacrilegious not to include their joint albums here. I have applied similar criteria to the other bands that Young has recorded with and co-credited on his albums over his career - everyone from the Shocking Pinks on *Everybody's Rockin'* and Promise of the Real on several of his most recent albums, to celebrity hook-ups with Pearl Jam on *Mirror Ball* and Booker T. and the M.G.'s on 2002's *Are You Passionate?* In all these cases, although the groups in question are integral to the album's sound, Young is the creative fulcrum of the record and the main songwriter, so while they may not strictly speaking be solo records, I feel comfortable categorising them as such.

Overall, there are 50 works included in my album-by-album guide. Most of these were released as studio albums shortly after they were recorded, but there are a few exceptions I would like to explain my rationale for also covering.

Firstly, I decided not to include live albums in my guide, although there is an Off The Beaten Track section focusing on these and some of Young's other non-core releases collectively towards the end of the book. However, I made an exception for 1973's *Time Fades Away*, as this was composed of new, previously unreleased material. That the album was recorded live rather than in the studio doesn't, in my view, exclude it from consideration as a bona fide original Young album. I did briefly toy with also including 1991's *Arc*, a 35-minute-long sound collage taken from multiple live performances which is technically an original composition. But despite it being arguably the most experimental, outright weird record Young has ever made, I slightly reluctantly concluded that its synthesis of guitar noise, feedback and fragments of already very familiar songs probably belonged in the aforementioned Off The Beaten Track section.

I experienced similar dilemmas when considering Young's occasional forays into film soundtracks. Upon reflection, I opted to leave out 1972's *Journey Through The Past* (due to the lack of original music and Buffalo Springfield/ CSN&Y involvement) and 1980's *Where The Buffalo Roam* (as only about a third of the tracks are actually performed by Young). But the soundtrack to *Dead Man*, Jim Jarmusch's postmodern Western, makes the cut, as does *Paradox*, his 2018 accompaniment to (his girlfriend and now wife) Darryl Hannah's film *Paradox* (with Promise of the Real) - both on the basis that they feature mostly original new Young music. It's worth adding a related point here regarding Young's peripatetic career as a film director. While undoubtedly a fascinating (if flawed) additional artistic side to Young and one often closely linked to his music, in the interests of time and space, I will not be discussing the movies of Young's alter ego Bernard Shakey in this book, nor will I be covering his output as an author, notably the autobiographies *Waging Heavy Peace* and *Special Deluxe*.

Compilations, such as 1977's still-definitive classic era retrospective *Decade*, will also be confined to the Off The Beaten Track 'wrap up' section; likewise, the Archives box sets, which while endlessly interesting for Young addicts, are nevertheless mostly made up of alternative and live versions of previously released songs - with four notable exceptions. These are 1974/75's *Homegrown*,

1976's *Hitchhiker,* 1977's *Chrome Dreams* and 2001's *Toast*, all planned as Young official releases before subsequently being ditched either by Young himself or by his record company. *Hitchhiker* finally emerged through the Archives series in 2017, with *Homegrown* following three years later and finally *Toast* in 2022 and *Chrome Dreams* in 2023. I believe these four albums form an essential part of Neil Young's artistic journey, and even though a substantial number of their songs ended up appearing on other albums long before the originals saw the light of day, they absolutely warrant inclusion here, as Young clearly viewed them as potential official releases when he recorded them. To ensure they are placed in an appropriate career context, I have inserted all four into my guide chronologically at the times they were originally recorded, while also adding their eventual release dates.

Ever unpredictable, Young threw me a last minute curveball with his most recent album, *Before and After*, in December 2023. Made up almost entirely of acoustic re-recordings of previously released material, with only one new song, it proved devilishly difficult to categorise, but in the end it made the final 50 as an official studio release.

Rather than allocate equal weighting to all the 50 albums I've decided upon, some are covered in a little more detail than others. While I've tried to spread the focus across his whole back catalogue as much as possible, I make no apology for the emphasis I've placed on Young's widely recognised classic era from 1969-79, beginning with *Everybody Knows This Is Nowhere* and ending with *Rust Never Sleeps*. Over forty years on, only the most diehard of revisionists would seriously challenge the view that Young produced the highest proportion of his finest records during this period, although of course there are other outstanding contributions to his canon released since.

At the end of the day though, we all enjoy a good old pub debate, so I've devoted the final section of my book to the somewhat daunting but very enjoyable task of ranking all Young's albums, from 50 -1! This will be a purely subjective, personal choice, and no doubt many fans reading my views will vehemently disagree! So, I'd invite you all to get in touch with me and share your own thoughts and rankings, either by posting on this book's Facebook page or by emailing me directly using the address provided.

PART 1

Setting the scene – Young's early years (1945-68)

Neil Percival Young was born in Toronto, Canada on 12 November 1945. His father Scott was one of Canada's leading sport writers, meaning that Young had a relatively comfortable upbringing, initially in the city of his birth before moving to the small Ontario village of Omemee at the age of four, where he experienced a near fatal brush with polio in 1951. A further move to the town of Pickering near Toronto followed, where the young Neil first fell in love with music, in particular, the exciting new sounds of rock and roll, doo wop and R&B that emerged in the mid-1950s. When asked by Paul Zollo when he first began playing the guitar, Young answered, "well, I started playing ukulele when I was eight or nine. I had a little plastic one, which I taught myself to play. It just went on from there."[1]

Scott Young's divorce from his wife Rassy in 1961 led to the teenage Neil moving with his mother to Winnipeg, Manitoba, where he would take his first steps in a musical career that would lead to him becoming one of the most successful and influential singer-songwriters of all time.

In early 1963, Young began performing around Winnipeg with his band The Squires, which he'd formed with school friends Ken Koblun, Ken Smythe and Allen Bates. Within five months, they'd recorded two instrumentals at a local studio, entitled 'The Sultan' and 'Aurora': primitive, murky-sounding Shadows-influenced numbers that gave little indication of their front man's potential. Young dropped out of school shortly afterwards and The Squires continued to perform mostly in Winnipeg and elsewhere in Manitoba, with various personnel changes, until Young left the band in 1965 to perform solo in folk clubs, sometimes on the same bill as another young Canadian with a huge future ahead - Joni Mitchell.

After a brief stint in 1966 with the Toronto-based R&B band The Mynah Birds, Young and the group's bassist Bruce Palmer took what would prove to be a life-changing decision: moving from Toronto to Los Angeles, driving all the way in Young's 1953 Pontiac Hearse - a vehicle funded by the pawning of the Mynah Birds' equipment. The two young arrivals sought out another folk musician whom Young had briefly met back in 1964 while performing with The Squires - Stephen Stills.

Shortly after locating Stills (via a chance meeting on Sunset Boulevard), Buffalo Springfield was born. Stills, Palmer and Young were joined by Stills' guitarist friend Richie Furay and drummer Dewey Martin, and before long the group were sharing LA club stages with fellow future legends The Byrds and The Doors. Springfield's combination of musical proficiency and a hip, highly potent blend of folk, country, psychedelia and pop influences meant they were quickly signed to Atlantic Records, and their first album followed less than a year after the band was formed.

---

1 Zollo, Songwriters on Songwriting, p.356

Buffalo Springfield's popular legacy is largely built on one hit single - the Stills-penned anti-violence anthem 'For What It's Worth' - and the band split up in 1968 after barely two years together. But their impact on popular music runs much deeper. Of course, Stills and Young would go on to have huge success in their later groups and solo work, but it shouldn't be overlooked that *Buffalo Springfield Again*, the band's second release, remains one of the classic albums of the late 1960s, full of lush textures, bold experimentation and song writing verve. Stephen Stills is at the absolute top of his game, and it's also here we see the first signs of the truly great songwriter Neil Young would become. The driving R&B of 'Mr Soul' features an early example of the searing guitar work that would later become a Young trademark, while 'Expecting to Fly', soaked in the summer of love ambience and spirit of invention that defined the era, showcases the wistful yet restless voice that we'd go on to hear on so many songs to come. 'Expecting to Fly 'also saw Young work for the first time with arranger Jack Nitzsche, who would go on to provide the orchestral arrangements on several future Young solo albums, most notably *Harvest*.

After an always fractious relationship with his fellow Buffalo Springfield members, which saw him quit and then re-join the band on several occasions, Young walked out for good in May 1968. He had become increasingly disillusioned by what he perceived as a lack of support for both his songs and singing, especially from Stills, with whom he had always had a keen rivalry. This culminated in Stills' reluctance to release 'Mr Soul' as a single, on the grounds that it sounded like The Rolling Stones' iconic 'Satisfaction' (which, it must be said, is not an unreasonable observation). The band went their separate ways, with Stills staying with Atlantic as a solo artist and Young signing for Warner/Reprise. Now able to pursue his own idiosyncratic direction unhindered by others, one of the greatest singer-songwriter careers of all time was about to begin.

Neil Young

Released 12 November 1968 (Reprise)

🎧　🎧　🎧

O ver 50 years after its release, Neil Young's self-titled debut album still sounds like nothing else in his solo career. In many ways, it's a little like the musical equivalent of a TV pilot: one that had some great ideas but needed something of a reboot before going on to be a highly successful series for many years.

Even before leaving Buffalo Springfield in May 1968, Young was already collaborating closely with the composer/arranger Jack Nitzsche, notably on the gliding, celestial 'Expecting to Fly', one of the standout tracks on *Buffalo Springfield Again*. *Neil Young* is essentially a continuation of the song writing style Young developed through working with Nitzsche - a slightly woozy concoction of country, folk, psychedelia and R&B that was ambitious, richly textured but often strangely toothless. It's very much a record of the late 1960s, where artists everywhere were seeking to emulate the stratospheric compositional heights achieved by The Beatles, The Beach Boys and Dylan, which had propelled popular music way beyond the simple beat group song structures of just three or four years before. The album's cover, a trippy image of Young's face protruding between mountain and urban landscapes painted by artist neighbour Roland Diehl, only serves to add to its caught in a time capsule feel.

Neil Young can therefore be considered as something of a transitional point in Young's evolution from Buffalo Springfield to established solo artist. The period around its recording also saw the formation of two other key relationships which would remain pivotal to Young's life and music for decades to come. Manager Elliot Roberts was already overseeing the emerging talent of Joni Mitchell when she introduced him to her fellow LA-based Canadian Young during the final days of Buffalo Springfield. The two men hit it off instantly and the partnership that followed lasted right through until Roberts' death in 2019. Likewise, producer David Briggs - who first met Young in 1968 while driving his army personnel carrier around LA, stopping to give the hitch-hiking Neil a lift - would go on to work with Young on many of his most iconic records until succumbing to lung cancer in 1994 at just 51 years old.

The album was recorded during the last few months of 1968 at Wally Heider and TTG studios in LA, with Young and co-producers Briggs and Nitzsche working alongside two distinct groups of musicians on different tracks. A rhythm section comprised of Buffalo Springfield's Jim Messina on bass and George Grantham, the drummer in Messina's new band, Poco, featured on seven of the ten songs, with seasoned session musicians, including a young Ry Cooder - later of Buena Vista Social Club fame - drafted in for the three Nitzsche-produced numbers: 'The Old Laughing Lady', 'String Quartet from Whiskey Boot Hill' and 'I've Loved Her So Long'. Like many albums of the era, *Neil Young* has a loose song cycle structure, with each half of the record beginning with a short instrumental and ending with a longer, more lyrically and musically complex track.

After opening with the jaunty but inconsequential orchestral country twang of 'The Emperor of Wyoming', *Neil Young* immediately shifts up a gear with second track 'The Loner'. The album's ubiquitous chamber-pop strings are still there, but they're joined by some squalling electric guitar work which hints at the far edgier, more fluid style Young would begin to favour in the near future. The insipid (if admittedly pretty) 'If I Could Have Her Tonight' is rather forgettable, but 'I've Been Waiting For You' returns to the more assertive, vigorous approach of 'The Loner', with Young opening the song by proclaiming "I'm looking for a woman to save my life" - a person he seemed to have found when he married restaurant owner Susan Acevedo in December 1968. 'I've Been Waiting For You' is also notable for featuring what is arguably the first of Young's long list of virtuoso guitar solos during his illustrious career, and while it's no 'Like A Hurricane' or 'On The Beach', once again, it's definitely a sign of what was to come.

Side one of *Neil Young* closes with perhaps the album's best-known song. 'The Old Laughing Lady'. A slow building slice of baroque folk-rock that has some similarities to the early work of Young's singer-songwriter contemporary Tim Buckley, it starts off promisingly before being overwhelmed by the arrival of a chorus of hollering backing singers who aggressively swamp the song's fragility. A shame, as 'The Old Laughing Lady's intriguing lyrics (possibly an allegory for the impact of alcoholism) and graceful melody deserve better, and indeed find it on later alternative versions, for example the one that opens Young's 1993 *MTV Unplugged* album.

Side two kicks off with 'String Quartet from Whiskey Boot Hill', another tasteful but ultimately decorative short orchestral passage composed by Nitzsche, before we get another intriguing precursor to Young's later direction with 'Here We Are In The Years'. A dreamy paean to the simple pleasures of rural life, its delicate piano, gentle groove and Young's wistful vocal create a recipe that he would soon go on to repeat with huge success on his two most iconic singer-songwriter albums - *After The Goldrush* and *Harvest*.

Neither 'What Did You Do To My Life?' or 'I've Loved You So Long' are ever likely to rank highly in the pantheon of great Neil Young songs, with the former hamstrung by a plodding melody and the latter once again falling prey to some over egged backing vocals, but *Neil Young*'s final track, 'Last Trip to Tulsa', is a bold if flawed attempt to end the record with a Dylan's 'Desolation Row'-style acoustic epic. More than nine minutes of surreal, fever dream imagery, in which Young inhabits a range of alter egos, it remains one of Young's most lyrically ambitious songs. Unfortunately, some of the scenes he depicts don't quite work - the song ends bizarrely with Young crushing a friend underneath a palm tree he's just felled - and his rather earnest strumming starts to grate a little towards the end. Even so, it's another example of the then 23-year old's willingness to stretch his songwriting craft from very early in his career.

The rather murky sound of *Neil Young* can be attributed to the use, without Young's knowledge, of an experimental mastering process, Heico CSG, by Reprise's engineers , which was intended to allow stereo recordings to be listened to on mono equipment, but only succeeded in muffling the singer's already rather thin vocals. The album bombed, failing to chart, and even though Young persuaded Reprise to release a new version in January 1969 that restored the original recordings (as well as adding Young's name to the previously untitled cover), the opportunity had been missed. Despite his status as a key former member of Buffalo Springfield and the meticulous steps he, David Briggs and Jack Nitzsche had taken to perfect the album's arrangements and sound, Neil Young's first outing as a solo artist ultimately ended in failure. As the Sixties drew to a close, he was about to make some important choices on where to take his music next.

⊙ TRACK LISTING   ⏮ ⏸ ⏭
(all written by Neil Young unless otherwise stated)

1. The Emperor of Wyoming ·· 2:14
2. The Loner ·· 3:55
3. If I Could Have Her Tonight ··· 2:15
4. I've Been Waiting for You ··· 2:30
5. The Old Laughing Lady ·· 5:05
6. String Quartet from Whiskey Boot Hill" (Jack Nitzsche) ············· 1:04
7. Here We Are in the Years ··· 3:27
8. What Did You Do to My Life? ··· 2:00
9. I've Loved Her So Long ·· 2:40
10. The Last Trip to Tulsa ··· 9:25

Length: 35:32

Timeline - Young's early years
(1945-68)

1945
12 November: Neil Percival Young born in Toronto General Hospital, Toronto, Ontario, the second son of Scott and Edna (Rassy) Young.

1948 - 1949
The Young family briefly moves to Jackson's Point, Ontario before settling in Omemee, Ontario.

1951
Autumn: Neil is hospitalised with severe polio during the Canadian epidemic that year.

1952
January - May: The Young family rent a cottage in New Smyrna, Florida, so Neil can convalesce in the warmer weather.

1953 - 54
The family moves again to Winnipeg, Manitoba and then back to Toronto before finally moving to Pickering, just east of the city.

1958
The family moves back to Toronto and that Christmas, Neil receives his first musical instrument - a ukulele - as a present from his parents.

1960
August: Scott and Rassy Young split up and Neil moves to Winnipeg with his mother, where he forms his first band, The Jades, with school friends at Earl Grey Junior High.

1961

January: Young plays his first ever gig with The Jades.

Autumn: Enrols at Kelvin High School. He also receives his first ever electric guitar, a Les Paul Junior, as a present from Rassy.

1962

October: Forms The Classic with a line up including Ken Koblun on bass. The group play just six dates before disbanding.

1963

February: Young forms The Squires with Koblun (bass), Allan Bates (guitar) and Jack Harper (drums), playing their first gig at Riverview Community Club, Fort Rouge. Harper is replaced by Ken Smyth.

November: The Squires' only single 'The Sultan/Aurora', featuring two instrumentals recorded at the CKRC radio station that July, is released by local label V Records.

1964

2 April: The Squires' second session at the CKRC studios includes Young's first ever vocal recording on 'I Wonder'.

September: Young leaves school to pursue a musical career.

October: The Squires secure a residency at the Flamingo Club in Fort William, Ontario.

1965

April: The Squires return to Fort William, where Young would meet Stephen Stills for the first time.

November: After unsuccessful auditions at Elektra Records in New York, Young returns to Toronto and disbands The Squires.

December: Young joins The Mynah Birds, an R&B band with future Buffalo Springfield member Bruce Palmer on bass.

1966

March: Young and Palmer left the Mynah Birds and relocated from Toronto to Los Angeles, driving all the way in Young's 1953 Pontiac Hearse.

April: After tracking down Stephen Stills, the trio form Buffalo Springfield with guitarist Richie Furay and drummer Dewey Martin, play their first gig in April

28 April - 22 May: Buffalo Springfield seven-week residency at Sunset Boulevard's Whisky a Go Go club.

8 June: Buffalo Springfield sign to Atlantic Records.

August: The band's first single 'Nowadays Clancy Can't Even Sing', written by Young, is released.

5 December: Debut album *Buffalo Springfield* is released on Atco, a subsidiary of Atlantic Records.

23 December: Single 'For What It's Worth', written by Stills, released. It would go on to become Buffalo Springfield's first top 10 single in early 1967.

1967

June: Young temporarily leaves Buffalo Springfield before rejoining a couple of months later.

30 October: *Buffalo Springfield Again* album released.

1968

5 May: Buffalo Springfield play their final gig at the Long Beach Arena before officially splitting up the following week.

July: Young signs a solo deal with Reprise Records.

18 July: Third and final Buffalo Springfield album, *Last Time Around*, is released.

12 November: Release of Young's debut solo album, *Neil Young*, on Reprise.

7 December: Young marries restaurant owner Susan Acevedo at his home in Topanga, California.

PART 2

The Classic Era (1969-79)

Neil Young with Crazy Horse - Everybody Knows This Is Nowhere

Released 14 May 1969 (Reprise)

🎧 🎧 🎧

It would not be an exaggeration to say that *Everybody Knows This Is Nowhere* is the single most important record of Neil Young's entire career. Perhaps not the best - although it undoubtedly has its advocates for that status - but in terms of setting the template for so much of what was to follow, its pivotal role is hard to dispute.

The album had its genesis in a chance meeting between Young and the members of a relatively unknown six-piece garage rock band called The Rockets during Young's Buffalo Springfield years. After jamming together a few times and loving their self-titled debut album, Young attended an August 1968 gig by The Rockets at LA's Whiskey A Go-Go club, in the words of his biographer Jimmy McDonough "armed with the weapons that have become crucial elements of his rock and roll sound: Old Black, a 1953 Gibson Les Paul plugged into a 1959 Fender Deluxe."[1] Excited by the possibilities of the gargantuan sound of his new guitar/amp combination backed by the Rockets' freeform, unstructured groove, Young soon booked studio time with three members of the group - guitarist Danny Whitten, bassist Billy Talbot and drummer Ralph Molina - who would soon evolve into the inimitable Crazy Horse.

In complete contrast to the painstaking development of *Neil Young*'s songs over several months to make them as polished as possible, *Everybody Knows This Is Nowhere* was essentially recorded in two sessions at Wally Heider's and Sunwest studios in January and March 1969, produced by Young and David Briggs. A far less cluttered affair than Young's debut, the album's seven tracks mostly featured just the core quartet of Whitten, Talbot, Molina and Young, with additional violin

---

1   Jimmy McDonough, Shakey (2002), p.298.

work from The Rockets' Bobby Notkoff and harmony vocals from LA folk singer Robin Lane. Gritty, intuitive, soulful, elemental and expansive, with far more confident, expressive singing from Young, it's a quantum leap forward from his over-produced debut.

In his autobiography *Waging Heavy Peace,* Young vividly described the unique role Crazy Horse has played in his music and his life: "You see, they are my window to the cosmic world where the muse lives and breathes. I can find myself there and go to the special area of my soul where those songs graze like buffalo. The herd is still there, and the plains are endless. Just getting there is the key thing, and Crazy Horse is my way of getting there."[2] Not all Young's contemporaries shared his enthusiasm for the raw and ramshackle sound of the Horse, with David Crosby in particular pulling no punches: "They should've never been allowed to be musicians at all. They should've been shot at birth. They can't play."[3] Others who knew Young suggested he was comfortable playing with Crazy Horse because their lack of accomplished musicianship meant they would happily play in whatever way he asked without challenging him.

With the exception of the title track, an earlier, much politer version of which had been recorded as part of the *Neil Young* sessions, *Everybody Knows This Is Nowhere* is made up entirely of new Young songs, mostly written while Young was holed up in his Topanga Canyon home with flu. Some of these remain among Young's most popular works to this day and have become perennial favourites in his live shows.

While there are no weak moments at all on *Everybody Knows This Is Nowhere,* a holy trinity of truly classic Young tracks provide the backbone of the record. It opens with 'Cinnamon Girl', one of his catchiest tunes ever, with the pop sensibilities of Young's Buffalo Springfield days dragged kicking and screaming into Crazy Horse's swampy blender. A straightforward expression of desiring a beautiful woman, from the irresistibly crunchy guitar riffs, handclaps and occasional whoops to the surging, joyous dual vocals of Young and Whitten, it's quite simply three minutes of rock near-perfection.

'Down By The River ', in contrast, is a smouldering nine-minute epic, an early example of the elegantly stoned, sprawling and unhurried sonic landscapes that would form an integral part of many a Neil Young and Crazy Horse album to come. Young's ostensibly troubling tale of shooting a love interest "down by the river" (he later claimed it was actually about blowing it with a woman, rather than actually murdering one) is punctuated by long passages of sinuously jagged, ominous guitar, which give the track a palpable atmosphere of portentous unease. Underpinning it all is the shuffling, hypnotic rhythm section of Talbot and Molina,

---

2   Neil Young, Waging Heavy Peace (2012), p.137
3   McDonough, p.269

based on the slowed down version of a James Brown beat they were taught by former Rockets bandmate George Whitsell.

Everybody Knows This Is Nowhere closes with the last of its immortal triumvirate, 'Cowgirl in the Sand'. Similar in length and approach to 'Down By The River', with its verse-chorus pattern interspersed with expansive, evocative instrumental sections featuring numerous tempo shifts and some scintillating interplay between Young and Whitten's guitars. In contrast to the outright menace of 'Down By The River', the mood of the song is angry and challenging, but tempered with an undertow of sadness. The stark lyrics appear to tell the story of an ageing prostitute, perhaps at a desert brothel - a 'cowgirl in the sand' whose life choice is called into question with the memorable couplet "old enough now to change your name/when so many love you, is it the same?" But it's Young and Crazy Horse's seemingly telepathic playing relationship and constantly shifting musical patterns that make 'Cowgirl in the Sand' one of the most enduring of all Neil Young songs.

Although the rest of the album doesn't quite hit the rarefied heights of its trio of best-known works, the standard of material is nevertheless consistently strong. The title track's world weary lyrics, seemingly a critique of LA's impersonal feel, are lent extra poignancy by the chorus's delicious vocal harmonies, while 'Round and Round (It Won't Be Long)''s mellow, hypnotic acoustic strum and the presence of Robin Lane's haunting female vocals as a counterpoint to the male voices create an intimate, campfire sound that reminds us of Young's folk roots.

'The Losing End (When You're On)' is the album's most country-influenced song, with its rolling, twanging guitars and mournful breakup lyrics straight out of the Nashville playbook - "It's so hard to make love pay/When you're on the losing end/And I feel that way again." And finally, 'Running Dry (Requiem for the Rockets)', which sounds unlike anything else Young has recorded before or since due to the eerie, piercing violin of Bobby Notkoff, the most distinctive element of a bleak, introspective song. 'Running Dry...' also provides an intriguing possible insight into Young's sometimes uncompromising, single-minded approach to his relationships with others, as he sings "I'm sorry for the things I've done/I've shamed myself with lies/But soon these things are overcome/And can't be recognized." Listening to these words would have been unlikely to have made George Whitsell feel much better: after assuming his fellow Rockets Whitten, Talbot and Molina were just 'on loan' with Young to make one record, the band had effectively been commandeered by their new frontman, and the Rockets were consigned to history.

Although it could scarcely be described as a hit record, *Everybody Knows This Is Nowhere* did reach number 32 in the U.S. album charts, which represented definite commercial success when compared to its predecessor. More importantly, Young himself was now happy with the music he was making, telling Jimmy McDonough: "I liked *Everybody Knows*. I knew it was a good record. I also knew that it was raw. I knew that it was us."[4]

⊙ TRACK LISTING   ◄◄ ⏸ ►►|

1. Cinnamon Girl ·· 2:58
2. Everybody Knows This Is Nowhere ·························· 2:26
3. Round & Round (It Won't Be Long) ························ 5:49
4. Down by the River ··· 9:13
5. The Losing End (When You're On) ························· 4:03
6. Running Dry (Requiem for the Rockets) ·················· 5:30
7. Cowgirl in the Sand ··· 10:03

Length: 40:02

---

4 McDonough, p.303

Neil Young - After The Gold Rush

Released 19 September 1970 (Reprise)

🎧　🎧　🎧

Although *Everybody Knows This Is Nowhere* was the record that heralded Neil Young's arrival as a solo artist of the first rank, it was its follow up *After The Gold Rush* that made him a star. Following the first outing of his Crazy Horse-backed, more unstructured garage rock sound on *Everybody Knows...*, *After The Gold Rush* also established what was to become Young's other trademark guise – that of the poetic, country and folk influenced acoustic singer-songwriter.

A key landmark in Young's journey between these two very different albums was his invitation to join the now-legendary super group Crosby, Stills and Nash (CSN&Y) during the summer of 1969. With their eponymous debut riding high in the charts, the trio were about to embark on a lucrative tour and Young's fellow Buffalo Springfield alumnus Stephen Stills felt they needed a fuller live rock sound than their meticulously crafted but delicate studio recordings. A number of additional musicians were discussed before Young was suggested, with Stills confident that the tensions that plagued their former band could be overcome this time. At first, Young was only envisaged as a sideman, but manager Elliot Roberts demanded equal song writing and partnership status, so Graham Nash, the ex-Hollies singer songwriter, former Byrd David Crosby and Stills were formally expanded to a quartet and CSN&Y were born.

It was on CSN&Y's hugely successful second album *Déjà Vu* that Young first displayed the effortlessly melodic, commercially appealing song writing voice that would go on to feature in his most popular future works like After The Goldrush and Harvest. 'Helpless' - Young's standout contribution to Déjà Vu - was originally recorded with Crazy Horse before the other members of CSN&Y convinced its owner that the song's fragile, aching beauty would be better suited to their smoother, less chaotic style. With its unforgettable opening words "there is a town in North Ontario..." - sung in Young's yearning, high voice accompanied by heartbreakingly mournful guitar - 'Helpless' remains one of Neil Young's best-known tracks, and helped *Déjà Vu* shift an incredible eight million copies worldwide, making it the best-selling record any of CSN&Y would ever be involved in.

The phenomenal success of CSN&Y created the perfect platform for each of the four individual members to push forward their own solo careers, and with *After The Gold Rush*, which he'd been working on alongside his CSN&Y commitments, Young came up with the ideal record to capitalise on his newfound fame. His decision to part ways with Crazy Horse - mainly due to the increasingly erratic behaviour of Danny Whitten, now fighting a losing battle with heroin addiction - meant he brought together a new band for the recordings, which mostly took place in a purpose-built studio in Young's Topanga canyon basement between December 1969 and June 1970. Young's musicians including Crazy Horse's Ralph Molina, CSN&Y bassist Greg Reeves and a teenage guitarist called Nils Lofgren, who Young, in typically wilful style, mostly asked to play piano, an instrument Lofgren had never previously played before, on the album.

First track 'Tell Me Why' draws the listener in instantly, with Young's vivid opening line "sailing heart-ships through broken harbors" immediately showcasing both the fragile, emotion-drenched vocals and idiosyncratic imagery that would characterise the whole album. Yet while its delicious harmonies and jangling guitar certainly set out the album's stall impressively, 'Tell Me Why' is a minor delight compared to what's to come.

After The Gold Rush's title track, which comes second in the running order, remains one of Young's best loved compositions, and with good reason. Boasting a melody that's undeniably gorgeous, delivered in a tremulous tenor and backed by cascades of rolling piano and a wonderful flugelhorn solo, it also has some of the most extraordinary lyrics in popular music. Based on an unpublished screenplay by the actor Dean Stockwell which Young had intended to write the soundtrack for, the song tells a surreal tale of time travel back to the Middle Ages culminating in a visit to another planet, with the refrain "look at mother nature on the run in the 1970s" perhaps a prescient reference to a future climate crisis that now seems all too accurate.

In comparison, 'Only Love Can Break Your Heart' is a simple, wistful country-tinged ballad, but once again, it has a melody to die for, with some soaring harmonies imbuing the song with an almost hymnal quality. Released as a single in October 1970, it became Young's first Top 40 hit as a solo artist, peaking at Number 33 in the U.S.

Things take an altogether more raucous turn on 'Southern Man', which as well as being one of only two predominantly electric tracks on the album, also embroiled Young in a well-documented controversy. The song's condemnation of racism in the Deep South of the U.S. pulled few punches, leading to accusations of broad-brush stereotyping and prompting proud Southerners Lynyrd Skynyrd to respond by penning the altogether more glowing appraisal of 'Sweet Home Alabama'. Featuring some searing guitar work from Young and a chorus dripping with passionate anger, its writer felt more ambivalent about it in later years, telling biographer Jimmy McDonough "Southern Man is a strange song. I don't sing it anymore. I don't feel like it's particularly relevant."[1]

After 'Southern Man' 's incendiary intervention, *After The Gold Rush* soon settles back into a gentler groove. 'Till The Morning Comes' is a brief but joyous union of piano, vocal harmonies and flugelhorn, while a cover of Don Gibson's 1958 country hit 'Oh Lonesome Me' features some wonderfully mournful harmonica work from Young. The piano ballad 'Birds' is one of the most hauntingly sad songs of Young's career, with its stark lyrics "when you see me fly away without you/ shadow on the things you know/feathers fall around you/and show you the way to go/it's over, it's over...." a lament for the breakdown of a relationship. Shortly after the completion of *After The Goldrush*, Young's own marriage to Susan Acevedo, strained for some time by the impact of his new-found fame post-CSN&Y, came to an end, with Young leaving Topanga Canyon to begin a new life at his Broken Arrow ranch near San Francisco - alone.

'When You Dance I Can Really Love' is one of only two songs on *After The Gold Rush* ('Southern Man' is the other) that's a more upbeat rock song, with the guitar playing louder and more ragged and some deliriously energetic piano playing from Jack Nitzsche, who joined the ensemble for this track along with Crazy Horse's Whitten and Talbot. In contrast, 'I Believe In You', is another magically tuneful, hymnal ballad examining the dynamics of a relationship, with Young's voice an instrument of soaring beauty as he sings "Now that you've made yourself love me do you think I can change it in a day?". The album ends with 'Cripple Creek Ferry', a rustic, lilting campfire singalong which, while frustratingly brief at just over 90 seconds, is a lovely way to close what's a truly outstanding album.

The critical reception for *After The Gold Rush* was mixed, with Langdon Winner of *Rolling Stone* magazine declaring that "Neil Young devotees will probably spend the next few weeks trying desperately to convince themselves that *After The Gold Rush* is good music. But they'll be kidding themselves...in my listening, the problem appears to be that most of this music was simply not ready to be recorded at the time of the sessions. It needed time to mature."[2] But the record buying public begged to differ, and the album made the top 10 in the U.S. and the U.K. charts, going on to achieve double platinum sales in both countries.

While he had certainly explored country and folk influences with both Buffalo Springfield and on his first two solo records, on *After The Gold Rush*, Young showed consistently for the first time his ability to mine traditional American music

---

1   McDonough, p.338
2   Rolling Stone magazine, 15 October 1970

and blend its sounds with rock's melodic immediacy to deliver songs that felt both organic and accessible. While not the most successful of his more pastoral albums (that would be its follow up, 1972's *Harvest*) nor his most rootsy (a close call between 1978's *Comes A Time* and 1985's *Old Ways*), there's a compelling argument that *After The Goldrush* is the most complete record of Young's entire career. This is partly because of the sheer quality of the songs, but also the beautifully judged musical textures, the restrained elegance of the performances and Young's lyrical versatility, which tackles subjects ranging from universal themes of love and loss to evocative depictions of a flawed America.

The 50th Anniversary Edition vinyl box set of *After The Gold Rush,* released in December 2020, features a variant of the album artwork, originally created by Neil's long-time art director Gary Burden, made in collaboration with Grammy Award-winning artist Jenice Heo. The set also includes a 7" single in a picture sleeve, with two agreeable versions of the infectious if slight album outtake 'Wonderin' '.

⊙ TRACK LISTING   ◄◄ ❚❚ ►►❘

1. Tell Me Why ··· 2:45
2. After the Gold Rush ··· 3:45
3. Only Love Can Break Your Heart ······················ 3:05
4. Southern Man ·· 5:41
5. Till the Morning Comes ···································· 1:17
6. Oh, Lonesome Me (Don Gibson) ························· 3:47
7. Don't Let It Bring You Down ···························· 2:56
8. Birds ··· 2:34
9. When You Dance I Can Really Love ·················· 3:44
10. Believe in You ··· 2:24
11. Cripple Creek Ferry··· 1:34

Length: 33:32

Neil Young - Harvest

Released 1 February 1972 (Reprise)

If *After The Gold Rush* was the album that made Neil Young a genuine solo star for the first time, its follow up briefly made him the most successful singer-songwriter on the planet. Even today, a full half century after its release, if asked to name one Neil Young record, the likelihood is the majority of people would go for *Harvest*.

In early 1971, with CSN&Y having broken up in July 1970 amidst a predictable flurry of rows between the group's members, Young was capitalising on the breakthrough success of *After The Goldrush* by embarking on a solo tour of the U.S., Canada, and the U.K. In the heady early days of a new relationship with the emerging Hollywood actress Carrie Snodgress, who he'd met the previous year, new songs were pouring out of Young, many expressing the contentment and joy of his blossoming romance. Several of these songs would go on to appear on *Harvest*, while others, like 'Journey Through The Past' and 'See The Sky About To Rain', would feature on other Young albums later that decade.

While in Nashville for an appearance on the Johnny Cash Show that February, Young met producer Elliot Mazer, who had opened Quadrafonic Sound Studios in the city. Recording sessions were swiftly arranged and a new band composed of veteran session musicians Kenny Buttrey on drums, Tim Drummond on bass and Ben Keith on pedal steel guitar was pulled together, christened The Stray Gators by Young. Also in town for the Johnny Cash show were A-listers James Taylor and Linda Ronstadt, who contributed backing vocals and (in Taylor's case) banjo. The end result was cuts of two of Young's most enduring songs - 'Old Man' and 'Heart of Gold'. The first seeds of Harvest had been sown.

Completing the album would take another few months, not least because of the ongoing back problems which plagued Young during 1971 and required an operation to remove two discs. Most of the remaining tracks were recorded with The Stray Gators and Mazer at Young's Broken Arrow ranch, with a return to Nashville to lay down the title track and a transatlantic flight to London for two songs with the London Symphony Orchestra, arranged once again by Jack Nitzsche. A live version of 'The Needle and the Damage Done' recorded at the University of California, Los Angeles, completed what appeared to be a rather fragmented line up of songs, but as has so often been the case in Young's long career, the chemistry somehow worked - for the record buying public at least.

At the risk of appearing to deliberately attack *Harvest* due to its status as the Neil Young album most beloved by non-Neil Young fans, upon closer scrutiny it does arguably lack the consistent top-drawer quality of *After The Gold Rush*, with the unquestionable highs counterbalanced by a few weaker moments that give it a slightly uneven feel overall. It was definitely the most relaxed and content-sounding record Young had made up to this point, with tight but characterful musicianship, although demons do still lurk in some of the songs.

Nowhere is this more the case than on 'The Needle and the Damage Done', one of the most devastatingly raw - and best - songs Young has ever written. The inspiration for the lyrics is well-documented - Danny Whitten's heroin addiction and the impact this had on Young - and it is hard to imagine any other artist capturing the horror and anguish of the situation with such a vivid combination of emotional intensity and unforgettable melody. From the gently cascading opening acoustic guitar chords to the stunning final line of "every junkie's like a setting sun" which abruptly ends the song and is left hanging as a stark reminder of its message, 'The Needle and the Damage Done' is two minutes of starkly beautiful brilliance.

Nothing else on *Harvest* quite scales the same lofty peaks, although there are other excellent songs amidst the comfortable blandness or over the top bombast that do sometimes dog the album. The title track (Young's personal favourite on the record) is a lovely ballad, with a languid, hypnotic swing that's hard not to nod along to. 'Old Man', with its thought-provoking lyrics apparently inspired by a conversation between Young and the elderly caretaker on his ranch - "Old man, look at my life/I'm a lot like you were," - is perhaps the most musically rich offering here, with a passionate chorus augmented by Taylor's fluttering banjo and some sinuous bass lines by Drummond.

Which leads us to 'Heart of Gold' - a slice of radio-friendly, impeccably crafted country-pop that gave Young his first and only U.S. number one single in April 1972. An undeniably catchy tune with Dylan-like harmonica, keening pedal steel and Ronstadt's soaring backing vocals, it's not hard to understand 'Heart of Gold's commercial appeal, as a great example of an emerging genre that would be epitomised by the work of The Eagles over the next few years. What it was not was the type of song Neil Young wanted to write again and again to achieve further chart success. As he wrote in the liner notes of his 1977 compilation album *Decade*:

"This song put me in the middle of the road. Travelling there soon became a bore so I headed for the ditch. A rougher ride but I saw more interesting people there."[1]

These four standout songs apart, the rest of *Harvest* is either unremarkable or in the case of a couple of tracks in particular, hasn't stood the test of time well. Opener 'Out on the Weekend', which sets out the album's primary lyrical theme of seeking and enjoying new relationships, has a similar mellow vibe to *Harvest*'s title track, but a less memorable melody, while 'Are You Ready For The Country', although an exuberant romp with some enjoyable bar room piano from Jack Nitzsche, feels somewhat throwaway. Likewise, the two heaviest rocking tunes - 'Words (Between the Lines of Age)' and 'Alabama' - are distinctly average when compared to the high bar Young had set on his previous two albums. The former outstays its welcome at nearly seven minutes, although there is an evocative guitar solo around two thirds of the way through that recalls the longer tracks on *Everybody Knows This Is Nowhere*. 'Alabama' sees Young renewing his assault on the American South, with lyrics like "I come to you and see all this ruin/What are you doing Alabama/ You got the rest of the union to help you along/What's going wrong?" unlikely to win any prizes for subtlety. As with the superior, more dynamic 'Southern Man', Young is far less comfortable with the views he expressed in Alabama these days, admitting in his 2012 autobiography *Waging Heavy Peace*, "I don't like my words when I listen to it today. They are accusatory and condescending, not fully thought out, and too easy to misconstrue."[2]

Probably the most divisive inclusions on *Harvest a*re the two tracks recorded with Jack Nitzsche and the London Symphony Orchestra - in particular, the perennially controversial A 'Man Needs A Maid'. What starts off as a pretty piano ballad - which was how it was originally performed in a medley with 'Heart of Gold' - the song is then swamped by a vast backdrop of cinematic strings and portentous, chiming percussion. But it's the lyrics that are constantly referred to when discussing the song, with the verse "I was thinking that maybe I'd get a maid/ Find a place nearby for her to stay/Just someone to keep my house clean/Fix my meals and go away" unsurprisingly generating accusations of hideously outdated chauvinism. An alternative, more sympathetic theory is that the song is intended to reflect on the sometimes painful emotional intensity of romantic relationships, and that the verse in question is the narrator pondering if it would be better to have a simple, transactional arrangement to spare himself the heartbreak of true love. Either way, 'A Man Needs A Maid' certainly isn't Neil's finest hour. The same can be said of 'There's A World', a mediocre song drenched in bombast and Young struggling to be heard above the incessant pounding drums and swirling harps.

---

1   Neil Young, Decade liner notes (1977)
2   Young, Waging Heavy Peace, p.417

Despite receiving a mixed critical reception, *Harvest*, buoyed by the success of 'Heart of Gold', went on to become the best-selling album of 1972 in the U.S., and has gone on to shift over 15 million copies worldwide. For Young, this newfound acclaim proved to be a mixed blessing. While he'd enjoyed the easy, swift, off the cuff flow of making *Harvest,* he had, as his reaction to 'Heart of Gold's chart-topping exploits showed, little interest in becoming a comfortable, commercially motivated mainstream musical figure. The ditch beckoned, and on his next three albums, Young would inhabit it like few other artists before or since.

⊙ TRACK LISTING   ⏮ ⏸ ⏭

1. Out on the Weekend ⋯⋯⋯⋯⋯⋯⋯⋯⋯⋯⋯⋯⋯⋯⋯⋯⋯⋯⋯ 4:35
2. Harvest ⋯⋯⋯⋯⋯⋯⋯⋯⋯⋯⋯⋯⋯⋯⋯⋯⋯⋯⋯⋯⋯⋯⋯⋯ 3:03
3. A Man Needs a Maid⋯⋯⋯⋯⋯⋯⋯⋯⋯⋯⋯⋯⋯⋯⋯⋯⋯⋯ 4:00
4. Heart of Gold⋯⋯⋯⋯⋯⋯⋯⋯⋯⋯⋯⋯⋯⋯⋯⋯⋯⋯⋯⋯⋯ 3:05
5. Are You Ready for the Country?⋯⋯⋯⋯⋯⋯⋯⋯⋯⋯⋯⋯ 3:21
6. Old Man ⋯⋯⋯⋯⋯⋯⋯⋯⋯⋯⋯⋯⋯⋯⋯⋯⋯⋯⋯⋯⋯⋯⋯ 3:22
7. There's a World ⋯⋯⋯⋯⋯⋯⋯⋯⋯⋯⋯⋯⋯⋯⋯⋯⋯⋯⋯⋯ 3:00
8. Alabama ⋯⋯⋯⋯⋯⋯⋯⋯⋯⋯⋯⋯⋯⋯⋯⋯⋯⋯⋯⋯⋯⋯⋯ 4:02
9. The Needle and the Damage Done⋯⋯⋯⋯⋯⋯⋯⋯⋯⋯⋯ 2:00
   (recorded in concert, 30 January 1971)
10. Words (Between the Lines of Age) ⋯⋯⋯⋯⋯⋯⋯⋯⋯⋯ 6:42

Length: 37:10

Neil Young - Time Fades Away

Released 15 October 1973 (Reprise)

🎧   🎧   🎧

*T*ime Fades Away remains one of the most intriguing, turbulent records of Neil Young's career. A collection of previously unreleased songs but recorded live at a series of concerts during 1973, it's an album Young hated so much it has only just, finally, been released on CD, yet it is undoubtedly an important landmark in his discography as the first instalment of the now-iconic 'ditch trilogy' (alongside 1974's *On The Beach* and 1975's *Tonight's The Night*).

In late 1972, Young, still squinting rather uncomfortably against the glare of *Harvest*'s enormous success, was planning to go back on the road again for the first time in nearly two years, during which time he had become one of the most popular singer-songwriters in the world. A 65-date tour of major U.S. arenas was planned, likely to be filled with audiences expecting to hear 'Heart of Gold' and 'Old Man'.

What they got was something very different indeed. While Young has always been a restless spirit, intrinsically opposed to ploughing the same furrow record after record, events leading up to the *Time Fades Away* tour had a major influence on the mood of the music performed there. Putting together a band for the tour, Young reached out to Crazy Horse's Danny Whitten, in the hope that the guitarist's heroin addiction days were behind him. Sadly, it quickly became clear that Whitten was still firmly in the grip of his drug demons and was soon sacked by Young, who put him on a flight to LA on 18 November 1972 with $50 in his pocket. Whitten proceeded to overdose on alcohol and valium and was found dead in the bathroom of a friend's house later the same day. Whitten's fate and his part in it was to haunt Young for many years, as well as leaving an indelible imprint upon his song writing.

The core of the live band was to be composed of the Stray Gators, who backed Young on *Harvest*, but before the tour had even begun, problems were emerging, with the musicians demanding more money. Young reluctantly backed down, but the animosity lingered on the road. Unlike Crazy Horse, the Stray Gators were polished session musicians at heart, and being asked to play Young's new, harder edged rock songs very loud pulled them out of the comfort zone of *Harvest*'s predominantly mellow country-folk vibe, although pedal steel player Ben Keith certainly made a valiant effort, adapting the cosy, homespun twang of his instrument into a piercing, visceral howl.

Young had explored the idea of recording an album of new songs in the studio between tour dates, but in the end abandoned this idea in favour of capturing them live on the road. Producer Elliott Mazer was tasked with securing a recording truck, which Young christened "His Master's Wheels" and seven songs were taken from the subsequent tour performances, with the eighth - 'Love In Mind' - a recording from a concert back in 1971.

The tour itself was predictably chaotic. Buttrey - persistently castigated by Young for not playing loud enough despite drumming so hard his hands bled - ended up being replaced by ex-Turtles and Jefferson Airplane member Johnny Barbata, while Jack Nitzsche regularly performed drunk to overcome his terrible stage fright. Young himself began consuming copious amounts of tequila, leading to some ill-tempered outbursts onstage, before his voice began to give out and old friends Graham Nash and David Crosby were called in as the cavalry, leading to even more personality clashes.

Yet despite these myriad issues, *Time Fades Away* has some great moments. There is a raw, ragged tension to the performances that's strangely compelling, and some real rough diamonds of songs, interspersed with flurries of crowd noise and on stage interjections that further add to the sense of simmering unease. The album starts out by going straight for the jugular, with the woozy country boogie of the title track lumbering out of the speakers as Young opens by belting out the bleakly poetic lyrics "Fourteen junkies too weak to work/One sells diamonds for what they're worth/Down on pain street, disappointment lurks." But the atmosphere then shifts effortlessly on the gorgeous piano ballad 'Journey Through The Past', with Young delivering one of his most vulnerable, plaintive vocal performances as he reflects on his Canadian youth from his new ranch.

The next three tracks vary in quality. 'Yonder Stands The Sinner' is an unremarkable, plodding rocker that's unquestionably the weakest offering on the album. Things go up a level on 'L.A', an acidic critique of the Californian metropolis as the "uptight city in the smog/Don't you wish that you could be here too?". Then we have 'Love in Mind', a solo piano performance which, as previously mentioned, predates the rest of *Time Fades Away* by two years and feels gentle and reflective, at odds with the weary, cynical tone of many of the other, later recordings.

Without doubt the most enduring track on *Time Fades Away* is 'Don't Be Denied'. One of the most starkly autobiographical of all Young's songs, it was written on the morning Young heard about Danny Whitten's death, and features a bruised, gut wrenching vocal of the kind that would go on to characterise the bleakest record of the ditch trilogy, 1975's *Tonight's The Night*. 'Don't Be Denied' tells the story of the teenage Young's parents' divorce, his move to Winnipeg with his mother, subsequent schoolyard scrapes and the forming of his first band. The narrative then seems to jump forward to the present day and addresses the challenges of musical fame with lyrics that would appear to directly reference Whitten: "Well, all that glitters isn't gold/I know you've heard that story told/And I'm a pauper in a naked disguise/A millionaire through a businessman's eyes/Oh, friend of mine/Don't be denied."

'The Bridge', another pretty piano ballad similar in feel to 'Journey Through The Past', is at its heart a simple love song, but *Time Fades Away*'s closing track, 'The Last Dance' is a feedback-drenched, sprawling 10-minute dirge, with Young singing flat above the squalling guitars swooping in and out of the pounding rhythm. Memorably described by biographer Jimmy McDonough as "an oil slick" of a song[1], it epitomises the album's status as the antithesis to its melodic, radio-friendly predecessors *After The Goldrush* and *Harvest*.

It probably came as little surprise to Young or anyone else that *Time Fades Away* was a comparative commercial failure, peaking at number 22 in the U.S. charts and being greeted by widespread bemusement from the music press, with the *NME*'s Nick Kent describing the album as "murky, sloppy attempts at rock n'roll, built around tiresome chord progressions and obscure nonsense lyrics."[2] But with the benefit of hindsight and framed in the context of the other albums that followed, *Time Fades Away* is an important album in Young's career, with at least two songs - 'Journey Through The Past' and 'Don't Be Denied' - that bear comparison with his finest work. It showed the world that here was an artist unwilling to compromise his artistic integrity for the sake of sales and paved the way for two more albums in which he would spiral towards even greater depths of existential despair.

⊙ TRACK LISTING   ◄◄ ❚❚ ►►|

1. Time Fades Away ·· 5:36
   (recorded at The Myriad in Oklahoma City, 1 March 1973)
2. Journey Through the Past ··· 3:19
   (recorded at the Public Hall in Cleveland, 11 February 111973)
3. Yonder Stands the Sinner ··· 3:17
   (recorded at the Seattle Center Coliseum in Seattle, 17 March 17 1973)
4. L.A. ··· 3:11
   (recorded at The Myriad in Oklahoma City 1 March 1973)

---

1 McDonough, p.398
2 NME, 13/10/1973

5. Love in Mind 1:58
   (recorded in Royce Hall at the University of California, Los Angeles,
   30 January 1971)
6. Don't Be Denied 5:16
   (recorded at The Coliseum in Phoenix, 28 March 1973)
7. The Bridge 3:05
   (recorded at the Memorial Auditorium in Sacramento, 1 April 1973)
8. Last Dance 8:47
   (recorded at the Sports Arena in San Diego, 29 March 1973)

Length: 34:33

Neil Young - On The Beach

Released 19 July 1974 (Reprise)

🎧　🎧　🎧

Although *On The Beach* is often considered the second of Neil Young's ditch trilogy based on its release date, this is misleading. In fact, it was recorded several months after *Tonight's The Night,* the sessions for which took place as early as August 1973, but that album was held back by Young for almost two years before it was eventually released. This order of events is important when listening to and reflecting upon *On The Beach*, as while still very much deserving of its 'ditch' status in terms of its mood and lyrical focus, it definitely feels more different in style from *Time Fades Away* and *Tonight's The Night* than they do from each other. While both these two records are characterised by a sense of boozy, raw boned tension, *On The Beach* feels, on the surface at least, a calmer, slower paced, more reflective record, often with a starkly hypnotic quality that sets it apart from the straight for the jugular intensity of much of *Time Fades Away* or *Tonight's The Night*.

After a frenetic 1973 of constant touring in North America and Europe, often in a state of drunkenness and on stage agitation, Young began recording new material with producer David Briggs in February 1974 at his Broken Arrow ranch. Some of these recordings, including versions of 'Walk On' and 'For The Turnstiles', formed the first building blocks for what would become *On The Beach*. The remaining tracks were cut at LA's Sunset Studios in April of that year, with Young joined by his trusted stalwarts Crazy Horse's Ralph Molina and Stray Gators Tim Drummond and Ben Keith, who played everything from bass and piano to dobro and Wurlitzer organ.

The core band were joined by a wide range of other players ranging from David Crosby and Graham Nash to The Band's Levon Helm and Rick Danko and even the ex-Rocket George Whitsell, who had long since lost the rest of his old group to Young. The ever-shifting line up was completed by the hellraising fiddle and steel guitar player Rudy Kershaw, who also became instrumental in the concoction of the now-infamous 'honey slides' - a mind blowing combination of honey and industrial strength fried marijuana imbibed by the musicians which played a big part in creating the palpably frazzled vibe that pervades the record. Not everyone involved with the record found the environment to their liking - veteran producer Al Schmidt quit halfway through the sessions due to frustration with the behaviour of the musicians and Young's choice of murky mixes and was replaced by the more amenable Mark Harmon.

On The Beach opens with the jauntily infectious 'Walk On', in which Young outlines his determination not to allow the negative views of others to affect him. Lyrics like "I hear some people been talkin' me down/bring up my name, pass it 'round/they don't mention happy times/they do their thing, I'll do mine," may have been a response to his record company's lack of enthusiasm for the unreleased *Tonight's The Night*, or perhaps even his ongoing feud with Lynyrd Skynyrd following the release of the Southern rockers' 'Sweet Home Alabama.' Musically, it's lithe and funky, with some punchy guitar work, and - perhaps due to the fact it was recorded at Broken Arrow ranch rather than the main album sessions in LA - the bleak alienation of many of the album's other tracks is largely absent.

'See The Sky About To Rain', unlike the rest of *On The Beach*, was written several years earlier, appearing in several live shows, but it's elegantly maudlin backdrop of electric piano, steel guitar and harmonica, together with Young's plaintive vocal and evocative lyrics, ensure it fits well. The song has a central theme focused on the different paths we are all inevitably destined for, just as rain will come from the sky, with Young concluding "Some are bound for happiness, some are bound to glory/Some are bound to live with less, who can tell your story?"

The relatively benign feel of the first two tracks of *On The Beach* comes to a screeching halt with 'Revolution Blues', a deeply unsettling aural assault stalked by the ghost of notorious cult leader Charles Manson. Young had known Manson when he was an aspiring musician in the late 60s LA scene, and the murderous acts committed in the name of the Manson Family's insane ideology inspired some of the most vivid, disturbing imagery in all his song writing. Framed by choppy, jerky guitars and intimidatingly relentless rhythms, Young sneers out his apocalyptic lyrics as he imagines Manson's followers preparing to wreak further carnage on the decadent population of California, with the memorable lines "I got the revolution blues, I see bloody fountains/And ten million dune buggies comin' down the mountains/Well, I hear that Laurel Canyon is full of famous stars/But I hate them worse than lepers and I'll kill them in their cars."

'For The Turnstiles', the other track recorded with David Briggs at Broken Arrow ranch, returns us to more mellow territory, although the troubled undertow remains. A rustic, banjo led campfire sing along, with Young and Ben Keith's high, harmonising vocals clearly strained and struggling to stay in tune, its lyrics are peppered with oblique references to the unsatisfactory nature of commercial success, "singin' songs for pimps with tailors/Who charge ten dollars at the door" with Young drawing a comparison with baseball players "left to die on the diamond... for the turnstiles." Next up is 'Vampire Blues' which sounds monumentally stoned, a woozy tapestry of off kilter guitar licks, shuffling percussion and wobbly organ stabs, with Young adopting the persona of an unscrupulous oil baron, singing "I'm a vampire, baby, suckin' blood from the earth/well, I'm a vampire, babe, I'll sell you twenty barrels worth."

But it's the second half of *On The Beach* that elevates the album to unquestionable greatness. The title track in particular, on which Young continues to contemplate the meaning of fame and the impact it has upon him psychologically, is one of his absolute classic songs. As a mood piece, it's absolutely peerless, with the shimmeringly wasted guitars, spectral electric piano and rolling hand drums soon joined by Young's anguished voice proclaiming, "I need a crowd of people, but I can't face them day to day/though my problems are meaningless, that don't make them go away." The pair of minute-long solo guitar passages, two and a half minutes and six minutes into the track respectively, are simply sublime, with Young coaxing a level of emotional intensity from his instrument that's rarely been matched, anchored perfectly by the rhythm section's funereal tempo which allows Young's arid, melancholy notes to cut like a knife.

'Motion Pictures (For Carrie)' is a gorgeously languid, unhurried ballad, with gentle strums of acoustic guitar, twangs of slide guitar and floating harmonica. Referencing his now tempestuous relationship with the movie actress Carrie Snodgress, who was often away making films, Young sings about "Motion pictures on my TV screen/A home away from home, livin' in between/But I hear some people have got their dream/I've got mine." He also returns again to his difficult relationship with fame, while at the same time offering a glimmer of hope that he can see a way to a better future - "Well, all those headlines, they just bore me now/I'm deep inside myself, but I'll get out somehow."

On The Beach ends with the almost nine minute long 'Ambulance Blues', another lyrical tour de force in which Young conjures up a dizzying array of metaphor, cultural references and reminiscences to create a dreamlike landscape of images, held together by a sparse but strangely peaceful musical accompaniment of guitar, harmonica and Rudy Kershaw's otherworldly fiddle. In the biography *Shakey*, Young confessed to having inadvertently borrowed the melody for 'Ambulance Blues' from Bert Jansch's harrowing 1965 song Needle of Death, saying "I loved that melody... when I went back and listened to that record (*On The Beach*) again I realised that I copied his thing...I felt really bad about that."[1] But even taking this admission into account, the lyrics and vibe are unmistakably, uniquely Young's own. 'Ambulance Blues' sees Young looking back on his past

---

1 McDonough, p.443

career while simultaneously trying to make sense of the present: "It's hard to say the meaning of this song/An ambulance can only go so fast/It's easy to get buried in the past/When you try to make a good thing last."

If *Time Fades Away* is the raucous, boozy party of the ditch trilogy and *Tonight's The Night* the early hours of the morning comedown session, then On The Beach is unquestionably the hangover. Even the album cover - which depicts a car part submerged in the sand next to empty beach furniture, with Young gazing out to sea in the distance - conveys a sense of emerging from emotional wreckage, starting to piece together what's happened and working out how to move forward.

Despite its lack of radio friendly material and introspective, sometimes challenging songs, *On The Beach* still reached a respectable chart position of 16 in the U.S., while at the same time providing further evidence that the Young who made *Harvest* wasn't coming back any time soon. For the man himself, *On The Beach* was the point at which Young decided to clamber out of the ditch and shift his musical direction again. But before the world got to see where he'd go next, there was still time for the last instalment of his legendary trilogy to stagger bleary eyed into view.

⊙ TRACK LISTING   ◄◄ ❚❚ ►►|

Length: 39:40

Neil Young - Tonight's The Night

Released 20 June 1975 (Reprise)

A fter *Time Fades Away* saw Neil Young veer off the middle of the road course that *Harvest* had set him on, *Tonight's The Night* saw him ploughing deeper still into the career ditch he'd consciously sought out.

In late summer 1973, a physically and emotionally exhausted Young, his voice shot to pieces from touring and still reeling from the deaths of Danny Whitten and (in June 1973) of much-loved CSN&Y roadie Bruce Berry, was in need of catharsis. In August, he brought together a core of trusted sidekicks - Ralph Molina and Billy Talbot of Crazy Horse, Stray Gator Ben Keith, Jack Nitzsche and Nils Lofgren - for a series of now legendary, crepuscular sessions at Instrument Rentals studio in Hollywood that resulted in one of the rawest but most powerful albums of Young's career. Further insight into the *Tonight's The Night* recording process was provided by Neil's father Scott, in his excellent memoir *Neil And Me,* which examines the respected writer's relationship with his famous son. Young senior explained that the band smoked and drank together during late afternoons and evenings to get high before playing late at night, so they could have some empathy with the frame of mind Danny Whitten and Bruce Berry might have been in just before they died.[1]

Although the unpolished, off the cuff feel of the *Tonight's The Night* sessions is absolutely fundamental to the record's impact, with many songs barely rehearsed and captured warts and all, it nevertheless has a clear structure, with considerable thought going into the track listing. Different versions of the title track open and close the album, and three additional tracks recorded separately were also added, including - fittingly - a performance of 'Come On Baby Let's Go Downtown' from March 1970 featuring the late Whitten on lead vocals. While the prevailing mood is unquestionably downbeat and desolate, the skilful flow of the record means there are also some highs among the lows. Producer David Briggs's original mix of

---

1   Scott Young, Neil And Me, p.179

Tonight's The Night, even starker with a different song order, audible conversations between tracks and some alternative songs including 'Walk On' and 'For The Turnstiles' - soon to appear on *On The Beach* - remains tantalisingly unreleased. Briggs himself described it to Scott Young as "unrelenting…it's like some guy having you by the throat from the first note, and all the way to the end."[2]

From the very first seconds, it's clear *Tonight's The Night* is going to be a special record. It opens with a gentle ripple of piano and tuning up guitar, then Young and his backing band, who he called the Santa Monica Flyers, begin to softly chant the line "tonight's the night", gradually building the volume before Young utters the immortal lines "Bruce Berry was a workin' man; he used to load that Econoline van/a sparkle was in his eye, but his life was in his hand." By beginning the record with such a direct reference to Berry, Young sets out his stall immediately: the gloves are off, and he is prepared to unflinchingly confront his demons. What follows is a touching tribute to Berry, whose life, like that of other jobbing musicians everywhere, received little or no recognition. The playing and harmonies are rough and ready but dripping with atmosphere.

'Speakin' Out', which arrives next, is an early album highlight. With the Santa Monica Flyers now settled into a delightfully languid, after hours groove, there's the opportunity for some of the individual musicians to really shine. Young's rolling saloon bar piano and Keith's ghostly pedal steel are fantastic, but the real star is Nils Lofgren, who, after suddenly being told by Young in the middle of the song to "'take it Nils" delivers a guitar solo of understated, mellifluous brilliance. Lyrically, it's one of the more optimistic songs on the album, with Young addressing partner Carrie Snodgress as he sings "I'm hopin' for your love to carry me through/You're holdin' my baby and I'm holdin' you/And it's alright."

'World On A String' is a more up-tempo, conventional rock song, all crunchy guitar riffs and thumping drums, with lyrics focusing on the search of meaning in a life "that's only real/in the way I feel from day to day." In contrast, 'Borrowed Tune', recorded by Young at his Broken Arrow ranch in late 1973, is stark and unadorned, just Young on piano and harmonica and back in solo singer-songwriter mode, questioning the meaning of fame: "I'm climbing this ladder/My head in the clouds/I hope that it matters/I'm having my doubts." Another verse brazenly explains the song's title, for those who haven't yet spotted the glaring similarity between Jagger and Richards' 'Lady Jane': "I'm singing this borrowed tune/I took from the Rolling Stones/Alone in this empty room/Too wasted to write my own."

Recorded live in 1970 at the legendary Lower East Side venue the Fillmore East, 'Come On Baby Let's Go Downtown' is a raucous blast of pure hedonism that also appeared on Crazy Horse's first album. Young takes a back seat, with Danny Whitten on lead vocals telling the tale of a late night drug deal. It showcases

---

2 Scott Young, p.195

Whitten as the owner of a rich, rasping rock voice and its inclusion here is a fitting testament to his talent, with the song's subject matter lending it added poignancy. Side one of *Tonight's The Night* concludes with the emotion drenched 'Mellow My Mind,' which features a vocal performance as compelling as any in Young's long career. The way his voice cracks with weariness as he sings the lines "I've been down the road and I've come back/Lonesome whistle on the railroad track/Ain't got nothing on those feelings that I had" is quietly devastating, and once again, Ben Keith's steel guitar provides the song with an evocative undercurrent of spectral weirdness.

Side two opens with 'Roll Another Number (For The Road)'. A woozy, off key slice of country-rock, it sees Young reinforce his determination to move on from what he sees as the now meaningless late 1960s/early 1970s musical scene where he first made his name, stating "I'm not goin' back to Woodstock for a while/ Though I long to hear that lonesome hippie smile/I'm a million miles away from that helicopter day/No, I don't believe I'll be goin' back again." 'Albuquerque', a road movie in a song that focuses on escaping from fame into anonymity, has an elegant sadness about it, emphasised by Young's lower than usual voice and yet more stellar work by Keith.

With its tight multi-voice harmonies and banjo-like acoustic guitar, 'New Mama' could almost be a lost CSN&Y track, a similarity noticed by Stephen Stills, who went on to cover the track. A tender celebration of new parenthood, the song is another example, like 'Speakin' Out', of how Young sought to imbue *Tonight's The Night* with some positivity amid the prevailing despair. 'Lookout Joe' is a Stray Gators recording dating back to 1972, but bizarrely sounds as far away from *Harvest*'s mellow vibe as any track here, with a strutting, sleazy swagger mirrored by the song's lyrics about American GIs returning from Vietnam to a small town America riddled with danger and vice.

Tonight's The Night reaches a late peak with the astonishing 'Tired Eyes.' An uncompromising portrait of a drug deal gone wrong, resulting in several fatal shootings, it seems to point a finger at the evils of the narcotics trade and how it can destroy lives in different ways, expanding the album's narrative beyond the very personal stories of Whitten and Berry. With Keith's pedal steel weeping more beautifully than ever, the soaring but desperately sad chorus, imploring the song's subject to "Please take my advice/open up the tired eyes" is among the most moving moments in Young's entire catalogue. A second, much rougher take of the title track effectively rounds off what has been a sometimes gruelling but utterly immersive listening experience.

Without a single weak track and boasting a remarkable cohesion that belies the inclusion of tracks from different times and sessions, *Tonight's The Night* is undoubtedly one of Neil Young's most impressive achievements, right down to the now iconic monochrome cover art. Yet despite its obvious quality, Reprise were nervous about what they saw as a lack of commercial appeal, and it was another two years before the album was finally released, with the alterations to the track listing and running order referred to previously, by which time Young had already toured and played most of the songs extensively.

Non-commercial it may have been, but *Tonight's The Night* still reached the top 30 in both the U.S. and U.K. album charts and drew a largely positive response from critics. Detractors usually dismissed the record's performances as ragged and under-produced, an accusation the writer Paul Williams neatly rebuffed in his January 1976 essay I Sing The Song Before I Love the Man with the retort "Slick is sloppy because it's superficial". Young himself would go on to describe *Tonight's The Night* as the most significant record he's ever made. While there are a few other contenders for that lofty accolade, its place in the pantheon is undisputed, and its reputation as one of popular music's most harrowing yet mesmerising albums continues to grow as every year goes by.

⊙ TRACK LISTING   ⏮ ⏸ ⏭

1. Tonight's the Night ⋯⋯⋯⋯⋯⋯⋯⋯⋯⋯⋯⋯⋯⋯⋯⋯⋯ 4:39
2. Speakin' Out ⋯⋯⋯⋯⋯⋯⋯⋯⋯⋯⋯⋯⋯⋯⋯⋯⋯⋯⋯ 4:56
3. World on a String ⋯⋯⋯⋯⋯⋯⋯⋯⋯⋯⋯⋯⋯⋯⋯⋯ 2:27
4. Borrowed Tune ⋯⋯⋯⋯⋯⋯⋯⋯⋯⋯⋯⋯⋯⋯⋯⋯⋯ 3:26
5. Come on Baby Let's Go Downtown ⋯⋯⋯⋯⋯⋯⋯⋯ 3:35
   (live at the Fillmore East, New York City, 7 March 1970)
6. Mellow My Mind ⋯⋯⋯⋯⋯⋯⋯⋯⋯⋯⋯⋯⋯⋯⋯⋯ 3:07
7. Roll Another Number (For the Road) ⋯⋯⋯⋯⋯⋯ 3:02
8. Albuquerque ⋯⋯⋯⋯⋯⋯⋯⋯⋯⋯⋯⋯⋯⋯⋯⋯⋯⋯ 4:02
9. New Mama ⋯⋯⋯⋯⋯⋯⋯⋯⋯⋯⋯⋯⋯⋯⋯⋯⋯⋯ 2:11
10. Lookout Joe ⋯⋯⋯⋯⋯⋯⋯⋯⋯⋯⋯⋯⋯⋯⋯⋯⋯ 3:57
11. Tired Eyes ⋯⋯⋯⋯⋯⋯⋯⋯⋯⋯⋯⋯⋯⋯⋯⋯⋯⋯ 4:38
12. Tonight's the Night" (Part II) ⋯⋯⋯⋯⋯⋯⋯⋯⋯ 4:52

Length: 44:52

Neil Young - Homegrown

Released 19 June 2020 (Reprise)

🎧 🎧 🎧

For over four decades, *Homegrown* occupied mythical status as the great lost Neil Young album, the Canadian's answer to Dylan's *Blood on the Tracks* with a collection of profoundly personal songs chronicling the disintegration of his tempestuous relationship with Carrie Snodgress.

As outlined in the previous chapter, *Homegrown* was originally intended to be released in 1975, before Young replaced it at the last minute with the rawer, in his view stronger and more powerful *Tonight's The Night* album. Over the ensuing years, intense speculation built up among Young's diehard fan base around whether *Homegrown* would ever be released, and what songs it included, with Young himself offering a few tantalising insights, albeit not always accurately (for example, in the liner notes for his retrospective *Decade*, he suggest 'Deep Forgotten Lake' was part of the lost album, when in fact it was part of another abandoned project). But despite the best efforts of Young aficionados and archivists, until recently, *Homegrown* seemed destined to be consigned to a list of frustrating 'lost' albums alongside the likes of The Beach Boys' legendary *Smile*.

The launch of the official *Neil Young Archives* series in 2009 brought new hope that *Homegrown* would finally see the light of day, and it made its long awaited appearance in June 2020, as part of Young's *Special Release Series*, also going on to form part of the *Neil Young Archives Vol. II: 1972-1976* box set released in November 2020.

Taken from a series of sessions recorded between June 1974 and January 1975, much of *Homegrown* was a relatively spartan affair, with only the ever-reliable multi-instrumentalist Ben Keith and bass player Tim Drummond joining Young on most of the tracks, although a range of eminent guests - including Levon Helm and Robbie Robertson from The Band and country legend Emmylou Harris on backing vocals - also contributed. Young was joined as co-producer by David Briggs, Elliot Mazer and Tim Mulligan, with the sessions taking place at Quadraphonic Sound

Studios in Nashville, Village Recorder Studios in LA and at Young's Broken Arrow ranch. One track - 'White Line' - was recorded at Ramport Studios in London, during a CSN&Y tour.

Of the 12 songs included on *Homegrown*, seven were previously unreleased – 'Separate Ways', 'Try', 'Mexico', 'Kansas', 'We Don't Smoke It No More', 'Vacancy' and 'Florida'. Also included are the first recordings of 'Star Of Bethlehem' and 'Homegrown' - which appeared on 1977's *American Stars n' Bars* (the latter re-recorded with Crazy Horse); 'White Line', which was revamped for 1991's *Ragged Glory*, 'Little Wing', which appeared unchanged on 1980's *Hawks and Doves* and finally 'Love Is A Rose', which appeared on *Decade*.

One of the defining characteristics of *Homegrown* is its unusually personal subject matter, from an artist whose songs often tell the stories of others, or focus on broad themes of alienation, injustice, despair and loss. Another often cited reason for Young's unwillingness to release *Homegrown*, or indeed to initially play tracks from it live, is that he felt uncomfortable sharing his emotions so directly and openly with the world. Right from the start of the record, the listener is starkly exposed to his pain.

'Separate Ways' sets the tone. A bittersweet country-rock ballad, it deals unflinchingly with the process of a relationship ending, with the lyrics "We go our separate ways/Looking for better days/Sharing our little boy/Who grew from joy back then" also referencing the impact the split would have on the couple's child Zeke, born in 1972. While 'Separate Ways' is tinged with regret, there is also acceptance and even cautious optimism for the future, with the final verse concluding "Me for me, you for you/Happiness is never through/It's only a change of ways/And that is nothing new."

Second track 'Try' is similar in feel; perhaps the track here that's most reminiscent of *Harvest* with its beautifully mellow pedal steel, rolling drums and piano and Harris's cooing backing vocals. In contrast to 'Separate Ways', the lyrics seem to yearn for reconciliation, with Young singing "Darlin', the door is open/To my heart, and I've been hopin'/That you won't be the one/To struggle with the key/We got lots of time/To get together if we try."

After a strong start, Homegrown gets patchier. 'Mexico' is pleasant enough; a heartfelt if slight piano ballad similar in style to 'Journey Through The Past' or 'Love In Mind' from *Time Fades Away,* with Young planning a trip across the Californian border while lamenting "Oh, the feeling's gone/Why is it so hard/To hang on to your love?" The likeably trite 'Love Is A Rose', meanwhile, is probably the closest to a pure country song Young had recorded up to this point, a precursor to his future *Comes A Time* and *Old Ways* albums, which would embrace the genre fully, and a hit single for Linda Ronstadt when she covered it shortly afterwards.

There is a strange lack of shape to *Homegrown* as an overall album which is perhaps indicative of the fact it was cobbled together from over 30 songs recorded across several sessions. This sense of unevenness increases towards the middle of the album, with the unexceptional title track, a rather clumpy ode to marijuana cultivation, followed by the bizarre, spoken word interlude 'Florida', in which Young describes walking through a city and after witnessing the accidental killing of a couple by a glider, rescuing their unharmed baby - a disturbing narrative accompanied by a wet finger being rubbed across a wine glass.

'Kansas', a simple acoustic song examining how a one night stand can provide solace to a wounded heart - "it doesn't matter if you're the one/We'll know before we're done"- is better, but we're back in underwhelming territory with the plodding boogie of 'We Don't Smoke It No More', which staggers and meanders rather aimlessly for almost five minutes, with the refrain of "we don't smoke it no more" delivered in a laconic slur that one can only assume deliberately undermines the veracity of the song's statement.

It's only in the final third of *Homegrown* that the quality threshold rises again. 'White Line' is delicate and wistful, a return to the confessional country-rock of the album's opening songs, with some lovely harmonica and guitar interplay and lyrics that hint at Young's hopes for a romantic life after Carrie: "And I'm rollin' down/ The open road/Where my true love, she lies waiting/Right now I'm thinking 'bout/ These things I know/But the daylight will soon be breaking." 'White Line' first emerged officially in another, far heavier garage rock guise on Young's superlative 1990 album *Ragged Glory*, but the original is equally compelling. In contrast, 'Vacancy' is undoubtedly the angriest song on *Homegrown*, a propulsive rocker on which Young questions the true nature of his former partner, asking "Are you my friend? Are you my enemy? Can we pretend/To live in harmony?"

Homegrown closes with two songs already familiar to Young fans from his earlier 'official' albums. The plaintive, sorrowful ballad 'Little Wing', with Young imploring the subject of the song "don't fly away/when the summer turns to fall/ don't you know some people say/the winter is the best time of them all" is a clear metaphor for pleading with a partner not to give up on a relationship too soon. 'Star of Bethlehem' is admittedly Young as his most syrupy and schmaltzy, but it's irresistible nonetheless, with its lilting rhythm and hymnal vocals (Emmylou Harris once again) giving the song a hypnotic, blissful quality, even though the lyrics once again focus on the vulnerability and loss Young felt after his breakup with Carrie. But amid all the pain, Young once again suggests there may be hope ahead, ending with the enigmatic words "Yet still a light is shining/From that lamp on down the hall/Maybe the star of Bethlehem/Wasn't a star at all."

Overall, it's hard to see *Homegrown* ultimately being evaluated as belonging in the ranks of Young's greatest work. There are undoubtedly some excellent songs, but most of these have been heard already in the intervening 45 years since they were first recorded, and with the honourable exceptions of 'Separate Ways' and 'Try', the previously unreleased tracks simply aren't - by Young's lofty standards - very good.

The relative lack of ripe new fruit is probably what makes *Homegrown* a slight disappointment based on the many years of feverish anticipation it generated, but its importance in Young's career history, and as a musical snapshot of a particularly turbulent period in his personal life, is beyond dispute. Its strong chart performance - reaching number 17 in the U.S. and number 2 in the U.K. - is indicative of both Young's enduring appeal and of *Homegrown*'s unique position in his back catalogue as a key 'missing link' from his classic era.

⊙ TRACK LISTING   ⏮ ⏸ ⏭

1. Separate Ways ·· 3:33
2. Try ·· 2:47
3. Mexico··· 1:40
4. Love Is a Rose ·· 2:16
5. Homegrown ··· 2:47
6. Florida ··· 2:58
7. Kansas ·· 2:12
8. We Don't Smoke It No More ·· 4:50
9. White Line··· 3:14
10. Vacancy ·· 3:59
11. Little Wing ·· 2:10
12. Star of Bethlehem·· 2:42

Length: 35:23

Neil Young - Zuma

Released 10 November 1975 (Reprise)

🎧　🎧　🎧

With the ditch trilogy now held in such reverence by critics and Young fans alike, the excellence of the album that immediately followed it is sometimes overlooked. Yet when assessing Neil Young's long career, in terms of songwriting quality, atmosphere and just sheer enjoyment, *Zuma* indisputably warrants inclusion among the very finest records he's ever made. Not only that, but it also saw the triumphant return of Crazy Horse as Young's backing band after six long years; an unexpected but joyous rebirth of one of the great musical unions which has continued to thrive ever since.

Although Crazy Horse bassist Billy Talbot and drummer Ralph Molina had continued to appear regularly on Young's albums since 1969's *Everybody Knows This Is Nowhere*, the increasingly wayward behaviour and then tragic death of guitarist Danny Whitten meant that the full band hadn't backed Young on a record since. This all changed with the arrival on the scene of Frank 'Poncho' Sampedro, a little known guitarist who had spent the late sixties and early seventies drifting between California and Mexico. Although he had never been in any groups of note, Sampredo was a Young and Crazy Horse obsessive who had been playing along to *Everybody Knows This Is Nowhere* for years and after meeting him and jamming together in early 1974, Billy Talbot was convinced he had found the missing ingredient needed to revive Crazy Horse.

An initial session with Young showed enough promise for the new line up to get together during spring 1975, with the sessions for *Zuma* taking place at a rented house in Malibu. With producer David Briggs also on board, the mood among the players was upbeat although also decidedly bacchanalian, with the copious quantities of drugs and alcohol flowing and a steady stream of girls coming and going making the atmosphere the very epitome of rock and roll excess. Briggs himself told Jimmy McDonough "Neil was the happiest I've ever known him during Zuma. He was a great guy to be around."

Neil Young - Zuma

Having purged his soul on the ditch trilogy and offered up his bleeding heart on the now-shelved *Homegrown,* Zuma saw Young finally get back to making music that was sunny, energised and optimistic again, although as ever with this most mercurial of songwriters, darker forces were also at work in some of the songs. The ghost of Carrie Snodgress still looms large and many of the tracks do retain a focus on the negative impacts of relationships - with a few sentiments and language choices concerning women that would be questionable today. But overall, this is Neil Young moving forward again, albeit with a few regrets.

Opener 'Don't Cry No Tears' is a catchy, uncomplicated rock song, instantly re-establishing that inimitable Crazy Horse groove, with Young clearly having a ball back on lead guitar and defiantly singing "Old true love ain't too hard to see/ Don't cry no tears around me." Interestingly, the roots of the song dated right back to Young's early days in The Squires back in Canada, with much of it a reworking of 1964's 'I Wonder'.

Next up is Danger Bird, which is an altogether heftier beast, a welcome return to the slow burning guitar dynamics of *Everybody Knows This Is Nowhere,* with the titular bird's turning to stone used as a metaphor for a failing relationship: "And he rides the wind back to his home/Although his wings have turned to stone." At seven minutes long, Danger Bird is a true epic, with constant shifts in tempo and mood, and the giant, soaring bird imagery of the lyrics can be applied just as aptly to Young's extraordinarily fluid, expressive guitar playing. Propelled skywards by Talbot and Molina's indomitable rhythm section and Sampedro's effortlessly intuitive accompaniment, it is by turns graceful, tortured and incendiary, prompting the great Lou Reed to describe Young's playing as some of the best he'd ever heard.

In contrast, 'Pardon My Heart' is a gentle acoustic ballad, in which Young seems to wrestle with the pros and cons of a relationship breaking down. Early in the song, he seems despondent, lamenting "You brought it all on/Oh, but it feels so wrong." But by the end, he is contradicting his earlier thoughts, singing "You brought it all on/Oh, and it feels so good." It's a compelling depiction of the contrasting, sometimes confusing feelings people can experience when love starts to fall apart at the seams, demonstrating that Young is often at his best as a lyricist when focusing directly on human emotions, rather than shrouding them in metaphor and allegory.

'Lookin' For A Love', meanwhile, is quite simply one of the most delightful, instantly hummable songs Young has ever written. The idea of a rambunctious force of nature like Crazy Horse doing jangle-pop is incongruous in the extreme, but they pull it off with aplomb here, adding in some gorgeous harmonies as Young's wide-eyed quest for a new romance is tempered by his concerns about whether the relationship will survive "when she starts to see the darker side of me."

The high watermark is maintained with 'Barstool Blues', which Young claims he wrote after a mammoth Malibu bar crawl and in such a state of drunkenness he couldn't even remember doing it. Intoxicated or not, it's another triumph, with a fantastic, yearning melody, a scintillating closing guitar solo and lyrics that adeptly capture the blurred workings of the inebriated mind: "If I could hold on to just one thought for long enough to know/Why my mind is moving so fast and the conversation so slow." But perhaps more than any other song Young wrote around the time of his breakup with Carrie Snodgress, 'Barstool Blues' also encapsulated the whole journey of hope, joy and pain he experienced, with the memorable lines: "He trusted in a woman/And on her he made his bets/Once there was a friend of mine/Who died a thousand deaths."

Unfortunately, Young's gift for lyrical perceptiveness promptly deserts him on the brusquely titled 'Stupid Girl', with its borderline offensive depiction of a supposedly misguided woman as "a beautiful fish, floppin' on the summer sand." Neither this track nor 'Drive Back', an unremarkable no frills, angry rocker in which Young seems determined to see the back of his former lover, hit the same heights as the rest of *Zuma*.

Quite the opposite is true of the towering 'Cortez The Killer', regarded universally as one of the truly great Neil Young songs. It would be possible to devote an entire chapter of this book to such an astonishingly rich, complex and evocative composition, equally compelling both musically and lyrically and entirely deserving of its exalted status in the rock pantheon. The first of several songs Young wrote about indigenous American peoples during this period of his career, it tells the devastating story of Spanish conquistador Hernán Cortez's decimation of the Aztec culture of what Mexico during the early 16th century is now, or, as Young unforgettably describes it "he came dancing across the water/with his galleons and guns." Clocking in at seven and a half minutes overall, the first half of 'Cortez the Killer' is instrumental only, with Young's mesmeric guitar building layer upon layer of atmosphere over Crazy Horse's smouldering tempo. While critics of the song have pointed out that the lyrics present an idyllic view of the Aztecs as a peaceful 'noble savages' which is historically inaccurate (as they had ruthlessly conquered neighbouring powers and practised human sacrifice), it's nevertheless a hugely ambitious, impactful choice of subject matter, matched by some of Young's finest, most distinctive guitar work. Interestingly, Scott Young claims in his memoir *Neil and Me* that 'Cortez The Killer' originally had a final verse that is missing from the recorded version because an electrical circuit blew, forcing the song to fade out instead. His son is said to have shrugged this off with the response "I never liked that verse anyway."[1]

After the drama and intensity of 'Cortez The Killer,' *Zuma* ends quietly with the wisp-like prettiness of 'Through My Sails', a throwback to the CSN&Y sound with delicate harmonies by Stephen Stills and Graham Nash. While it's a slightly

---

1   Scott Young, p.149-50

anti-climactic conclusion to an album with some scintillating highs, the reflective tone of the lyrics and music provide a sense of calm after the storm, suggesting that Young may have finally exorcised his remaining demons.

Despite being Young's most accessible and commercial album since *Harvest*, *Zuma* was only a moderate success with the record buying public, reaching number 25 in the U.S. Billboard charts. But its importance to Young's career journey, heralding both his re-emergence from the harrowing depths of his post-*Harvest* albums and the resurrection of Crazy Horse, together with some absolutely outstanding songs, means it deserves to be considered in the same league as the more celebrated records that immediately preceded it.

⊙ TRACK LISTING   ⏮ ⏸ ⏭

1. Don't Cry No Tears ⋯⋯⋯⋯⋯⋯⋯⋯⋯⋯⋯⋯⋯⋯⋯⋯ 2:34
2. Danger Bird ⋯⋯⋯⋯⋯⋯⋯⋯⋯⋯⋯⋯⋯⋯⋯⋯⋯⋯ 6:54
3. Pardon My Heart ⋯⋯⋯⋯⋯⋯⋯⋯⋯⋯⋯⋯⋯⋯⋯⋯ 3:49
4. Lookin' for a Love ⋯⋯⋯⋯⋯⋯⋯⋯⋯⋯⋯⋯⋯⋯⋯ 3:17
5. Barstool Blues ⋯⋯⋯⋯⋯⋯⋯⋯⋯⋯⋯⋯⋯⋯⋯⋯ 3:02
6. Stupid Girl ⋯⋯⋯⋯⋯⋯⋯⋯⋯⋯⋯⋯⋯⋯⋯⋯⋯⋯ 3:13
7. Drive Back ⋯⋯⋯⋯⋯⋯⋯⋯⋯⋯⋯⋯⋯⋯⋯⋯⋯⋯ 3:32
8. Cortez the Killer ⋯⋯⋯⋯⋯⋯⋯⋯⋯⋯⋯⋯⋯⋯⋯ 7:29
9. Through My Sails ⋯⋯⋯⋯⋯⋯⋯⋯⋯⋯⋯⋯⋯⋯⋯ 2:41

Length: 36:34

Neil Young - Hitchhiker

Released 4 August 2017 (Reprise)

🎧 🎧 🎧

With the ditch trilogy completed, Crazy Horse back in the saddle on *Zuma* and the breakup of his relationship with Carrie Snodgress mostly navigated, by 1976 Neil Young was in his best frame of mind for years. He had even found time to record an album with his old bandmate and sparring partner Stephen Stills (the admittedly underwhelming *Long May You Run)* although he blotted his copybook by abandoning the duo's sold out summer tour only a few dates in, apparently deliberately redirecting his tour bus to Nashville, Tennessee when the next gig was in Atlanta, Georgia.

Although he was continuing to collaborate regularly with other artists, Young was also constantly writing and recording songs alone during this period. Perhaps the best example of his astonishingly prolific output during 1975-77 is the acoustic solo album he recorded on August 11, 1976 at Indigo Ranch Recording Studio in Malibu, California, built close to the site of a former Native American burial ground, which Young booked regularly to coincide with the full moon.

On the night in question, Young and producer David Briggs went up to Indigo from their beach home and, as Briggs put it, Young said "guess I'll just turn on the tap."[1] The following 33 minutes provide a fascinating insight into a great songwriter at the peak of his powers. Young intended to release the album shortly after it was recorded, but executives at Reprise dismissed it as a collection of demos, advising him to record the songs with a band instead. Unsurprisingly, Young declined to do so, and the album remained locked in the vaults for the next 40 years before finally appearing as the first of the *Neil Young Archives Special Release* series with the title 'Hitchhiker'. By this point, eight of the ten songs had been released on other studio albums during the intervening three decades, a testament to the formidable strength of the material.

---

1   McDonough, p.508

Hitchhiker begins with Young nonchalantly enquiring "you ready Briggs?" before seamlessly launching into a flawless rendition of 'Pocahontas', one of his most strange but beautiful songs, which would go on to appear in an almost identical version on 1979's classic *Rust Never Sleeps*. This and the other songs here that were first released on other Young albums will be covered in more detail in those chapters but suffice to say it sets a high bar for *Hitchhiker* which it by and large goes on to maintain.

Another early cut of an iconic track from *Rust Never Sleeps*, 'Powderfinger', arrives next, and in contrast to 'Pocahontas' it sounds markedly different to its more familiar version. With the Crazy Horse juggernaut absent, the song is stripped right back, transforming it from ragged rock into a haunting murder ballad with its desperate lyrics telling the tale of a young man who attempts to protect his family against an approaching gunboat. Although the sense of drama and urgency seeps through more powerfully in the full band *Rust Never Sleeps* recording, the *Hitchhiker* take is nevertheless a compelling alternative.

'Captain Kennedy', which emerged on 1980's *Hawks and Doves,* is, like 'Pocahontas', almost identical on *Hitchhiker* to the version released a few years later, in other words, pleasant but hardly essential. Much more interesting are 'Hawaii' and 'Give Me Strength' the two previously unreleased songs on the album. Young gives a stoned chuckle before beginning 'Hawaii', a cryptic story of an unnamed acquaintance asking for a loan "On an overdose of vitamins, trying to explain/Something that I already knew." Similar in style to some of the quirkier tracks on *Homegrown*, with a gently burbling melody and a slightly sinister undertow, it's an understated little gem of a song. 'Give Me Strength' is a more conventional acoustic ballad, with its maudlin tone mirroring the song's heartfelt reflections on the challenges of recovering from a failed relationship. When Young sings "The happier you fly/The sadder you fall…Give me strength to move along/Give me strength to realise she's gone" it's pretty clear who he's talking about. Although he was enjoying life again, the spectre of Carrie Snodgress still occasionally loomed large in Young's writing.

The second half of *Hitchhiker* begins with a third track that would end up on *Rust Never Sleeps* - the sweet but slight 'Ride My Llama', sounding very similar to its officially released version. In contrast, 'Hitchhiker' had to wait until 2010's incendiary *Le Noise* album for its debut, and sounds radically different here to the murky, feedback-drenched assault on the senses of its later incarnation. In many ways, the song's hallucinatory lyrics, describing Young's drug use during different periods of his life, feel a better fit for the woozy late night acoustic vibe here. Young himself begged to differ however, judging the song as unfinished when he revisited it for *Le Noise* despite having played it live several times, and adding an extra verse to bring the lyrics up to date.

'Campaigner', which was included on Young's 1977 *Decade* compilation but not on any other album before now, is one of Young's most explicitly political songs, focusing on an unnamed, disillusioned figure who has apparently been campaigning for the by then disgraced ex-U.S. president Richard Nixon. Lyrically complex, with an unconventional rhyme scheme, its slightly eerie refrain of "even Richard Nixon has got soul" can be read as either a sympathetic assessment of the beleaguered Republican or a sarcastic indictment of tribal political loyalties, depending on how the listener chooses to interpret it.

The last two tracks on *Hitchhiker* were the first to appear on other albums. 'Human Highway' and 'The Old Country Waltz' both seem stark and unadorned compared to their more fleshed out, country rock versions on 1978's *Comes A Time* and 1977's *American Stars n'Bars* respectively. 'Human Highway' feels a little ponderous without the joyous jangle and Nicolette Larsen's deliciously subtle harmony vocals, but Young's piano and harmonica-only rendition of 'The Old Country Waltz' brings out the song's elegant sadness, which is rather lost among the much richer instrumental textures on *American Stars n'Bars*.

Amidst the many captivating solo performances recorded at concert venues during his career, *Hitchhiker* stands alone as an example of Young playing new material live in the studio, alone and with no other musicians involved. His sheer natural talent can be appreciated here in its purest form, with some truly great songs flowing through his body to his guitar and voice with seemingly effortless ease. Even though most of the tracks ended up being heard on other records prior to its eventual release, *Hitchhiker* is still an absolutely essential addition to any Neil Young fan's collection.

⊙ TRACK LISTING   ◄◄ ❚❚ ►►❙

1. Pocahontas ··· 3:27
2. Powderfinger ··· 3:22
3. Captain Kennedy ·· 2:51
4. Hawaii ··· 2:38
5. Give Me Strength ·· 3:40
6. Ride My Llama ·· 1:50
7. Hitchhiker ·· 4:37
8. Campaigner ·· 4:19
9. Human Highway ·· 3:16
10. The Old Country Waltz ·· 3:37

Length: 33:44

Neil Young - Chrome Dreams

Released 11 August 2023 (Reprise)

🎧　🎧　🎧

*C*hrome Dreams, believed to have been originally planned for a 1977 release, had long been alleged to exist on a bootlegged acetate disc before Young finally ended the speculation in August 2023 by making the album officially available as part of his Special Release series. Named after a title shared in a purported Warner Bros memo that supposedly accompanied the bootleg disc (which Young archivist Joel Bernstein dismissed as a fake), *Chrome Dreams*, like *Homegrown*, steadily grew in mystique over the decades that followed, another great lost masterpiece from Young's most fertile creative period.

The track listing - a combination of songs to emerge later in 1977 on *American Stars 'n Bars* and on other subsequent records including 1979's *Rust Never Sleeps, 1989's Freedom* and even 1993's *MTV Unplugged* live album - undoubtedly features several Young classics, and is consistently strong throughout. However, experiencing *Chrome Dreams* as an official release over 45 years after it was recorded means it has a very different impact than it would have created had it emerged in 1977. With this chronology in mind, more detailed analysis of most of the individual tracks has been included in the reviews of the albums on which they first 'officially' appeared.

Chrome Dreams opens with 'Pocahontas', the same solo acoustic version taken from the 1976 Indigo Ranch Recording Studio session captured on *Hitchhiker,* and its stark, poetic beauty provides a mesmerising start to both albums. But the decision to put the seven minute long, meandering late night atmospherics of 'Will to Love' up second rather than later in the record - where it featured much more compellingly on *American Stars n'Bars* - means the melodic urgency created by 'Pocahontas' swiftly evaporates. Next up is 'Star of Bethlehem', the oldest track here dating back to the 1974 *Homegrown* sessions. It's one of Young's prettiest songs, but again, the tonal shift, this time from 'Will to Love's lo-fi crackle to gentle country-rock, is a little jarring. The same thing happens again when the epic 'Like A Hurricane' - another track destined to become one of Young's greatest after appearing on *American Stars n'Bars* - blasts like a force of nature from the speakers, with Crazy Horse now firmly in the saddle.

The album then briefly settles into a more consistent country rock style. 'Too Far Gone' didn't appear on record until a more muscular version was included on 1989's *Freedom,* but it dated back to 1975's *Zuma* sessions and the gentler recording here feels very much representative of Young's mid-70s acoustic songwriting. 'Hold Back The Tears', meanwhile, received the full country treatment on *American Stars n'Bars*, but it arguably works better in its more intimate setting on *Chrome Dreams*, a Young home demo shorn of its exuberant fiddle and female harmonies. But the contemplative vibe is rudely shattered by the same lumbering recording of 'Homegrown' that would go on to feature on *American Stars n'Bars*.

Two lesser known songs appear next - the *Hitchhiker* recording of the unexceptional 'Captain Kennedy' (also included on 1980's *Hawks and Doves*) and the more intriguing 'Stringman'. The latter, performed occasionally in Young's live sets from 1976 onwards including on his 1993 *MTV Unplugged* album, is an elegantly sad piano ballad that recalls some of his early '70s work like 'Journey Through The Past' or 'After The Goldrush'. 'Stringman's lyrics are some of Young's most poignant, depicting a lonely figure struggling to cope with the losses he's experienced: "On his shoulder rests a violin/For his head where chaos reigns/ But his heart can't find a simple way/To live with all those things." Recorded live in London with overdubs added a day later by Young at CBS Studios, it's perhaps the most interesting inclusion on *Chrome Dreams*, otherwise only available in the *Archives Volume II: 1972–1976* box set.

As well as 'Pocahontas', *Chrome Dreams* features earlier versions of two other pivotal *Rust Never Sleeps* tracks - 'Sedan Delivery' and 'Powderfinger'. The recording of 'Sedan Delivery' with Crazy Horse dates from 1975's *Zuma* sessions and is notably slower than the better known, punk-influenced 1978 version included on *Rust Never Sleeps*, while 'Powderfinger' is the same acoustic take included on *Hitchhiker.* The *Chrome Dreams* track listing ends with 'Look Out For My Love', originally recorded with Crazy Horse in 1976 and the sole song here to resurface on 1978's *Comes A Time*.

Even if it had been released back in 1977 as a new, fresh collection of often outstanding songs rather than the repackaging of familiar favourites it has inevitably become today, overall *Chrome Dreams* still lacks the cohesion of Young's very best albums. The track order feels unevenly sequenced, with the predominantly acoustic vibe suddenly lurching into the full band electric maelstrom of 'Like A Hurricane' or the messy stomps of 'Homegrown' *and* 'Sedan Delivery'.

Had it been more sympathetically curated, *Chrome Dreams* could have flowed better and ranked higher in the Young pantheon, even allowing for the passing of the years and drip feeding of its material inevitably diluting its power. Ultimately though, it feels like a collection randomly thrown together by an artist writing and recording songs at such an astonishingly productive rate he was struggling to focus his output. This remained evident when *American Stars n'Bars* was released later in 1977, with Young choosing to combine several tracks from *Chrome Dreams* with the country-flavoured outputs from a hastily convened series of sessions at Young's Broken Arrow ranch in April 1977.

There is a strong argument though that had Young released *Chrome Dreams* in 1977, one of his most iconic albums of all might never have seen the light of day, at least not in the form we recognise today. A *Rust Never Sleeps* without 'Pocahontas', 'Powderfinger' and 'Sedan Delivery' feels unimaginable, although Young being Young, who's to say he wouldn't have come up with three different songs that would have proven equally enduring?

⊙ TRACK LISTING　　　　　　　⏮ ⏸ ⏭

1. Pocahontas ·· 3:23
2. Will To Love ·· 7.11
3. Star Of Bethlehem ·· 2.43
4. Like A Hurricane ·· 8.24
5. Too Far Gone ··· 2.44
6. Hold Back The Tears ··· 5.15
7. Homegrown ·· 2.23
8. Captain Kennedy ··· 2.54
9. Stringman ·· 3.32
10. Sedan Delivery ··· 5.21
11. Powderfinger ··· 3.23
12. Look Out For My Love ··· 4.01

Length: 50:28

Neil Young - American Stars 'n Bars

Released 27 May 1977 (Reprise)

🎧 🎧 🎧

Even by his own formidable standards, the mid 1970s was a period of astonishing song writing productivity for Neil Young. As well as releasing official albums with impressive regularity, entire unreleased records were also left tantalisingly stored away in his vaults, discarded at the last minute due to differences of opinion with record company bosses or Young's own capricious tendency to change his mind at short notice. *Homegrown*, *Hitchhiker* and *Chrome Dreams*, all now finally revealed for the world to hear through the *Neil Young Archives* series, are three prominent examples of his haphazard approach during this time.

To some extent, *American Stars 'n Bars* sounds like what it is - a disparate, uneven collection of songs taken from a range of sessions spanning several years. This has led to the record being disregarded by some critics as by far the least essential of Young's stellar run of 1970s albums. While it's hard to dispute this position too vigorously, particularly bearing in mind the strength of the competition, in terms of the individual tracks, there are some first rate Young compositions here.

The first side of *American Stars 'n Bars* is taken from a series of sessions at Young's Broken Arrow ranch in April 1977. Young and Crazy Horse were joined by Ben Keith on pedal steel, fiddler Carole Mayedo and two outstanding backing vocalists: Linda Ronstadt, already one of the best-selling female artists in the U.S., and Nicolette Larson, an emerging young country singer who would go on to appear on several more Young albums. Their harmonies add real authenticity and emotional heft to the songs, most of which are unsurprisingly pitched firmly towards the country-rock end of Young's range.

'The Old Country Waltz', 'Hey Babe' and 'Hold Back The Tears' could all feasibly appear on albums by more explicitly country artists, with the latter in particular echoing the solo work of Gram Parsons. These may not number among Young's most iconic songs, but they are nevertheless beautifully played, with

Young himself sounding as relaxed as we've ever heard him and Mayedo's fiddle and Keith's pedal steel dovetailing wonderfully.

'Saddle Up The Palomino' - a relatively rare Young co-credit with Tim Drummond and Cajun singer-songwriter Bobby Charles - and 'Bite the Bullet' are more up-tempo, raucous performances, but neither really hits the spot. Crazy Horse's rumbling stomp doesn't sit easily with the former's country leanings, while on the latter Ronstadt and Larson's vocals, consistently excellent and well-judged elsewhere on the album, become distractingly loud as they strive to match the song's rock dynamics by abandoning delicacy in favour of an overpowering bellow.

The second half of *American Stars 'n Bars* begins with 'Star of Bethlehem', one of the standout tracks from the shelved *Homegrown* album (see earlier review), which although recorded back in 1974, has a similar country-rock style to most of the first half, with Emmylou Harris's backing vocals every bit as strong as Ronstadt and Larson's, and shares the same relaxed, homely vibe.

The remaining three tracks are an altogether different proposition. 'Will to Love' was a Young home recording, on which he overdubbed himself playing various instruments over the top of a simple acoustic melody, apparently all in one night. Young rates the song as one of his finest, perhaps in part because he enjoyed the process of making it so self-sufficiently, and it certainly has a sense of atmosphere - you can clearly hear the fireplace crackling in the background, and its intriguing to hear the different instruments fading in and out of the mix, sometimes almost imperceptibly. But the bare bones of the song itself are unremarkable, and the recording is so muffled it sometimes sounds like Young is underwater.

Unremarkable is not a word that comes to mind when describing 'Like A Hurricane,' which can be regarded as the third in the holy trinity of Young's most revered electric guitar epics, alongside 'Cortez The Killer' and 'On The Beach'. Indeed, 'Like A Hurricane' could almost be described as one eight minute long guitar solo, so completely does Old Black dominate the song. The incendiary impact is instant, with the searing opening chords setting up the tortured yet euphoric mood of the track masterfully. Young's lyrics - which apparently began with just the two lines "You are like a hurricane, there's calm in yer eye" written on an envelope - deal with an intense desire to recapture a fleeting encounter with a passionate, elusive woman. The towering chorus, built upon wave upon wave of coruscating, jagged spikes of melody and feedback, is rock music at its most elementally powerful.

Interestingly, the version of the song used here was originally recorded without vocals, as Young was recovering from an operation to remove nodes from his vocal chords and barely able to speak, let alone sing. As was so often the way, Young went with his gut, abandoning later attempts to re-record the song with vocals in favour of the earlier take he felt worked best musically, adding his voice recordings separately. His decision was undoubtedly vindicated. While some (this author included) may have a personal preference for Young and Crazy Horse's slower burning grooves like the aforementioned 'Cortez The Killer' and 'On The Beach', as a pure rock anthem, "Like A Hurricane' is perhaps their finest hour. To this day, it remains a regular highlight of Young's live shows, testament to its enduring status in his canon.

American Stars 'n Bars ends rather disappointingly with 'Homegrown', another track Young picked up from the cutting room floor of his aborted album of the same name before re-recording it with Crazy Horse. An unsophisticated, bluesy romp extolling the virtues of domestic marijuana production, it feels rather throwaway and flat when compared to the fireworks that preceded it.

Initial reviews of the album upon its release in May 1977 were generally positive, with the variety of musical styles identified as a strength rather than a weakness. Young himself seemed keen to highlight that *American Stars 'n Bars* wasn't a single planned, cohesive endeavour by listing the recording dates for each song. Once again, the album sold respectably well, reaching number 21 on the Billboard chart.

But with the benefit of hindsight and a present day understanding of the other completed projects Young had chosen to hold back during this period, the record feels like a series of mismatched ingredients thrown together a little carelessly into a slightly disappointing stew, with some tantalising morsels that could have been savoured even more had they been served up as part of a more thoughtful overall recipe.

⊙ TRACK LISTING   ⏮ ‖ ⏭

1. The Old Country Waltz ·· 2:58
2. Saddle Up the Palomino ·· 3:00
   (Neil Young, Tim Drummond, Bobby Charles)
3. Hey Babe ·· 3:35
4. Hold Back the Tears ··· 4:18
5. Bite the Bullet ·· 3:30
6. Star of Bethlehem ··· 2:42
7. Will to Love ·· 7:11
8. Like a Hurricane ·· 8:20
9. Homegrown ··· 2:20

Length: 37:54

Neil Young - Comes A Time

Released 21 October 1978 (Reprise)

If there were an award for Neil Young's most upbeat, instantly accessible record, then *Comes A Time* would probably be the leading contender. With its warm, lush musical textures, relaxed, contented mood and wealth of easy on the ear melodies, it is - with one or two exceptions - an absolute delight from start to finish.

Following the release of his monumental greatest hits compilation, *Decade*, it seemed Neil Young was ready to move on from the restless shape shifting of his past half dozen albums and fully embrace the polished, tasteful country rock style he had flirted with on *Harvest*, *Homegrown* and most recently on the first side of *American Stars n'Bars*.

While the finished album flows serenely, *Comes A Time*'s gestation was in fact far from straightforward. Originally planned as a Young acoustic solo album, Reprise - as they had done with *Hitchhiker* - suggested that he add rhythm tracks to beef up the sound, and on this occasion Young agreed. He took the recordings he had made at Florida's Triad studio up to Nashville, where he assembled a formidably large pool of musicians Young christened The Gone With The Wind Orchestra to overdub onto the originals, ranging from perennial collaborators Ben Keith and Tim Drummond to new faces including Cajun fiddler Rufus Thibodeaux, Alabaman keyboard player Spooner Oldham and the influential Oklahoman singer-songwriter JJ Cale, as well as a full string section and (due to double bookings) no fewer than eight acoustic guitarists (Young, when he found out, apparently said "let's just use 'em all anyway"). But perhaps the most significant presence was Nicolette Larson - by now Young's girlfriend - who provided pitch perfect harmonies that gelled instinctively with her lover's lead vocals.

Young took the Florida/Nashville material and added two Crazy Horse tracks - 'Look Out For My Love' and 'Lotta Love' (which became a top 10 hit single for Larson when she covered it shortly afterwards). Due to uncharacteristically restrained performances by Sampedro, Talbot and Molina, both fitted seamlessly alongside the mellower country rock songs, yet there were still further barriers to overcome before *Comes A Time* would finally be released in October 1978, despite the core content essentially being ready by the end of the previous year. After several changes to the title, mixing and artwork, a series of sequencing and pressing problems so infuriated Young that he bought back 200,000 copies of the record from Reprise to prevent them being circulated, and according to biographer Johnny Rogan, took them to his ranch and shot a single bullet through each case of albums with a rifle.[1]

The finished album was undoubtedly worth the wait. *Comes A Time* draws the listener in instantly with its two outstanding opening tracks. 'Goin' Back' begins with a gentle acoustic guitar strum, reprised throughout, before very gradually building momentum with the unobtrusive addition of the rhythm section and strings. It's all so beautifully graceful and unhurried it can be easy to overlook the occasionally bizarre and troubling lyrics, which describe mysterious creatures "driven to the mountains high/sunken in the cities deep/livin' in our sleep."

The title track is a sheer joy. Built around Thibodeaux's irresistibly catchy fiddle playing, which dovetails beautifully with the full string section during the song's instrumental passages, 'Comes A Time' is a paean to finding contentment amid life's challenges as time passes by, with Young and Larson's voices melting into one as they sing "Oh, this old world keeps spinnin' 'round/It's a wonder, tall trees ain't layin' down. Comes a time."

'Look Out For My Love', which focuses on the contrasting emotions of a troubled relationship, is another standout. As you'd expect with Crazy Horse on board, it's a little less polished than the Nashville tracks, but it succeeds by maintaining the restrained, predominantly acoustic vibe of the overall album (although they are allowed to cut loose a little towards the end of the song). One of Young's best vocal performances, the backing vocals of the Horse really shine too - notably when they amplify Young's anguished "was I hurt too bad" just over a minute into the song in a way that's simple but highly impactful. 'Lotta Love', the other Crazy Horse collaboration, follows a similar pattern, eschewing the band's usual fireworks for a more subtle, bittersweet groove, anchored by Sampedro's lolloping barroom piano. On 'Lotta Love,' we find Young tentatively searching for a new partner, with lyrics like "So if you look in my direction/and we don't see eye

---

1   Johnny Rogan, Neil Young Zero to Sixty (2000)

to eye/my heart needs protection/and so do I" illustrating the vulnerability he felt after his breakup with Carrie.

'Peace Of Mind' is as blissfully calm as its title suggests, with Young's voice gliding over elegantly sweeping strings and hypnotic drum rolls, although the lyrics tell a slightly different story of trying to come to terms with the implications of leaving a partner. 'Human Highway' had been written a few years earlier and was originally planned as title track for CSN&Y's abandoned follow up to *Déjà Vu*. With Larson's gorgeous harmonies more than adequately standing in for Crosby, Still and Nash and a delightful bubbling brook of a melody flecked with banjo and steel guitar, it's another album highlight. 'Already One' sounds utterly timeless, with the mature, reflective beauty that Young would later recapture so charmingly on 1992's superb *Harvest Moon* album. It's also one of the most poignant songs Young had written to this point, acknowledging that while he and Carrie were no longer romantically involved, their shared love for their child Zeke meant they retained an important, permanent bond: "'Cause we're already one/Our little son won't let us forget."

After a pretty stellar first seven tracks, at this point in proceedings *Comes A Time* is arguably as consistent an album as Young has ever made, but unfortunately it starts to flag alarmingly in its latter stages. 'Field of Opportunity' lazily rehashes the title track's fiddle riff as Young indulges in a series of unconvincing farming metaphors, delivered in a gratingly mannered country drawl which he would revisit more extensively on 1985's *Old Ways*. 'Motorcycle Mama' is even worse, a tuneless, clodhopping dirge on which Young invites the two wheeled female in question to "lay your big spike down." It's right up there as one of Young's very worst songs, but thankfully, the album recovers its wits at the end with an elegant, wistful cover of Canadian folk duo Ian and Sylvia's 1963 single 'Four Strong Winds', which Young had loved since his teens.

Perhaps unsurprisingly given the high quality but relatively conventional and unchallenging nature of its songs compared to most of his mid-1970s work, *Comes A Time* became Young's best-selling album since *Harvest*, making the top 10 of the U.S. charts. Young himself was unimpressed by his newly restored popularity. "I like it when people enjoy what I'm doing, but if they don't I also like it. I sometimes like aggravating people with what I do," he said.[2] He knew he could make records in the style of *Harvest* and *Comes A Time* over and over again but remained determined to resist the temptation. And the tumultuous arrival of punk, the most transformational, confrontational musical style to emerge for many, many years, gave Young the ideal inspiration to change direction once again.

---

2 Rogan, p.429

⊙ TRACK LISTING ⏮ ⏸ ⏭

Length: 37:15

Neil Young - Rust Never Sleeps

Released 22 June 1979 (Reprise Records)

🎧   🎧   🎧

The 18-month period between the completion of the *Comes A Time* sessions and the release of *Rust Never Sleeps* was hugely significant for Neil Young both personally and musically.

After writing about his hopes of finding new romance on 'Lotta Love' and briefly finding it with Nicolette Larson, 1978 saw the beginning of the third and at this stage the longest of the key relationships in Young's life, following first wife Susan Acevedo and Carrie Snodgress. Pegi Morton was a waitress in a couple of California hangouts he frequented and after knowing each other for a while before Neil made his move, their romance developed at whirlwind speed, and they were married in August 1978. Son Ben was born in November of that year with severe cerebral palsy, meaning he would be quadriplegic and unable to speak. With first son Zeke, born to a different mother, also having the condition, Young understandably questioned whether there was some connection to him personally, only to be reassured that it was a fluke occurrence.

During the delays to the release of *Comes A Time*, Young became increasingly intrigued by the emergence of punk rock and new wave. While working on second movie *Human Highway* (which would not end up seeing the light of day until 1982), Young and actor friend Dean Stockwell attended a concert by Ohio art rockers Devo, whose spiky, anarchic songs and stage presence greatly impressed Young. They ended up joining him on stage at a show at San Francisco punk venue Mabuhay Gardens, where Young told them that if they couldn't remember the words, they should just make them up instead. This resulted in the immortal line "it's better to burn out because rust never sleeps" being uttered during a performance of Young's new song 'My, My, Hey Hey (Out of the Blue)' - the inspiration for the classic album that was to follow.

There is probably no single record that Neil Young has made that better demonstrates his phenomenal musical versatility than *Rust Never Sleeps*. Similar to *American Stars n'Bars*, it is a record divided into two distinct sides with different recording dates, personnel and styles. But while the earlier album feels uneven both in terms of song writing quality and overall cohesiveness, *Rust Never Sleeps'* straight down the line split between acoustic and electric halves - the latter with Crazy Horse - together with a higher proportion of great songs, mean it's a far greater achievement.

Three of the five acoustic tracks - 'My, My, Hey Hey (Out of the Blue),' 'Thrasher' and 'Ride My Llama' were recorded at The Boarding House, San Francisco between May 24 and May 28, 1978, where Young performed a series of solo gigs. 'Pocahontas' was the 1976 *Hitchhiker* version with additional overdubs, while 'Sail Away' was taken from the *Comes A Time* sessions, with Nicolette Larson on backing vocals, Karl T. Himmel on drums and Joe Talbot on bass.

Rust Never Sleeps begins with 'My, My, Hey Hey (Out of the Blue)', which - as with the *Tonight's The Night* title track - appears in two different versions with slightly amended titles and lyrics bookending the album. My, My, Hey Hey (Out of the Blue)' was jointly credited to Jack Blackburn, whom Young briefly performed with in the band the Ducks in a series of gigs in Santa Cruz during the summer of 1977. The two shared ideas on each other's new material during this time, leading to Blackburn's co-credit here.

One of Young's defining songs, the acoustic 'My, My, Hey Hey (Out of the Blue)' is starkly beautiful, with Young's urgent, mournful guitar and harmonica playing framing perhaps his most quotable lyric of all: "It's better to burn out than to fade away." This line became legendary when Kurt Cobain quoted it in his suicide note in 1994, but despite some suggestions that the words were intended to glorify rock and roll suicide, Young actually wrote the song about the challenges of staying artistically relevant as a musician as your career went on.

Young explores similar themes on 'Thrasher,' which is as musically gorgeous as it is lyrically complex. Boasting one of his very prettiest melodies, accompanied by chiming cascades of guitar, the song employs a range of farming and geological references to emphasise the impact of the passing of time. Large sections of the song, for example the lines "They were lost in rock formations/Or became park bench mutations... So I got bored and left them there/They were just dead weight to me" focus on Young's frustration with Crosby, Still and Nash, who he felt were unwilling to take any risks artistically and had therefore become "lost in crystal canyons."

'Ride My Llama,' another song first recorded in the 1976 *Hitchhiker* session, is a quirky little song that sees the narrator meet a Martian before travelling from Peru to Texas onboard the trusty steed referred to in the title, which feels rather insubstantial compared to the lofty heights of brilliance scaled around it. 'Pocahontas', meanwhile, is another example of Young's song writing at its absolute zenith. Also dating back to 1976, the song's subject matter is dazzlingly ambitious, leaping between different points in history to first tell the story of the massacre of a tribe of Native Americans by early New World settlers before Marlon Brando joins Young and Pocahontas round a campfire for the final verse. The images in the song - whether it be the elegantly sad "Paddles cut the water/In a long and hurried flight" or the more brutal "they killed us in our tepee/and they cut our women down/they might have left some babies/cryin' on the ground" are among the most vivid and arresting in all Young's work. The hypnotic rhythm of 'Pocahontas,' together with Young's heart wrenching vocal, combine to make this track pretty much the complete package.

Side one of *Rust Never Sleeps* ends with 'Sail Away', which although slightly fuller in sound than the previous four songs with the presence of other musicians, doesn't feel out of place due to the gently swaying accompaniment and lyrics that also touch on Native American life and the concept of time shift, opening with "I could live inside a tepee/I could die In penthouse thirty-five." But like 'Ride My Llama', the song is pleasant rather than exceptional.

The electric side of the record was made up of four performances from Young's autumn 1978 tour with Crazy Horse, which proved to be one of the most memorable of his entire career, spawning both a concert film (also entitled *Rust Never Sleeps*) and a live album (*Live Rust*). Just a few weeks before the tour was due to start, Young came up with the bizarre idea of dressing his roadies as 'Road Eyes' - imaginary creatures in flowing robes with glowing red eyes similar to the Jawas made famous by the recent *Star Wars* film. This elaborate gimmick, together with the use of an occasionally problematic pioneering new wireless microphone system, and the distribution of 'Rust-O-Vision' cardboard glasses to the audience (which Young had mischievously claimed would enable certain lucky wearers to "see the rust fall off" the band during certain performances) all combined to give the shows a somewhat chaotic, surreal air - but the shows saw Young and the Horse at the peak of their powers.

'Powderfinger' kicks off the electric side of *Rust Never Sleeps* in exhilarating fashion. Voted Young's best ever song by *Rolling Stone* magazine in 2021, it is a distillation of many of his finest writing qualities. It tells the story of a boat of armed men coming up the river "who don't look like they're here to deliver the mail," from the perspective of a 22 year old left alone to defend his family because "Daddy's gone, my brother's out huntin' in the mountains". It is almost cinematic in scope, while at the same examining the emotions of one individual as he realises his fate: "Then I saw black and my face flash in the sky." The interplay between Young and Crazy Horse is superb, instinctively complementing the dramatic tension of the lyrics, with a guitar solo towards the end that's so coruscating it threatens to leave a trail of smoke in its wake.

'Welfare Mothers' and 'Sedan Delivery' both pale in comparison as exemplars of Young's songcraft but do effectively showcase the sheer rock energy and muscularity of Crazy Horse, who - encouraged by Young - were now playing louder than ever. However, the former track's lyrics - "welfare mothers make better lovers/hard to believe that love is free now" are probably not Young's finest attempt at social commentary.

Rust Never Sleeps ends with the cacophonous 'Hey Hey, My My (Into the Black)' which provides a compelling, distorted mirror image of the near-identical 'My, My, Hey Hey (Out of the Blue).' It begins with a monstrous guitar riff, heavier and more feedback drenched than any yet played by Young and captures the raw aggression of punk better than any thirtysomething veteran of 1960s California had any right to do. With some subtle lyrical shifts - the removal of the line "it's better to burn out than to fade away" and questioning "is this the story of Johnny Rotten?" Young casts doubt on the 'boom and bust' message of the earlier version, instead suggesting defiant survival is possible. More than any other of his songs, 'Hey Hey, My My (Into the Black)' made Young an icon and key influence for a host of noise-pop and grunge bands in the late 1980s and early 1990s.

⊙ TRACK LISTING   ⏮ ⏸ ⏭

1. My My, Hey Hey (Out of the Blue) (Neil Young, Jeff Blackburn) ········· 3:45
2. Thrasher ·· 5:38
3. Ride My Llama ·· 2:29
4. Pocahontas ·· 3:22
5. Sail Away ··· 3:46
6. Powderfinger ·· 5:30
7. Welfare Mothers ·· 3:48
8. Sedan Delivery ·· 4:40
9. Hey Hey, My My (Into the Black) ······································· 5:18

Length: 38:16

Timeline - The Classic Era (1968–79)

🎧 🎧 🎧

1969

January - March: Young spends the first three months of the year in the studio with his new backing band, Crazy Horse, recording *Everybody Knows This Is Nowhere*, his follow-up to *Neil Young*.

12 February - 22 June: A series of club residences with Crazy Horse take place.

14 May: Second album and first Young and Crazy Horse collaboration *Everybody Knows This Is Nowhere* released.

July: Young joins forces with David Crosby, Stephen Stills and Graham Nash to form Crosby, Stills, Nash & Young (CSN&Y), taking part in a series of live dates across the U.S. over the remainder of the year, including the Woodstock Festival on 18 August.

August - December: Young works with CSN&Y on recording their *Deja Vu* album while simultaneously beginning sessions for his own *After The Goldrush* album.

1970

6-11 January: Young tours with CSN&Y in Europe.

25 February - 28 March: Tour with Crazy Horse in the U.S.

11 March: CSN&Y's *Deja Vu* album released.

12 May - 9 July: Tour of the U.S. with CSN&Y.

19 September: Young's third album, *After The Goldrush*, released.

September: Young buys the Broken Arrow ranch in La Honda, California.

9 October: Young's wife Susan files for divorce. In December, Young meets his new partner, the actress Carrie Snodgress.

30 November - 5 December: Short solo acoustic tour.

1971

6 January - 1 February: Young's *Journey Through The Past* solo tour of the U.S. and Canada.

February: Begins recording *Harvest* with the Stray Gators.

1972

17 January: Young's single 'Heart of Gold' released. It goes on to be his only U.S. number one.

1 February: *Harvest* released; goes on to top both the U.S. and U.K. album charts.

8 September: Carrie Snodgress gives birth to her and Young's son Zeke.

18 November: Crazy Horse guitarist Danny Whitten dies from a combination of valium and alcohol.

1973

5 January - 3 April: Young's *Time Fades Away* tour with the Stray Gators takes place.

8 April: Young's *Journey Through The Past* movie opens at the U.S. Film Festival in Dallas. Young's soundtrack had already been released the previous November.

August - September: The *Tonight's The Night* album is recorded with Young's new band The Santa Monica Flyers.

11 August - 23 November: The unreleased material from the *Tonight's The Night* sessions is played on the band's tour of the U.S., Canada and U.K.

15 October: *Time Fades Away* album, featuring live performances from the recent tour, is released.

1974

April: Young finishes recording his *On The Beach* album.

June: Begins work on *Zuma*, with guitarist Frank 'Poncho' Sampedro joining Crazy Horse for the first time.

19 July: *On The Beach* album released.

November - January 1975: *Homegrown* album sessions.

Autumn 1974: Young separates from Carrie Snodgress, and Zeke Young is diagnosed with mild cerebral palsy.

1975

20 June: *Tonight's The Night* released, almost two years after it was recorded.

10 November: *Zuma* released. A tour of small venues across Northern California, known as the Rolling Zuma Revue, follows between 7 - 21 December.

1976

3 March - 2 April: Tour of Europe and Japan with Crazy Horse.

23 June - 20 July: Tours the U.S. with Stephen Stills as the Stills-Young band. The tour is curtailed when Young unexpectedly pulls out with several dates still remaining. The duo's *Long May You Run* album is released on 20 September.

1 - 24 November: U.S. tour with Crazy Horse

1977

27 May: *American Stars 'n Bars* album released.

15 July - 2 September: Plays a series of small venues in Santa Cruz alongside local band The Ducks.

28 October: Three disc career to date retrospective *Decade* released.

1978

February: Following a brief relationship with backing vocalist Nicolette Larson, Young begins dating Pegi Morton, a waitress at a diner near his Broken Arrow ranch.

24-28 May: Young plays 10 shows - two per night - at the Boarding House, San Francisco, guesting with avant-garde rock group Devo at the nearby Mabuhay Gardens club after one gig.

2 August: Young marries Pegi Morton at his Malibu home.

16 September - 24 October: *Rust Never Sleeps* U.S. tour with Crazy Horse.

28 October: *Comes A Time* album released.

28 November: Birth of Neil and Pegi's first child, Ben. Shortly afterwards, Ben is diagnosed with a severe form of cerebral palsy.

1979

22 June: *Rust Never Sleeps* album released.

14 November: Release of *Live Rust* double album. The concert movie *Rust Never Sleeps*, directed by Young, is also released that day.

December: Young is named 'Artist of the Decade' by the Village Voice newspaper.

PART 3

The Wilderness Years
(1980-1988)

Neil Young - Hawks and Doves

Released 29 October 1980 (Reprise Records)

🎧 🎧 🎧

With *Rust Never Sleeps,* Neil Young had ended the 1970s on a high, with one of the most successful, critically acclaimed records of his career. With its unpolished urgency, energy and huge slabs of guitar noise, it also ensured that unlike most of his peers, he remained relevant in a musical world turned upside down by punk. Yet in retrospect, *Rust Never Sleeps* also marked the end of what had been a decade-long winning streak of albums dating back to 1969's *Everybody Knows This Is Nowhere.* His first release of the 1980s, *Hawks and Doves,* now has to be seen as the beginning of a new, less triumphant phase of Young's career, which would last almost as long as the classic era that preceded it.

Before coming down too hard on *Hawks and Doves*, it's important to understand the magnitude of the personal challenges Young was experiencing during 1980-81. It had become increasingly clear to him and Pegi that little Ben Young was going to require very extensive therapy and support for his cerebral palsy, which was more complex and severe than his elder half-brother Zeke's, leaving him confined to a wheelchair and unable to speak. A programme developed by Philadelphia's Institute for the Achievement of Human Potential meant Young, Pegi and additional friends and volunteers were required to spend up to 14 hours a day, seven days a week working with Ben, for a total period of 18 months. This daunting commitment, together with Pegi needing brain surgery to treat an arteriovenous malformation in the head area - which she thankfully made a full recovery from - meant Young's focus on his music during this period of his life was understandably not a priority.

Similar to *American Stars n'Bars*, the other Young album it most closely resembles, *Hawks & Doves'* two sides are very separate entities. Side one is a series of acoustic recordings dating from Young's rich seam of creativity between 1974 and 1977, while side two's prosaic country-rock is the output of sessions that took place specifically for the album in early 1980, featuring a band of musicians mostly made up of established wingmen including Ben Keith on pedal steel, Tim Drummond on bass and fiddler Rufus Thibodeaux.

The first side of *Hawks & Doves* is the stronger of the two. It opens with 'Little Wing', taken from 1975's at this stage unreleased *Homegrown* album. It's a delicately pretty, sparse ballad which, although a good song, feels a strangely understated choice to kick off an album and sits much more comfortably as one of the later tracks on *Homegrown*. Next up is 'The Old Homestead', probably the highlight of the record. Also dating from the *Homegrown* sessions, it's a quiet, languid, strangely hypnotic song, with a slightly sinister undercurrent amplified by the use of a ghostly hand saw that occasionally hovers in the background. The lyrics are intriguing and seem to focus on Young's own musical career. It begins with the lines "Up and down the old homestead/the naked rider gallops through his head/and although the moon isn't full/he still feels the pull" which references his restless creativity, as well as his preference for recording during a full moon. The later depiction of three 'prehistoric birds' and the line "Why do you ride that crazy horse? Inquires the shadow with little remorse" appear to be clear references to Crosby, Stills and Nash, and the frustration some people around Young - 'the naked rider' - felt about his choice to work with Crazy Horse rather than concentrate on much more lucrative ventures with his former supergroup partners.

'Lost in Space' and 'Captain Kennedy', the last two of the four songs on the first side of *Hawks & Doves,* both date from 1977. 'Lost in Space' is one of the oddest songs in Young's catalogue, a winsome, childlike lullaby which switches setting between outer space and the ocean, its true meaning impenetrable. 'Captain Kennedy' was originally intended for the aborted *Chrome Dreams* album. A much more conventional narrative than the previous three songs, with an almost bluegrass feel to the accompanying guitar playing, it tells the story of a U.S. marine heading to war "thinking about my family and what it was for" while reflecting on the life of his father, a World War 2 captain.

So far, *Hawks and Doves* has been pleasant, if hardly vintage Young, but its second side is by some distance the worst music Young had released as a solo artist up to this point. A brash, charmless and clumsy bar room brawl of songs, they chug along inanely, with Thibodeax's fiddle, so joyous on *Comes A Time*, now a grating irritant. 'Stayin' Power' is a plodding, cliche-ridden homage to enduring love, while 'Coastline' is vapid honky-tonk and 'Union Man' is a witless satire targeting the American Federation of Musicians, who had attracted Young's ire for reasons that remain a mystery.

The last two tracks see Young stepping into political and social commentary and can be interpreted as signalling his unexpected shift to supporting the Republican party, about to regain the presidency through the charismatic former actor Ronald Reagan. On 'Comin' Apart At Every Nail' he bemoans the plight of the working man in modern America (then led by Democrat Jimmy Carter) "It's awful hard to find a job/on one side the government, the other the mob." But on the closing title track, Young is suddenly "proud to be living in the U.S.A," painting a picture of "people here down on their knees and prayin'/hawks and doves are circlin' in the rain/got rock and roll, got country music playin'/if you hate us, you just don't know what you're sayin'". It's open to debate whether the song is meant to be taken as an endorsement of the values of traditional Republican voters or is simply mocking redneck patriots in the style of 'Southern Man' or 'Alabama'. What is beyond doubt is that Young expressed regular support for Reagan and his policies during the coming years, as well as making other comments very much at odds with his earlier, much more liberal voice.

With its short length, minimal promotion, the throwaway feel of most of the songs and a bizarre running order, it's little surprise that *Hawks and Doves* was Young's poorest performing album for over a decade, peaking at number 30 in the U.S. chart. While little tweaks here and there - for example reversing the order of the sides with the more upbeat tracks up first, may have marginally improved matters, ultimately *Hawks and Doves* is what it is - an uninspired stopgap, released during a time of huge family pressures, that remains one of Neil Young's most underwhelming records.

⏵ TRACK LISTING   ⏮ ⏸ ⏭

1. Little Wing 2:10
2. The Old Homestead 7:38
3. Lost in Space 4:13
4. Captain Kennedy 2:50
5. Stayin' Power 2:17
6. Coastline 2:24
7. Union Man 2:08
8. Comin' Apart at Every Nail 2:33
9. Hawks & Doves 3:27

Length: 29:47

Neil Young - Re.ac.tor

Released 2 November 1981 (Reprise Records)

🎧　🎧　🎧

During the last few months of 1980 and into 1981, Neil Young was spending most of his time at home consumed with son Ben's 18 month therapy programme designed by Philadelphia's Institute for the Achievement of Human Potential, meaning he had extremely limited opportunity to work on his music.

Typically for Young though, despite the huge demands upon him personally, he managed to find sufficient bandwidth to work on an album of new material with Crazy Horse, recorded at Modern Recorders, Redwood City, California (Young's ranch) and released in November 1981 with the title *Re.ac.tor*. Perhaps the most uncompromisingly loud and brutish rock record that Young and Crazy Horse ever made together, its forceful, repetitive rhythms perhaps reflected the relentlessly arduous daily routine Young and his family were experiencing during this period. At times a tough listen with its sense of emotional detachment and lack of trademark melodies, *Re.ac.tor* focuses instead on a simple driving intensity. Its recording was frequently frustrating for Crazy Horse, used to far greater engagement and focus from Young, with Ralph Molina pithily describing the album as "a turkey. A one-legged turkey."[1]

Re.ac.tor kicks off with 'Opera Star', the tale of a rock musician who loses his girlfriend to an opera aficionado. Built around a swashbuckling but soulless boogie riff that sounds more like ZZ Top than Crazy Horse, with some equally uncharacteristically jaunty backing vocals, it feels like a completely different band to the unpredictable force of nature that backed Young on Everybody *Knows This Is Nowhere*, *Zuma* and *Rust Never Sleeps*.

'Surfer Joe and Moe The Sleaze' feels a little more like having the old Horse back in the saddle, with Young a more vibrant voice, soaring harmonies and some vigorous lead guitar playing. In contrast, 'T-Bone' is nine minutes of Young and his band on autopilot, endlessly repeating the bone-headed line "Got mashed potatoes/

---

1 McDonough, p.549

Ain't got no T-bone" above a cacophony of electric guitar and clunking percussion. Young himself identified this track as his favourite from *Re.ac.tor,* as he felt it musically mirrored the grinding monotony of his personal life at the time, but for the average listener it's a hard, deafening slog. Next up is 'Get Back On It', an uninspiring slice of honky-tonk that provides an unwelcome foretaste of 1983's egregious rockabilly folly *Everybody's Rockin'*.

'Southern Pacific' is markedly better. The lyrics tell the story of a railway worker, Casey Jones, who loses his sense of purpose after being forced to retire from his job at 65: "I put in my time/I put in my time/Now I'm left to roll/Down the long decline." With an infectious, rolling rhythm from Crazy Horse and a (by the standards of this album at least) breezily catchy melody, it's about as accessible as *Re.ac.tor* gets. Unfortunately, the bar drops low again immediately with the cartoonish opening guitar riff and boorish ranting of 'Motor City' which extols the virtues of American cars while simultaneously deriding the Japanese competition.

The transport theme continues with the spiky garage rock of 'Rapid Transit', one of the most peculiar vocal performances of Young's career with its combination of garbled single line utterances and what appear to be car noises. Like 'Motor City', it's a song with very little to recommend it.

Re.ac.tor ends with the assault on the senses that is 'Shots', a scarily intense onslaught of squalling heavy rock guitars, frenetic military beats and unnerving gunshot and plane noises. The song's lyrics are a notable departure from the unsophisticated, even banal subject matter of most of the tracks that preceded it, with the ominous single word introductions ("Children," "Machines", "Men" etc) followed by streams of apocalyptic imagery. Originally performed live and acoustic back in 1978, this new, beefed up version also saw Young experimenting with a new computerised synthesiser, the Synclavier, giving a first hint of the bold new direction he would take his music in on the forthcoming *Trans*. While *Re.ac.tor* was hardly vintage Young and Crazy Horse, it would feel comfortably mainstream compared to what was coming next.

⊙ TRACK LISTING ⏮ ⏸ ⏭

1. Opera Star ⋯⋯⋯⋯⋯⋯⋯⋯⋯⋯⋯⋯⋯⋯⋯⋯⋯⋯⋯⋯⋯⋯⋯⋯⋯⋯⋯⋯⋯⋯⋯ 3:31
2. Surfer Joe and Moe the Sleaze ⋯⋯⋯⋯⋯⋯⋯⋯⋯⋯⋯⋯⋯⋯⋯⋯ 4:15
3. T-Bone ⋯⋯⋯⋯⋯⋯⋯⋯⋯⋯⋯⋯⋯⋯⋯⋯⋯⋯⋯⋯⋯⋯⋯⋯⋯⋯⋯⋯⋯⋯⋯⋯ 9:10
4. Get Back on It ⋯⋯⋯⋯⋯⋯⋯⋯⋯⋯⋯⋯⋯⋯⋯⋯⋯⋯⋯⋯⋯⋯⋯⋯⋯⋯ 2:14
5. Southern Pacific ⋯⋯⋯⋯⋯⋯⋯⋯⋯⋯⋯⋯⋯⋯⋯⋯⋯⋯⋯⋯⋯⋯⋯⋯ 4:07
6. Motor City ⋯⋯⋯⋯⋯⋯⋯⋯⋯⋯⋯⋯⋯⋯⋯⋯⋯⋯⋯⋯⋯⋯⋯⋯⋯⋯⋯⋯ 3:11
7. Rapid Transit ⋯⋯⋯⋯⋯⋯⋯⋯⋯⋯⋯⋯⋯⋯⋯⋯⋯⋯⋯⋯⋯⋯⋯⋯⋯⋯ 4:35
8. Shots ⋯⋯⋯⋯⋯⋯⋯⋯⋯⋯⋯⋯⋯⋯⋯⋯⋯⋯⋯⋯⋯⋯⋯⋯⋯⋯⋯⋯⋯⋯⋯ 7:42

Length: 38.45

Neil Young - Trans

Released 10 January 1983 (Geffen)

When things are said and written about Neil Young's perceived loss of direction during the 1980s, more often than not *Trans* is the album identified as epitomising his wayward artistic choices in this period. It was also the first album of his mostly unhappy six year period at Geffen, following his decision to leave Reprise after spending his entire solo career to date with the same label.

Young had been frustrated by the reception and sales of *Hawks and Doves* and *Re.ac.tor*, so eager to try a refreshed approach after so many years with Reprise, he and manager Elliot Roberts signed with Geffen in favour of a more lucrative offer from RCA, attracted by David Geffen's promise of complete artistic control. Around the same time that the Geffen deal was being finalised, Young's son Ben's hugely time-consuming therapy programme through the Institute for the Achievement of Human Potential was replaced by a more manageable course focusing on mental and communicative skills rather than extensive physical activity, meaning Young was now able to focus more on his music again.

With the use of a synthesiser on 'Shots,' *Re.ac.tor's* final track, Young had given the first indications of perhaps his most radical musical shift yet. He invested in a wider range of electronic equipment, including a vocoder, and continued recording songs at his La Honda ranch with a slightly bemused but still game Crazy Horse using the new technology now at his disposal. But once he was no longer so constrained by his son's therapy programme, Young relocated the sessions to Hawaii and - as had been so often the case before - began to work on a different album idea entirely, a collection of less challenging acoustic material provisionally entitled *Island In The Sun*. After an eventful 1982 involving his first tour in three years with a backing group dubbed the Trans Band, which included his old Canada and Buffalo Springfield friend Bruce Palmer, and the disappointment of his long-awaited film *Human Highway* failing to secure a distribution deal, the new Young album that finally emerged in January 1983 ended up being a combination of the electronic compositions and Hawaiian songs, but with the former style very much in the ascendancy. As well as Crazy Horse, Palmer and the omnipresent Ben Keith, Nils Lofgren also joined the supporting musicians, playing his usual impressive range of instruments.

Just how bold and divisive a record *Trans* would be isn't immediately apparent on the opening track 'Little Thing Called Love', a breezily inconsequential slice of straightforward light rock from the *Island In The Sun* sessions that, some nice harmonies apart, is one of Young's most forgettable songs. It leaves the listener completely unprepared for what comes next: the five minutes plus journey to a brave new world of futuristic synthesisers and distorted robotic voices that is 'Computer Age.' A depiction of a mechanised, science-fiction world clearly inspired by the pioneering electronic music of Kraftwerk, it is a surprisingly successful first attempt by Young to capture the rhythms and textures of a genre wildly different from anything he had done before; atmospheric, subtly funky and with organic instruments effectively integrated into the song towards the end.

Unfortunately, 'Computer Age' is followed by the execrable 'We R In Control', which abruptly shatters the initial promise of Young's electronic experiment. A lumbering, tuneless, migraine-inducing mess of monotonous guitar riffs and portentous vocoder pronouncements, its dystopian vision of a society ruled by machines is considerably less terrifying than the prospect of having to hear the song for a second time. 'Transformer Man' is thankfully much better, even though the electronic treatment of Young's falsetto is piercingly high at times. Exploring how technology enabled the severely disabled Ben Young to communicate with the world, its sweetly melodic timbre and heartfelt lyrics give the song an emotional resonance that the rest of *Trans* lacks. When Young sings "Every morning when I look in your eyes/I feel electrified by you" the connection between father and son is palpable. The first half of *Trans* ends with 'Computer Cowboy (AKA Syscrusher)', a pounding, ominous-sounding futuristic cowboy story, during which the occasional clip clop of a horse's hooves can be heard among the frenetic flurries of guitar and vocoder.

The second of the Hawaiian songs, 'Hold On To Your Love' is a wistfully pretty, uncomplicated paean to the benefits of sticking with a relationship through hard times, similar in feel to 'Little Thing Called Love', although markedly superior. It's a low key, undemanding start to the second side of *Trans*, but the return of the synthesisers and vocoders isn't delayed long. 'Sample and Hold' is another no holds barred journey into a future world, this time a portrayal of a robot dating agency. As with much of *Trans*, it's so unrecognisable from anything else in Young's canon it will anathema to many fans, but it's hard not be impressed by the uncompromising shift to Krautrock rhythms and mechanical vocals, which wouldn't sound out of place on a Daft Punk record.

Young then springs a surprise with a new version of Buffalo Springfield favourite 'Mr Soul', which is given a full *Trans* makeover and is - by and large - none the worse for it, with the electronically manipulated backwards guitar especially effective. The album ends with the sprawling, eight minutes plus 'Like An Inca', the final and most intriguing remnant of the Hawaiian *Island In The Sun* project. With its length and lyrics revisiting his earlier fascination with the ancient empires of the Aztecs and Incas, there are some similarities to 'Cortez The Killer', but tonally 'Like An Inca' is very different, with its upbeat groove, rolling congas and soaring chorus a million miles from the smouldering tension of Young's *Zuma* classic.

Despite sounding like nothing else Young had ever released, *Trans* sold relatively respectably, making the U.S. top 20 and receiving some positive reviews while at the same time baffling and enraging many diehards - a divisive status the album retains to this day. What no one knew at the time was that the album's use of technology - in particular the vocoder - was partially inspired by Young's attempts to communicate with his son. At this point, Ben's condition, the programme in place to treat it and the impact this had on his parents' lives was not in the public domain, as Young had understandably chosen to keep the details private. Knowing the truth today, it is possible to view Trans through a very different lens, and while it is unlikely to ever be the album of choice for the vast majority of Young aficionados, for all its flaws it is nevertheless a work of commendable courage and no little ingenuity.

⊙ TRACK LISTING   ◄◄ ❚❚ ►►◄

1. Little Thing Called Love ··· 3:13
2. Computer Age ··· 5:24
3. We R in Control ·· 3:31
4. Transformer Man ·· 3:23
5. Computer Cowboy (AKA Syscrusher)······························· 4:13
6. Hold On to Your Love ·· 3:28
7. Sample and Hold ··· 5:09
8. Mr. Soul ··· 3:19
9. Like an Inca ·· 8:08

Length: 39:48

Neil Young and the Shocking Pinks - Everybody's Rockin'

Released 1 August 1983 (Geffen)

After his bold journey into the future of music on the synthesiser-dominated *Trans*, Neil Young's next move was predictably unpredictable. Released less than eight months later, *Everybody's Rockin'* saw him travelling in a polar opposite direction, revisiting the early years of rock and roll on a collection of 1950s covers and original compositions performed in the same throwback style.

The reasons behind Young's latest shift were linked to his already challenging relations with his new label, Geffen. Young had originally planned to follow up *Trans* with another acoustic album similar to *Harvest* or *Comes A Time,* and the results of his 1983 Nashville sessions, entitled *Old Ways*, were presented to Geffen but rejected as "too country" - a genre Young's bosses felt was completely unfashionable. They claimed to want a "more rock and roll album" and Young - furious at what he felt was unreasonable interference in the artistic process - duly obliged in his own inimitable way.

Young - who appeared on the album cover sporting a vile pink suit and tie and quiff while clutching a vintage Gretsch guitar - pulled together a backing band featuring regular collaborators Karl T.Himmel (drums), Tim Drummond (upright bass) and Ben Keith (bizarrely asked to play lead guitar and alto saxophone), together with three doo wop backing singers (Larry Byrom, Anthony Crawford and Ricky Palumbi). Recorded at Modern Recorders in Redwood City, California and credited to Neil Young and the Shocking Pinks, the resulting *Everybody's Rockin'*, clocking in at an almost insultingly brief 25 minutes, is perhaps the most carefree but throwaway album of Young's career.

Taken in context - in other words, as a simple pastiche with no pretensions of creative ambition - Everybody's *Rockin'* can perversely at times come close to being enjoyable. Young and the Shocking Pinks are clearly having a ball, which is reflected in the exuberance of the performances, effectively mimicking the classic rock n'roll vibe without ever threatening to do anything remotely interesting. It's almost like Young is moonlighting as the frontman of a very competent wedding covers band.

The album kicks off with a very forgettable cover of Bobby Freeman's very forgettable 1958 song 'Betty Lou Got A New Pair Of Shoes', which introduces us to Young's admittedly serviceable 50s croon. 'Rainin' in My Heart', a similarly obscure minor hit by Slim Harpo, is dashed off in similarly inoffensive fashion. The quality bar does go up a notch with 'Payola Blues,' an enjoyable romp co-written with Ben Keith, which Young also uses as a platform to launch a less than subtle broadside at Geffen. The term "Payola" refers to the controversial 1950s practice of DJs accepting money from labels and record companies to play certain songs or records on the radio. The song's lyrics, for example "Listen to me Mr. DJ, hear what I've got to say/If a man is making music, they ought to let his record play/ Payola blues/No matter where I go I never hear my record on the radio" have a thinly disguised double meaning that showed Young was still smarting, albeit with a mischievous glint in his eye.

In what was another sign of his waning song writing inspiration, Young reached back over a decade and revived 'Wonderin'', an amiable little tune dating from his *After The Goldrush* period. Its transition from folk-rock to doo-wop is reasonably smooth, but it was never more than an average song in the first place. 'Wonderin'' did however become Young's first ever promotional video, a most peculiar outing directed by Englishman Tim Pope in which the singer, almost spreadeagled on the camera lens, seems oddly out of sync with the Shocking Pinks and various LA locations behind him. It's followed by the outright silliness of 'Kinda Fonda Wanda', which name drops a host of famous females in classic rock 'n' roll era songs, from Peggy Sue and Barbara Ann to Long Tall Sally. If there was more evidence needed that Young saw the whole *Everybody's Rockin'* project as one big joke, this sheer cheese was it.

The second half of the album continues in a similarly tossed off, rapid fire vein. 'Jellyroll Man,' another Young original, is a hollow honk of a song with some of the inanest lyrics imaginable, while a cover of Jimmy Reed's blues standard 'Bright Lights, Big City' just goes through the motions. By the time we get to Young's insipid 'Cry Cry Cry' there's a sense of all the songs merging into one inoffensive but inconsequential background track to a long forgotten coming of age drama set in mid-20th century Iowa. A cover of the 1956 Elvis classic 'Mystery Train' is faithful enough, but always likely to pale in comparison to the awesome, ageless original.

Everybody's Rockin' closes with the Young-composed title track, which encapsulates everything that has gone before - good natured fun, executed smoothly but soullessly, with absolutely nothing to say other than a big "fuck you" to Young's paymasters at Geffen. The man himself even admitted "I almost vindictively gave Geffen *Everybody's Rockin'* "1, with producer Elliot Mazer estimating that recording the album took a grand total of "about two hours". Unsurprisingly, the album was Young's poorest seller since his debut back in 1968 and was roundly panned by the critics.

Tensions between Young and his label bosses were now close to boiling point, with David Geffen convinced the A-list artist he had brought on board as a flagship signing was deliberately giving him sub-standard, wilfully eccentric material. Geffen took the decision to sue Young for damages of $3.3 million, citing *Trans* and *Everybody's Rockin'* 'as "not commercial" and "musically uncharacteristic of Young's previous recordings". Young countersued, claiming he had been promised complete creative control in his contract with Geffen. The label eventually backed down, but the relationship never recovered, and nor did *Everybody's Rockin's* reputation as a cringe-inducing low point in Neil Young's long, often illustrious career.

⊙ TRACK LISTING ◄◄ ❚❚ ►►

1. Betty Lou's Got a New Pair of Shoes (Bobby Freeman) ⸳⸳⸳⸳⸳⸳⸳⸳⸳⸳⸳⸳⸳⸳⸳⸳⸳⸳⸳⸳⸳ 3:02
2. Rainin' in My Heart (Slim Harpo, Jerry West) ⸳⸳⸳⸳⸳⸳⸳⸳⸳⸳⸳⸳⸳⸳⸳⸳⸳⸳⸳⸳⸳⸳⸳⸳⸳ 2:11
3. Payola Blues (Ben Keith, Young) ⸳⸳⸳⸳⸳⸳⸳⸳⸳⸳⸳⸳⸳⸳⸳⸳⸳⸳⸳⸳⸳⸳⸳⸳⸳⸳⸳⸳⸳⸳⸳⸳⸳⸳ 3:09
4. Wonderin' ⸳⸳⸳ 2:59
5. Kinda Fonda Wanda (Tim Drummond, Young) ⸳⸳⸳⸳⸳⸳⸳⸳⸳⸳⸳⸳⸳⸳⸳⸳⸳⸳⸳⸳⸳ 1:51
6. Jellyroll Man ⸳⸳ 2:00
7. Bright Lights, Big City (Jimmy Reed) ⸳⸳⸳⸳⸳⸳⸳⸳⸳⸳⸳⸳⸳⸳⸳⸳⸳⸳⸳⸳⸳⸳⸳⸳⸳⸳⸳⸳ 2:18
8. Cry, Cry, Cry ⸳⸳ 2:39
9. Mystery Train (Junior Parker, Sam Phillips) ⸳⸳⸳⸳⸳⸳⸳⸳⸳⸳⸳⸳⸳⸳⸳⸳⸳⸳⸳⸳⸳ 2:47
10. Everybody's Rockin' ⸳⸳⸳ 1:57

Length: 24:55

---

1 McDonough, p.571

Neil Young - Old Ways

Released 12 August 1985 (Geffen)

🎧 🎧 🎧

In early 1984, the threat of a lawsuit from his record label following the *Everybody's Rockin'* fallout not yet resolved, Neil Young was back in the studio with Crazy Horse, hoping he could recapture his rock mojo by rekindling his most enduring musical relationship. Unfortunately, Young's insistence on meddling with their usual simple, natural recipe - bringing in a horn section and utilising state of the art 'click' studio technology to regulate their playing - meant the sessions soon collapsed.

With his personal life once again eventful - in addition to the ongoing Geffen conflict, third child Amber Jean was born that year, thankfully without any complications - Young retreated into his new comfort zone of country music. A band of top musicians, including Ben Keith, Tim Drummond, Karl T. Himmel, fiddler Rufus Thibodeaux and multi-instrumentalist Anthony Crawford, began touring around the U.S. and Canada with Young as the wryly named International Harvesters. Claiming to be ready to embrace the genre permanently, praising its warmer, kinder nature than the cutthroat world of rock, Young began to cultivate a good ol' boy image, complete with bandana, a suspect Southern twang and performing with Waylon Jennings, as well as expressing strong pro-Ronald Reagan views, speaking in favour of controversial U.S. interventionist foreign policy in Latin America and attacking welfare dependency - utterances that would have been unthinkable earlier in his career. Whether Young truly had changed or was instead carefully constructing another alter ego to fit a new musical direction, is as always hard to know for sure.

After touring intermittently with the Harvesters throughout 1984 and 1985, during which time the Geffen dispute was resolved (Young agreed to return half of his $1 million per album deal in exchange for making the music he wanted) and Young appeared at Live Aid in Philadelphia, *Old Ways* finally emerged in August 1985. Although the genesis of the album was the Geffen-rejected original *Old Ways* from 1983, the new version (sometimes referred to by Young as 'Old Ways 2') had several new songs and alternative versions of most of the others. Recorded in Tennessee and Texas, it saw most of Young's usual supporting cast replaced by a host of seasoned Nashville session musicians. As with *Comes A Time* a few years before, the cast list was unusually expansive, including numerous backing singers and a string section, as well as country legends Jennings and Willie Nelson. Young had always had a strong country influence in his work, going right back to his earliest records, but even his most significant flirtations - *American Stars n'Bars*, *Comes A Time* and *Hawks and Doves* - had also included some rock material. *Old Ways* was the real deal.

To prove the point, Young opened the album with a cover of country classic 'The Wayward Wind,' previously a U.S. and U.K. number one hit for Gogi Grant and Frank Ifield respectively. With a sweepingly cinematic string arrangement by Chuck Conran, and Young sharing vocals with the talented Denise Draper, the latest in a succession of excellent female singers he'd worked with, it's an accomplished if slightly saccharine introduction. In contrast, the twee, fiddle-heavy hoedown of 'Get Back To The Country' feels a step too far, with Terry McMillan's frantically bouncy jew's harp an unwelcome distraction.

'Are There Any More Real Cowboys' brings us back to the realms of gentle country-rock. A wistful reflection on the loss of the old time cowboys from the landscape of the American West, it has an easy grace and some elegant harmonica work, although guest Willie Nelson's vocals and Young's don't blend well. Next up is 'Once An Angel', an over-sentimental ballad with a pace so languid it's almost as if the record is being played at the wrong speed. Much more engaging is 'Misfits,' one of the most intriguing songs Young had released in years. Lyrically, it recalls much of Young's late 70s work, with a kaleidoscopic cast of characters ranging from a space station crew watching Muhammad Ali fights to an alcoholic rodeo rider and a prostitute suffering a seizure. It provides a welcome mid-album shift in atmosphere, with the swirling strings and anchoring upright bass forming a hypnotic backdrop to Young's enigmatic storytelling.

However, we're straight back to the country again on side two, with the pleasant but unexceptional 'California Sunset', a live recording of the original Harvesters line-up playing at Austin's City Limits. It's followed by the title track, another example of Young's take on traditional country straying too far into cosy cliche, although his latest warning on the dangers of stagnation is done neatly enough, notably on the lyrics: "It's hard to teach a dinosaur a new trick/Lately I've been finding out/I'm set in my ways/Old ways, can be your ball and chain."

'My Boy,' a touching tribute to Young's oldest son Zeke as he entered his teens, is slightly mawkish but undeniably pretty, with a heartfelt vocal augmented by graceful fiddle and fluttering banjo, also played by Young. 'Bound For Glory' is another mid-tempo, likeable but slightly too comfortable ballad, with Waylon

Jennings sharing vocal duties, while 'Where Is The Highway Tonight' ends the record rather underwhelmingly in a similar vein, with Jennings on board again as Young laments the loss of happier times, crooning "Where is the highway tonight? Where are those old days and crazy nights?"

Compared to the radical electronic sound of *Trans* or the sheer vacuous banality of *Everybody's Rockin'*, *Old Ways* is at least recognisably a Neil Young record, with a handful of standout tracks and a relaxed, undemanding feel throughout that makes it a mostly agreeable although hardly essential listen. Once again and to Geffen's dismay, it was a commercial failure, peaking at a lowly 75 in the U.S. album charts, with the critics mostly bemused or indifferent. Not that Young cared, defiantly stating "I don't care what people think of my country music. They can stick it up their ass if they don't like it."[1]

⊙ TRACK LISTING   ◄◄ ❚❚ ►►❘

1. The Wayward Wind (Herb Newman, Stanley Lebowsky) ·················· 3:12
2. Get Back to the Country ··· 2:50
3. Are There Any More Real Cowboys? ···································· 3:03
4. Once an Angel ··· 3:55
5. Misfits ·· 5:07
6. California Sunset ·· 2:56
7. Old Ways ··· 3:08
8. My Boy ··· 3:37
9. Bound for Glory ··· 5:48
10. Where Is the Highway Tonight? ·· 3:02

Length: 36:43

---

1 McDonough, p.598

Neil Young - Landing On Water

Released 21 July 1986 (Geffen)

🎧 🎧 🎧

Despite the lukewarm reception for *Old Ways*, Neil Young continued to tour material from the album for the next few months, while at the same time busying himself with other projects, notably co-organising the first two Farm Aid benefit concerts to raise money to support family farmers in the United States, whose parlous financial plight had been highlighted by Bob Dylan. Then one morning, he claimed to wake up hearing a booming noise in his head - the sound of rock and roll.

However, the rock and roll Young had in mind was not his long-established Crazy Horse template. Instead, with the MTV age now in full swing, he opted to make what he perceived to be a modern-sounding rock record, with usual producer David Briggs replaced by Danny Kortchmar, a seasoned collaborator with artists including Crosby, Stills and Nash, Carly Simon and Carole King. Kortchmar also played guitars and synthesisers on the album, with him and Young joined by experienced session drummer Steve Jordan to form a tight trio for the sessions recorded at Young's Broken Arrow Ranch and at Record One studios in Los Angeles.

The end result was another low point in Young's troubled Geffen career. While he undoubtedly succeeded in creating an album that sounded current, unfortunately the combination of tinny, artificial textures and weak songwriting makes *Landing On Water* one of the least enjoyable listening experiences of any Young album. *Trans* and *Old Ways* both had their moments amid the missteps, and *Everybody's Rockin'* at least gave a sense that Young and his bandmates had great fun making it. *Landing On Water* just feels turgid throughout.

The album kicks off with 'The Weight Of The World', by no means the worst offering here, but straight away, the clattering electronic drumming, squalling guitars and frenetic synthesisers create a sonic backdrop that has aged horribly, with Young's vocals stripped of all their usual emotion and buried deep in the muddy mire of the mixing. Lyrically, it's pretty banal, with Young extolling the virtues of a new romance that has caused all his troubles to fade away. 'Violent Side' once again completely buries Young, this time beneath the massed voices of San Francisco Boys Chorus, with the lyrics - this time focused on urban violence - feeling formulaic and lacking any subtlety or depth.

'Hippie Dream' is possibly the pick of *Landing On Water*'s bad bunch, with Young taking his latest pot shots at the late 60s/early 70s folk-rock scene he had long sought to distance himself from. The lyric "but the wooden ships were just a hippie dream/Capsized in excess, if you know what I mean" is a particularly pointed barb at the now ruinously drug addled David Crosby with its sly use of a Crosby, Stills and Nash song title , but far more powerful is the scathing "Another flower child goes to seed/In an ether-filled room of meat-hooks." Regrettably, 'Bad News Beat' is as inane as the previous track was clever, with wordplay more characteristic of manufactured boy bands than one of rock's greatest singer songwriters, "I've got the bad news beat/And my reception is loud and clear" being just one risible example. The first side of the album ends with the overblown but not completely unenjoyable heavy rock of 'Touch The Night', with Young's guitar work taking centre stage for the first time.

'People On The Street', a commentary on big city homelessness, is dominated by relentlessly driving synthesisers, with some additional, cringeworthy vocal contributions from Kortchmar and Jordan. It sounds utterly of its time but could be by anyone. 'Hard Luck Stories' is a feeble slice of funk rock, with a particularly watery vocal from Young, while 'I Got A Problem' and 'Pressure' are both jerky, anxious songs focusing on emotional distress, themes hammered home by Jordan's thumping drums. Last track 'Drifter' is the pick of the album's otherwise lamentable second half. Framed by menacing stabs of guitar and keyboards, Young paints an unapologetic self-portrait that sums up how he's approached his musical career. Lines like "I'm just a drifter/I'll stay until you try to tie me down" and "I like to feel the wheel" neatly address his free spirited, restless character and unwillingness to be pigeonholed or controlled.

Landing On Water performed marginally better on release than *Old Ways*, reaching number 46 in the U.S. album charts, but was critically panned, with Adam Sweeting describing it in Melody Maker as "a strange combination of numbskull hard rock and electronics... God only knows what co-producer Danny Kortchmar was doing."[1] Even Young himself didn't take long to acknowledge the record's failings, telling British DJ Dave Ferrin in 1987 "It's a piece of crap...If I was going to give one of my records to someone, I don't think this would be the one."[2]

---

1   Melody Maker, 02/08/1986
2   BBC2 FM Radio interview with Dave Ferrin, 05/06/1987

▶ TRACK LISTING ◀◀ ❚❚ ▶▶

1. Weight of the World ⋯⋯⋯⋯⋯⋯⋯⋯⋯⋯⋯⋯⋯⋯⋯⋯⋯⋯⋯ 3:40
2. Violent Side ⋯⋯⋯⋯⋯⋯⋯⋯⋯⋯⋯⋯⋯⋯⋯⋯⋯⋯⋯⋯⋯⋯ 4:22
3. Hippie Dream ⋯⋯⋯⋯⋯⋯⋯⋯⋯⋯⋯⋯⋯⋯⋯⋯⋯⋯⋯⋯⋯ 4:11
4. Bad News Beat ⋯⋯⋯⋯⋯⋯⋯⋯⋯⋯⋯⋯⋯⋯⋯⋯⋯⋯⋯⋯ 3:18
5. Touch the Night ⋯⋯⋯⋯⋯⋯⋯⋯⋯⋯⋯⋯⋯⋯⋯⋯⋯⋯⋯ 4:30
6. People on the Street ⋯⋯⋯⋯⋯⋯⋯⋯⋯⋯⋯⋯⋯⋯⋯⋯⋯ 4:33
7. Hard Luck Stories ⋯⋯⋯⋯⋯⋯⋯⋯⋯⋯⋯⋯⋯⋯⋯⋯⋯⋯ 4:06
8. I Got a Problem ⋯⋯⋯⋯⋯⋯⋯⋯⋯⋯⋯⋯⋯⋯⋯⋯⋯⋯⋯ 3:16
9. Pressure ⋯⋯⋯⋯⋯⋯⋯⋯⋯⋯⋯⋯⋯⋯⋯⋯⋯⋯⋯⋯⋯⋯⋯ 2:46
10. Drifter ⋯⋯⋯⋯⋯⋯⋯⋯⋯⋯⋯⋯⋯⋯⋯⋯⋯⋯⋯⋯⋯⋯⋯⋯ 5:05

Length: 40:04

Neil Young & Crazy Horse - Life

Released 30 June 1987 (Geffen)

A lthough *Life* will never go down in history as one of Neil Young's finest albums, it nevertheless occupies a pivotal place in his career. After spending the past half decade wilfully stumbling between different genres, to increasing bemusement and ultimately apathy from his audience, Young's final record in his troubled Geffen tenure offered up the first green shoots of creative recovery. Reunited with Crazy Horse for the first time since 1981's *Re·ac·tor,* the material on *Life* sees Young begin his transition away from the experimentation of his past few records and back towards a more classic rock style: a journey which would be triumphantly completed at the end of the decade with *Freedom* and *Ragged Glory*.

Young had begun touring with Crazy Horse again during the autumn of 1986, with the thankless task of promoting the mostly risible *Landing On Water* album. Attempts to recreate its sterile synthetic textures live using the latest computer technology inevitably clashed with the Horse's instinctive, raw ethos, but what did emerge from the carnage were some new and previously unreleased Young songs that were markedly superior to *Landing On Water's* vapid, grating fare. Recordings of these from concerts at the Universal Amphitheatre in Universal City, CA on November 18 and 19, 1986 formed the core of *Life,* with two additional tracks recorded at LA's Record One studio in February and March 1987.

While the twin challenges of 1980s production techniques unsympathetic to Young and Crazy Horse's sound and Young's continuing flirtation with right wing patriotism mean *Life* has some uncomfortable moments, overall, it can be classed as a cautiously encouraging return to form.

The album kicks off with 'Mideast Vacation', the first of three tracks celebrating the U.S. military and foreign policy of the period. A soft rock song with a stately pace and pounding beat, like much of *Life* its production does bear the scars of *Landing On Water*, and the lyrics - about a rogue U.S. soldier who ends up massacring Arabs while on holiday - are worryingly gung-ho, although one can alternatively give Young the benefit of the doubt and conclude he is actually satirising the hawkish attitudes of the period towards regimes like Colonel Gadafi's Libya.

'Long Walk Home' starts out prettily with a harmonica and piano accompaniment that harks back to Young's early singer-songwriter days but builds into what appears initially to be a hymnal celebration of America's recent role as a global policeman, complete with gospel-like backing vocals and sounds of explosions and gunshots. However, on closer examination it seems the song may actually be questioning the purpose of overseas interventions, with lines like "America, America/Where have we gone? It's such a long walk home" suggesting the country had lost its way. The opening trilogy of military-themed compositions is completed by 'Around The World', a tubthumping blend of snarling guitars and burbling synths over which Young rather glibly proclaims "Why do we have to hate/Why do we incinerate/ Why don't we illuminate/Around the world."

The mood of the record changes completely with the arrival of 'Inca Queen', a serene, gliding ballad on which Young once again explores the cultures of pre-Columbian civilisations against an unfamiliar backdrop of flamenco guitar and Amazonian bird noises. But the calm mood is only brief, as next track 'Too Lonely' sees Crazy Horse lumber back to take centre stage. A straightforward, uncomplicated rocker, with Young sounding more animated than for years, like Buffalo Springfield's 'Mr Soul' many years before, its riff bears more than a passing resemblance to the Stones' 'Satisfaction.'

'Prisoners of Rock 'N' Roll', is another middling chunk of comfort zone garage rock, with Young cocking a snook at long standing criticisms of Crazy Horse's lack of musical sophistication. The on the nose lyrics leave little possibility of misinterpretation: "People tell us that we're playing too loud/But they don't know what our music's about/We never listen to the record company man/They try to change us and ruin our band... that's why we don't wanna be good." 'Cryin' Eyes' dated back to Young's days playing small Californian venues in The Ducks a decade previously, but the version here, recorded at LA's Record One studio, has a completely different feel to the rest of 'Life', with its throbbing bassline, murky guitars and urgent vocals recalling the post-punk bands of the late 70s and early 80s rather than the sleek, stadium rock sounds of the mainstream.

The final two tracks of the album see Young switching styles again, this time to the kind of lush, tinkling power ballads that were so popular during this era. While the sound again feels a little overproduced, dated and frankly very un-Neil Young, the songs themselves are strong, providing further evidence that Young was beginning to recover his writing mojo. 'When Your Lonely Heart Breaks' is an elegant but defiant call to move on from failed relationships, while 'We Never Danced' is a wistfully sad depiction of love in the afterlife. The latter was produced by Jack Nitzsche, in his first collaboration with Young for many years, and was originally recorded for the fantasy romance film *Made In Heaven* but was ultimately rejected and then re-recorded in a much more up-tempo version by Martha Davis of American new wave band The Motels.

Despite being perhaps Young's most accessible album of the decade so far, his artistic reputation had by now fallen so far *Life* sank without trace among the record buying public, becoming his lowest charting release ever on both sides of the Atlantic. It also finally brought an end to Young's unhappy and undistinguished relationship with Geffen, after manager Elliott Roberts thrashed out a deal for his client to return to his old home at Reprise. After spending most of the 1980s fighting with his record company, Young was now back on familiar territory, a return that raised hopes his ailing career might now finally reignite.

⊙ TRACK LISTING   ◄◄ ❚❚ ►►

1. Mideast Vacation ⸱⸱ 4:20
2. Long Walk Home ⸱⸱⸱ 4:56
3. Around the World ⸱⸱ 5:25
4. Inca Queen ⸱⸱ 7:58
5. Too Lonely ⸱⸱⸱ 2:48
6. Prisoners of Rock 'N' Roll ⸱⸱⸱ 3:12
7. Cryin' Eyes ⸱⸱⸱ 2:52
8. When Your Lonely Heart Breaks ⸱⸱⸱⸱⸱⸱⸱⸱⸱⸱⸱⸱⸱⸱⸱⸱⸱⸱⸱⸱⸱⸱⸱⸱⸱⸱⸱⸱⸱⸱⸱⸱⸱ 5:16
9. We Never Danced ⸱⸱⸱ 3:37

Length: 40:40

Neil Young & The Bluenotes - This Note's For You

Released 11 April 1988 (Reprise)

🎧 🎧 🎧

Following his return to Reprise Records and the first signs of a return to more familiar musical territory on *Life,* it was perhaps a surprise to many that Neil Young's next album, *This Note's For You,* was another foray into the kind of genre dalliance that had frustrated so many fans and critics during his Geffen years. But unlike most of his early to mid-1980s work, Young's record with the Bluenotes - a confident blend of blues, big band and soul - was a surprisingly consistent, enjoyable collection, characterised by excellent musicianship and further evidence of a song writing renaissance.

Young had first experimented with the use of horns in his music while touring with Crazy Horse in late 1987, when Young performed a trio of songs with Poncho Sampedro on organ and guitar technician Larry Cragg on saxophone. Soon afterwards, Young recruited a six strong horn section, mostly members of the East LA Horns group introduced to Young by Horse bassist Billy Talbot. As well as retaining Cragg, the ubiquitous Ben Keith, usually a pedal steel player, was also brought in on alto sax. Performing as the Bluenotes, the new band played a series of Californian club dates, with the intention of building a new album from a series of live recordings. However, concerns regarding the Crazy Horse rhythm section's ability to cope with the more sophisticated blues and soul-influenced material Young had written led to Talbot and Ralph Molina being unceremoniously sacked, with drummer Chad Cromwell and bassist Rick Rosas, who were part of singer songwriter/guitarist Joe Walsh's band, eventually brought in as replacements.

The resulting album, recorded in LA, San Francisco and Oakland, while lacking a little of the energy of the Bluenotes' live performances, was nevertheless a tight, polished collection, with Young sounding much more comfortable and assured than on most of his previous ventures outside of his established style. Opening track 'Ten Men Workin' sets the tone from the start with its vibrant horn riff and swaggering rhythm, although it's a tad overlong at more than six minutes, and the hollered backing vocals sound slightly pained.

The title track of *This Note's For You* ended up providing Young with his most positive publicity for several years through an irreverent promotional video directed by Julien Temple, later to become known for the film Absolute Beginners and the Sex Pistols rockumentary *The Filth and the Fury*. A ruthless satire of the corporate sponsorship deals many major stars of the time were signing, it featured a Michael Jackson lookalike setting fire to his hair - a reference to an infamous Pepsi ad mishap - while a Whitney Houston doppelganger douses him with Coke. The song's title was a play on Eric Clapton's "This Bud's For You" slogan. An unimpressed MTV banned the clip, in doing so giving Young his biggest PR boost in years, and the outcry gathered so much momentum that MTV eventually not only reinstated it, but also gave it its "Best Video Of The Year" award. Musically, it's one of the more rock oriented songs on the album, with some similarities to Dire Straits, particularly in Young's slick guitar work.

This Note's For You shifts its mood totally on its third track, 'Coupe de Ville', an elegant jazz lounge ballad with some beautifully textured, understated trumpet and saxophone contributions from Tom Bray and Steve Lawrence. The song's lyrics contrast Young's passion for his Coupe de Ville Cadillac with his longing for a lost lover, reflecting that material possessions, however luxurious, never really end up fulfilling you, with Young concluding "If I can't have you/I don't want nothin' else."

The horns are back at full blast on 'Life In The City', a slightly frantic critique of urban deprivation which pulls no punches lyrically as Young laments the "people sleepin' on the sidewalks/on a rainy day/family livin' under freeways/it's the American way." The tempo then slows again on the atmospheric 'Twilight'. Underpinned by a portentous ticking clock, Young delivers some of his most emotive guitar work in many years, perfectly contrasted by Bray's trumpet and Lawrence's saxophone. It's arguably the high point of the album, with Young back on top form as a sensitive chronicler of the human heart, singing "Making love to you while time stands still/I may be dreamin', but I always will/'cause I'll be holding you/when the twilight falls."

Unfortunately, *This Note's For You*'s quality then dips significantly on 'Married Man', a charmless, headache-inducing stomp, while 'Sunny Inside' although adeptly arranged and performed with gusto, feels like a hollow pastiche of classic soul, with Young's reedy voice stretched too far from its comfort zone. But 'Can't Believe You're Lyin'' is sultry, crepuscular blues, with Young's guitar once again to the fore, this time gently finger picking rather than cutting loose. Other than some subtle, drifting trumpet from guest player John Fumo, the backdrop is sparse, anchored by Rosas and Campbell's exemplary rhythm section. Penultimate track

'Hey Hey' is another vivacious blow out, with the juxtaposition of squalling horns and guitars and a rockabilly shuffle giving the song a strong 1950s flavour.

The album ends with 'One Thing', another delicate, smouldering ballad on which Young tells the tale of a doomed relationship over six unhurried minutes, with the repeating line "I think we're headed for a heartache." Surprisingly, the song features the otherwise side-lined Ralph Molina on drums, as well as former Rockets guitarist George Whitsell on bass, and like the other slower songs on the record, the horn section is used judiciously, allowing Young's guitar and vocals all the space they need.

Although not all its songs are great, and it's occasionally guilty of trying too hard to emulate the genre templates it aspires to, overall, *This Note's For You* is one of Neil Young's most successful attempts to embrace an unfamiliar sound. The playing, arrangements and production are impressive throughout, with the slower tracks particularly well handled, and Young inhabits the material with an easy self-assurance. Regrettably, the album was another commercial failure, falling short of the Top 50 in both the U.S. and the U.K., although one critic, the NME's Fred Dellar, went as far as describing it as "Record of the Year territory."[1] But as the decade drew towards its close, it would not be long before Young's burgeoning second coming as a major artist would be more widely recognised.

⊙ TRACK LISTING   ⏮ ⏸ ⏭

1. Ten Men Workin' ··· 6:28
2. This Note's for You ·· 2:05
3. Coupe de Ville ··· 4:18
4. Life in the City ··· 3:13
5. Twilight ··· 5:54
6. Married Man ··· 2:38
7. Sunny Inside ·· 2:36
8. Can't Believe Your Lyin' ·· 2:58
9. Hey Hey ·· 3:05
10. One Thing ·· 6:02

Length: 39:25

---

1 NME, 30 April 1988

Timeline - The Wilderness Years (1980 - 88)

1980

February: Records the new songs that would become side two of his Hawks and Doves album.

1 March: Release of *Where The Buffalo Roam* soundtrack, directed by Art Linson and starring Bill Murray. Young contributes seven of the 15 tracks on a score also featuring Bob Dylan and Jimi Hendrix.

October: Neil and Pegi enrol their son Ben on a highly demanding programme run by Philadelphia's Institute of Human Potential for a total period of 18 months, meaning Young was mostly home-based during this period.

October - July 1981: Recording sessions for *Re.ac.tor* album take place at Young's Redwood City, California ranch.

3 November: Release of *Hawks and Doves*.

1981

September - May 1982: Recording sessions for Young's *Trans* album take place.

28 October: Release of *Re.ac.tor* album.

1982

September: *Human Highway*, a comedy film Young had been working on since 1978, is finally released, co-directed by Young and the actor Dean Stockwell.

31 August - 19 October: Young's *Trans* tour of Europe with his Trans band takes place.

29 December: *Trans* album released, Young's first for the Geffen label.

1983

5 January - 4 March: Young tours his *Trans* album solo around the U.S. and Canada. The tour ends early when Young collapses backstage in Louisville due to exhaustion.

January: The initial songs recorded for Young's *Old Ways* album are rejected by Geffen as "too country."

April - May: *Everybody's Rockin'* album recorded by Neil Young and the Shocking Pinks.

1 July - 1 October: A second solo Trans tour of the U.S. takes place, this time with the Shocking Pinks providing the encores.

27 July: Release of *Everybody's Rockin'*.

1 December: Geffen Records sue Young for making records that are "musically uncharacteristic of Young's previous recordings." Young countersues.

1984

15 May: Neil and Pegi's second child, Amber Jean, is born.

23 August - 26 October: Young tours country music venues in the U.S. and Canada with his group The International Harvesters.

1985

22 February - 22 March: Young's first ever tour of Australia and New Zealand, with The International Harvesters and Crazy Horse.

1 April: Geffen and Young's lawsuits dismissals filed in Los Angeles Superior Court after David Geffen apologises and Young proposes reduced album payments in return for a guarantee of artistic freedom.

13 July: Appears at Live Aid in Philadelphia, playing both a solo set and alongside Crosby, Stills and Nash.

9 August - 21 September: Tour of the U.S. with The International Harvesters.

12 August: Old Ways album released.

22 September: Organises the first Farm Aid concert in Champaign, Illinois with fellow musicians Willie Nelson and John Cougar Mellencamp.

1986

March: Recording of most of the *Landing on Water* album at Record One studios in Los Angeles.

21 July: *Landing On Water* released.

15 September - 21 November: Live in a Rusted Out Garage tour of the U.S. and Canada with Crazy Horse.

13 October: Neil and Pegi organise the first ever benefit concert for the Bridge School, which supports children with severe physical impairments and complex communication needs. Held at the Shoreline Amphitheatre in Mountain View, California, the event would continue annually until 2016.

18-19 November: Recordings of two concerts from the Rusted Out Garage tour at the Universal Amphitheatre, Los Angeles, for use on Young and Crazy Horse's next album.

1987

24 April - 6 June: Young tours Europe with Crazy Horse.

30 June: Release of *Life*, the last of Young's five albums with Geffen, mostly made up of the November 1986 concert recordings with Crazy Horse.

13 August - 4 September: Young tours the U.S. and Canada with Crazy Horse to promote the *Life* album.

7 October: Young's return to former label Reprise is confirmed.

November - January 1988: Young records *This Note's For You*, his first album back on Reprise, alongside his new band The Bluenotes.

1988

February: Reunites with Crosby, Stills and Nash to record the *American Dream* album.

11 April: *This Note's For You* is released.

12 August - 8 September: Young and the Bluenotes' *Sponsored By Nobody* tour of the U.S.

22 November: Release of CSN&Y's *American Dream* album.

13-15 December: Young records songs at New York's Hit Factory studio with Rick Rosas and Chad Cromwell as The Restless, using amps to project feedback and paving the way for the hard rock sound of *Freedom* and *Ragged Glory*.

PART 4
Rebirth (1989-2000)

Neil Young - Freedom

Released 2 October 1989 (Reprise)

🎧　🎧　🎧

Over 30 years after its release, *Freedom* remains one of the most pivotal records Neil Young has ever made. While *Life* and *This Note's For You* had shown signs of an artist rediscovering his vigour and creativity after several years of frustrating, often wilful missteps, neither had significantly restored his reputational or commercial standing, which had reached an all-time low by the late 1980s. With *Freedom*, Young recovered both, at the same time heralding the beginning of a genuinely vital mid-career renaissance which would result in work on a par with his very finest 1970s records and see him revered as an icon by many of the next generation of alternative rock and grunge musicians.

By late 1988, Young was immersed in a period of restless invention and relentless productivity unequalled since the middle of the previous decade. As well as touring with The Bluenotes, he also revived his love-hate relationship with Crosby, Stills and Nash, recording the disappointingly lacklustre *American Dream*, while at the same time penning a number of long, lyrically ambitious new songs that were clearly influenced by Bob Dylan, who Young had stay at his ranch and performed with during this period. The outputs from a highly productive session at New York's Hit Factory, including several new songs, formed the basis of an album provisionally entitled *Times Square*.

In early 1989, Young returned to the road on a global tour with a slimmed down Bluenotes line up including Poncho Sampedro, Ben Keith, bassist Rick Rosas and drummer Chad Cromwell. Increasingly experimenting with a heavier, feedback-drenched guitar sound, bridged by machine noise between songs, a limited edition EP, *Eldorado*, was released in Australasia and the Far East only, giving a tantalising glimpse of Young's newfound vibrancy to those Western fans able to secure imports. After further studio work, including re-recording several abandoned earlier songs, Young then cemented his comeback with a scintillating performance of what was to become his flagship new anthem 'Rockin' In The Free World' on U.S. television's *Saturday Night Live*.

When it was released in October 1989, *Freedom*, as the new Young album was now titled, lived up to expectations and more. Recordings from sessions at the Hit Factory and Young's Broken Arrow ranch featured the established core of Sampedro, Keith, Rosas and Campbell, as well as the wider Bluenotes horn section and a returning Linda Ronstadt on backing vocals. Essentially a distillation of many of the best elements of Young's career to date, albeit with a sheen of contemporary stadium rock polish that robbed it of a little of the rawness of some of his earlier work, it had a bit of everything: fierce guitar workouts, fragile country-influenced ballads, strong melodies and above all, a sense of energy and outrage that had been missing from Young's music since *Rust Never Sleeps*.

Just as he'd done so successfully on his last truly great album a decade before, Young bookended *Freedom* with acoustic and electric versions of the same song, this time the towering 'Rockin' In The Free World'. Starting off life as a tongue in cheek slogan on Young's tour bus, it soon evolved into a serious critique of the political changes going on at the time, including George Bush Senior's new presidency, which Young seemed to view far less favourably than that of fellow Republican Ronald Reagan. The opening acoustic version, recorded live at Jones Beach, Long Island, sets out its stall right from the start, with Young passionately strumming his guitar as he spews out the lyrics "There's colors on the street/Red, white and blue/People shufflin' their feet/People sleepin' in their shoes." Further, even more pointed references to Bush's politics follow, with the line "We got a thousand points of light/For the homeless man" a deliberately ironic parody of comments made in the president's inaugural address about the country's community organisations.

'Crime in the City (Sixty to Zero Part I)' is another bona fide Young classic. Although almost nine minutes long, the song - originally called just 'Sixty To Zero' - started out as an eleven verse epic of double the duration, which Young performed live with the Bluenotes in late 1988. Scaled down to a more manageable five verses, it remains dazzlingly ambitious, propelled by a subtly funky rhythm and with a dash of extra colour provided by Keith's ever-effective pedal steel and the horn section carried over from *This Note's For You*. Featuring a cast of characters including a beleaguered inner city cop, a soulless record producer and the child of separated parents - almost certainly referencing Young's own experience - the lyrics focus on different forms of alienation, frustration with authority and the flaws of the perceived status quo.

'Don't Cry' gives the listener their first experience of Young's formidable new guitar sound, with some mighty moments of ear splitting volume and screeching intensity punctuating an otherwise simple song exploring the emotions involved with an acrimonious break up. Lyrics like "My sweet love/Your disappointed eyes/ Are haunting me like my big lies/I see you glaring now" suggest the fault lies with the song's narrator, and the haunting end, with a ghostly Young singing "Don't cry, my sweet girl/You won't really be alone" is pointedly laced with ambiguity. Then without warning, we are effortlessly transported back to Young's earlier singer-songwriter days with 'Hangin' On A Limb', a divinely pretty acoustic ballad featuring a gorgeous harmony vocal from Ronstadt and bucolic lyrics about flowing rivers and melodies floating through windows that sounded more 1969 than 1989.

'Eldorado', which originally appeared on the limited edition EP of the same name, is included here in a re-recorded version. An atmospheric tale of a Mexican town inhabited by mariachi bands, bandits and bullfighters, it features some evocative, Latin-tinged guitar playing from Young and Sampedro, with a smattering of castanets adding to the mood. We're then firmly back in country-rock territory with the lilting, dreamy 'The Ways of Love', which was written back in the late 1970s and once again sees Ronstadt's vocals come to the fore, sighing wistfully above Ben Keith's timeless pedal steel. It's another example of Young's seemingly inexhaustible seam of effortlessly melodic, instantly accessible songs that for some fans made his wilful stylistic meandering of the past decade all the more galling.

The second half of *Freedom* isn't quite as strong as the first. With its cascades of synthetic keyboards, saxophone solos and laboured, grunting backing vocals, 'Someday' feels dated, a hangover from his recent underwhelming attempts to capture the contemporary sounds of the mid-1980s. The formidably loud, discordant guitar sound is back on a cover of 'On Broadway', originally a hit for The Drifters back in 1963., but now radically transformed into a menacing indictment of the poverty that exists among glamour. The track ends with a tumult of guitar noise that sounds like tectonic plates shifting, a technique Young would experiment with further over the next couple of years, notably on the live album *Weld* and sound collage *Arc*.

The altogether gentler 'Wrecking Ball' is a slightly plodding soft rock ballad, on which Young wrestles with the destructive nature of relationships, using a dance as a metaphor. Later covered by Emmylou Harris, the lyrics - "We got nowhere to hide/We got nowhere to go

But if you still decide/That you want to take a ride/Meet me at the wrecking ball" - effectively capture the way romantic passion can lead to ill-advised life decisions. 'No More' is a perfectly serviceable mid-tempo rock tune, with Young's guitar a keening presence throughout, but the harrowing lyrics about the desperate nature of drug addiction deserve better, with lines like "Livin' on the edge of night/You know the sun won't go down slow/You don't know which drug is right/Can't decide which way you wanna go" recalling the stark honesty of his Ditch Trilogy albums.

'Too Far Gone', the penultimate track, is another tasteful acoustic offering revived from the mid-70s, hindered a little by an over-sprightly mandolin part. Lyrically though, it's a heart breaking tale of a fleeting love affair, opening with the killer lines "When I woke up you were gone/And the sun was on the lawn/

Empty pillow with perfume on." *Freedom* ends with an incendiary electric version of 'Rockin' In The Free World', with its surging guitar riffs and propulsive rhythm epitomising Young's rediscovered dynamism and making it ideally suited to a single release. The song's defiant message and crowd pleasing, titular chorus helped 'Rockin' In The Free World' become one of Young's most enduringly popular compositions, not least in the political arena, where its use by Donald Trump in his 2016 and 2020 presidential campaigns led to an unimpressed Young filing a lawsuit for breach of copyright.

With the generally high calibre of its material and as a long awaited return to a more 'typical' Neil Young sound, it was little surprise that *Freedom* became its creator's most successful album of the decade, reaching number 17 in the U.K. and number 35 in the U.S. charts. But even more importantly, it paved the way for two of the finest records he would ever make during the next three years, each perfectly encapsulating the opposing musical forces that make Young such a uniquely captivating artist.

⊙ TRACK LISTING ◖◖ ‖ ▶◖

1. Rockin' in the Free World" (Live acoustic) ··· 3:38
2. Crime in the City (Sixty to Zero Part I) ·· 8:45
3. Don't Cry ··· 4:14
4. Hangin' on a Limb ·· 4:18
5. Eldorado ··· 6:03
6. The Ways of Love ··· 4:29
7. Someday ·· 5:40
8. On Broadway (Barry Mann, Cynthia Weil, Jerry Leiber, Mike Stoller) ······ 4:57
9. Wrecking Ball ·· 5:08
10. No More ··· 6:03
11. Too Far Gone··· 2:47
12. Rockin' in the Free World ·· 4:41

Length: 61:11

Neil Young & Crazy Horse - Ragged Glory

Released 9 September 1990 (Reprise)

With his artistic credibility and popularity restored by the success of *Freedom*, Neil Young entered the 1990s in the enviable position of being a survivor from the 1960s who was both revered for his imperious back catalogue and respected as a musician who remained relevant to a modern audience. Sadly, his personal life began the decade less positively, as he spent several months at the bedside of his terminally ill mother Rassy in Florida, who passed away from cancer the day before her 73rd birthday in October 1990.

Young had also now embarked on his behemoth *Neil Young Archives* project, which would see a plethora of previously unreleased material become available to Young's fans through a series of categorised releases and box sets. It would be several years before the Archives began to bear fruit, with Young initially envisaging a *Decade 2* box set compilation, but even at this early stage, revisiting his old audio and video performances gave him food for thought - in particular with regard to Crazy Horse.

The tensions on the 1987 *Life* album tour and Young's decision to fire Billy Talbot and Ralph Molina during 1988's *This Note's For You* Bluenotes tour had led to Talbot and Molina forming a new Horse line up with two new members - Matt Piucci and Sonny Mone - while Poncho Sampedro had continued to work with Young. Keen to recapture the original band's elemental force after watching recordings of their mid-70s *Zuma* period peak, peace talks were arranged in February 1990 between Talbot, Molina, Sampedro and Young, with producer David Briggs as mediator. Young apologised unreservedly for his previous behaviour - whether this was purely to grease the wheels of the reunion we will never know - and recordings for *Ragged Glory* went ahead at the Broken Arrow ranch, with only guitar technician Larry Cragg authorised to join the core quartet and Briggs.

The resulting album was quite simply spectacular. Playing together warts and all, with no other musicians or experimental influences and armed with a clutch of first rate songs, Neil Young and Crazy Horse not only succeeded in recapturing the zeitgeist of their halcyon days but emerged with a record that was fit to stand alongside *Zuma* and *Everybody Knows This Is Nowhere* as one of their trio of crowning achievements.

Right from the first coruscating notes that Young spews out from Old Black at the beginning of 'Country Home', it's clear *Ragged Glory* is going to be one hell of a ride. With Molina thumping out a monstrous beat and the band singing in unison with Young on the soaring chorus, 'Country Home' is a magnificent opener. A song dating back to the mid-1970s, with a lyrical theme of escaping from an urban environment to a calmer rural lifestyle, it sets the tone for the record: a big, brash and unadorned sound, unpolished but passionate. Young's guitar work is the loosest and most expressive it's been for years, with several passages of soloing on 'Country Home' demonstrating the almost telepathic groove he and the Horse can summon up when allowed to roam free.

'White Line' also traces its roots back to around 1974/75, with a very different acoustic version appearing on *Homegrown*. Due to this album being shelved for over four decades, the first official appearance of 'White Line' arrived on *Ragged Glory*, with the mournful harmonica and country-folk twang of its earlier incarnation replaced by majestically chugging electric guitars and crashing cymbals. Originally written - like most of *Homegrown* - about Young's breakup with girlfriend Carrie Snodgress, the song's second verse could equally apply to both his failed relationship and the ups and downs of his musical career: "I was adrift on a river of pride/It seemed like such a long easy ride/You were my raft but I let you slide/I've been down but I'm coming back up again."

'F*! #in' Up' is built around a titanic guitar riff, while Molina's drums thump with a power that threatens to penetrate the earth's crust as Young howls "why do I keep fuckin'up?", in doing so referencing his own self-destructive tendencies. The last minute of the track is a maelstrom of squalling guitar noise and feedback, every bit as edgy and innovative as anything much younger bands were creating at the time. 'Over and Over' is again built around a muscular guitar line, although the song itself is - by the standards of *Ragged Glory* - a little more mellow, as Young sings "I love the way you open up and let me in/So I go running back to you/Over and over again" with Crazy Horse's combined voices joining him on the "Over and over again" refrain. Another great example of the irresistible chemistry of Young and Crazy Horse at work, Young coaxes a superb solo from Old Black, magically capturing both the melancholy and energy of the song.

At 10 minutes, 'Love To Burn' feels a tad overstretched, but the sound is still tremendous, with the sparse lyrics allowing Young and the Horse to roam the wide open spaces with abandon. Young is playing guitar like a man reborn, and while the longer tracks on *Ragged Glory* don't have the same light and shade as a 'Down By The River' or 'Cortez The Killer' they demonstrate the sheer elemental force of Neil Young and Crazy Horse's musical telepathy more thrillingly than any other record.

The second half of *Ragged Glory* opens with a cover of The Premieres' 1964 U.S. hit 'Farmer John', a favourite of Young's since his Squires days. Young and Crazy Horse successfully recapture the ramshackle energy of the original while simultaneously ramping up the volume a few notches, meaning the only non-original track on the album fits well alongside the Young-penned material. But arguably the high point of the record comes next with 'Mansion On The Hill' - also released as a single - which is up there with 'Cinnamon Girl' and 'Powderfinger' as one of his finest ever straight up rock songs. With lyrics that revisit a popular theme for Young, reflecting on the supposedly idyllic '60s and his troubled relationship with that period, its irresistible, propulsive guitar riff and a knockout chorus sung with tremendous gusto by the whole band combine to make 'Mansion on The Hill' Young's best track for more than a decade. The lines "There's a mansion on the hill/ Psychedelic music fills the air/Peace and love live there still/In that mansion on the hill" make Young's feelings clear - the world of the '60s has passed, and only still exists for those who shut themselves off from moving forward.

Young had shown in the past he was more than happy to blatantly appropriate the melodies of his most illustrious contemporaries - notably on *Tonight's The Night*'s 'Borrowed Tune', which was based on the Rolling Stones' song 'Lady Jane'. This time it's Dylan's 'My Back Pages' that gets the magpie treatment on 'Days That Used To Be', another nostalgic song that laments the fraying of once-happy relationships. Lyrics like "I wish that I could talk to you, and you could talk to me/'Cause there's very few of us left my friend" are clear references to Crosby, Stills and Nash. It's followed by 'Love And Only Love', the second 10-minute long track on Ragged Glory and like 'Love to Burn' a real showcase for Young and Crazy Horse to let rip, with more coruscating Young solos anchored by the juggernaut rhythm section and Poncho Sampedro's underrated second guitar. Hypnotic in its intensity, it's hard to believe this is the work of the same man who had been written off by many as a directionless has-been just a few years earlier.

Final track 'Mother Earth (Natural Anthem)', with a melody adapted from the traditional folk ballad 'The Water Is Wide' was recorded live at Farm Aid IV, the now annual benefit concert for U.S. farmers co-founded by Young. Noticeably less furious in pace than the rest of *Ragged Glory*, with the hymnal group vocals taking centre stage, it feels rather a disappointing end to such a strong album, but it does highlight Young's growing interest in environmental issues, which would become a more and more prominent theme in his work. Lyrics like "Respect Mother Earth/ And her giving ways/Or trade away/Our children's days", while they may seem a little trite today, arguably shared sentiments that were ahead of their time in 1990.

Released in September 1990 to critical acclaim, *Ragged Glory* maintained the improved sales of *Freedom*, reaching number 31 in the U.S. charts and 15 in the U.K. But the record represented so much more than that. As well as resurrecting Crazy Horse to match their past heights, it also cemented Young's reputation as a lodestar for a new generation of alternative artists, leading to him to be dubbed 'the godfather of grunge'. The previous year's *The Bridge: A Tribute to Neil Young* saw his songs covered by The Pixies, Sonic Youth and Nick Cave, and the influence of *Ragged Glory's* guitar pyrotechnics could be heard loud and clear in the music of everyone from Nirvana and Pearl Jam to Radiohead and The Smashing Pumpkins. But Young being Young, he refused to rest on his laurels, and his next great album would be completely different once again.

⊙ TRACK LISTING   ◀◀ ▌▌ ▶▶

1. Country Home ·· 7:05
2. White Line ·· 2:57
3. F*! #in' Up (Neil Young, Frank "Poncho" Sampedro) ············ 5:54
4. Over and Over ·· 8:28
5. Love to Burn ··· 10:00
6. Farmer John" (Don Harris, Dewey Terry) ··················· 4:14
7. Mansion on the Hill ·· 4:48
8. Days That Used to Be ··· 3:42
9. Love and Only Love··· 10:18
10. Mother Earth (Natural Anthem) ······························ 5:11

Length: 62:43

Neil Young - Harvest Moon

Released 2 November 1992 (Reprise)

🎧   🎧   🎧

Following the triumphant return to the peak of their powers on *Ragged Glory*, Neil Young and Crazy Horse began 1991 by kicking off what became known as the 'Smell The Horse' tour, a mammoth 54 date undertaking, with Sonic Youth as the main support. The gruelling schedule and demanding, ear splittingly loud performances led to severe band tensions, producer David Briggs being sent home following a major bust up, and Young suffering from hyperacusis, a condition when everyday sounds seem much louder than they should.

Despite these challenges, the tour itself was a big success, with Young and Crazy Horse's outstanding live shows - some of the best they ever did - vividly captured on the live album and concert film *Weld*. This was initially released as a limited edition three-disc set entitled *Arc-Weld*, with the *Arc* portion being a single disc consisting in its entirety of a sound collage of guitar noise and feedback, another example of Young's fearless experimentation during this period.

"Playing that hard and that loud for that long is like spending the winter in the Arctic and then spending the summer in the Arctic and then finally deciding 'Well, let's go to Florida this winter," Young told Greg Kot of the Chicago Tribune. "You gotta have relief. That's what acoustic music is like to me." While he had released other albums since *Harvest* that felt similar in style to what remained his most popular album of all, *Comes A Time* and in particular *Old Ways* travelled even further towards pure country territory. With *Harvest Moon*, Young was finally delivering the bona fide follow up to *Harvest* fans had spent the past two decades hoping for, even reassembling most of the original Stray Gators line-up from the 1972 record - Ben Keith on steel guitar, Tim Drummond on bass and Kenny Buttrey on drums, together with the harmony vocals of James Taylor and Linda Ronstadt. Jack Nitzsche was replaced on keyboards by Spooner Oldham (although Nitzsche did arrange one track) and additional harmony vocals were provided by Nicolette Larsen and Young's half-sister Astrid, the daughter of Scott Young.

In a departure from his usual off the cuff, rough and ready approach to making albums, Young worked on perfecting *Harvest Moon* for many months, building on a series of original demos - some new songs, others dating back as far as 1971. Similar to *Harvest,* the subject matter is largely about relationships, but now written from the perspective of a middle-aged man, rather than the wide eyed twenty-something of 20 years before. While a few critics would go on to accuse Young of slipping into an unadventurous comfort zone when *Harvest Moon* was released - rather ironically, given the fact many had been calling for him to make 'Harvest II' when he was releasing 'difficult' material and experimenting wildly with unfamiliar genres - the album's meticulous craftsmanship, beautifully understated playing and some wonderfully elegant, timeless songs made it a delightfully mellow, if occasionally over-cosy listen.

Harvest Moon's best tracks appear early on. It opens with *Unknown Legend*, which instantly sets the tone for the record with Young's wistful vocal, Keith's gliding steel guitar, the unhurried rhythm and some gorgeous harmonies on the gently soaring chorus from Ronstadt. Partly inspired by Young's then wife Pegi Morton, who he had met in a diner back in 1974, it tells the tale of a mother of two looking back at the carefree life of her youth. Young's love for his wife shines through - especially the line "I used to order just to watch her glide across the floor" and the chorus of "Somewhere on a desert highway/She rides a Harley-Davidson/ Her long blonde hair flyin' in the wind" is sentimental yet exultant.

'From Hank To Hendrix' is equally wonderful, this time framing the challenges of maintaining a long-term relationship with a series of nostalgic references to cultural icons, ranging from Hank Marvin and Jimi Hendrix to Marilyn Monroe and Madonna, to reflect the passing of time. Musically it's like a warm bath, with some sublimely evocative harmonica and steel guitar work, and the bittersweet lyrics - "I always expected/That you should see me through/I never believed in much/But I believed in you" are both poignant and universal. 'You and Me' doesn't quite maintain the lofty standards of the first two tracks, but it's still utterly lovely, with the ghostly harmony vocals of Nicolette Larson and simple acoustic guitar accompaniment wrapped around another emotionally literate reflection from Young on the importance of keeping the spark of love alive. The first three lines - "Open up your eyes/See how lifetime flies/Open up and let the light back in '' - beautifully capture the sentiment of not allowing age to dim the feelings two people have for each other.

Harvest Moon's title track divides opinion among some listeners. Young's biographer Jimmy McDonough describes it as "bland", with "scattershot lyrics that careen from the cliche to the indelible, sometimes in the same verse."[1] The similarities to the Everly Brothers' 1961 hit 'Walk Right Back' are also

---

1 McDonough, p.663

well-documented. Yet 'Harvest Moon's' blissful serenity, built around a gossamer-light, lilting guitar line, swooning melody and lyrics that celebrate enduring love make it irresistible for those willing to accept Young at his most saccharine. The evergreen chorus "Because I'm still in love with you/I want to see you dance again/Because I'm still in love with you/On this harvest moon" has helped make it one of his best known songs, even giving Young a rare top 40 single in the U.K. charts.

'War of Man' temporarily shelves the laid back vibe to allow Young to make the point that while the world's media was focusing on human deaths in the Gulf War, animals were being routinely killed by mankind polluting the waters and the air. It's well-intentioned but a little overwrought, especially the portentous chorus, and feels somewhat out of place alongside the gentler material that otherwise predominates. But we're back on tried and tested ground with the plaintive 'One of These Days', on which Young remembers the many friends he's made during his now near-30 years in the music business, observing "I never tried to burn any bridges/Though I know I let some good things go." He pledges "to write a long letter to all the good friends I've known", acknowledging that "My friends are scattered/Like leaves from an old maple/Some are weak, some are strong."

The graceful but glacially paced 'Such A Woman', a heartfelt tribute from Young to his wife Pegi, has a quietly epic quality with the massed voices on the chorus and the presence of an 18-strong string section, arranged by Jack Nitzsche. While it thankfully lacks the unwelcome bombast of the London Symphony Orchestra's two contributions to *Harvest*, there is still a slight sense that this fragile song would work better with a little less melodrama, as the core message of the power and uniqueness of a long-term relationship's bond is most eloquently expressed by Young's yearning vocal with just piano and harmonica. In contrast, 'Old King', an affectionate, good humoured tribute to Young's late dog Elvis, is by some distance the most up-tempo track on the album, an exuberant, rootsy singalong with Young's banjo the most prominent instrument. 'Dreamin' Man' operates on two levels - on one hand, it's another wispy, pretty country rock ballad, with cooing female backing vocals, yet on the other, it has some genuinely disturbing lyrics suggesting the narrator is imagining murdering his love interest: "I park my Aerostar/With a loaded gun and sweet dreams of you."

Harvest Moon ends with the 10 minute long 'Natural Beauty', recorded live at The Civic Auditorium, in Portland, Oregon in January 1992. Mostly a solo performance by Young played on acoustic guitar and harmonica, it meanders gracefully without ever really going anywhere, with lyrics comparing the purity of nature with the greed of humankind, including a dig at modern music technology - soon to become another of his pet hates - with the line "I heard a perfect echo die/Into an anonymous wall/Of digital sound." The crowd applause at the end fades into a dawn chorus of wildlife noise, emphasising the contrast between the modern and natural worlds.

Probably unsurprisingly given its expertly crafted, easy on the ear material, *Harvest Moon* became Young's best-selling album since *Harvest,* showing that although his days of topping the charts remained behind him in year where Whitney Houston's *The Bodyguard* soundtrack sold a mind boggling 45 million copies worldwide, he nevertheless remained an artist with enduring appeal.

As an overall album, Young's long awaited 'Harvest II' is actually more consistent than its more celebrated but uneven predecessor, with a reflective, rich warmth that makes it one of the most accessible (if admittedly undemanding) and instantly enjoyable records he has ever made.

⊙ TRACK LISTING   ◄◄ ‖ ►►

1. Unknown Legend ⋯⋯⋯⋯⋯⋯⋯⋯⋯⋯⋯⋯⋯⋯⋯⋯ 4:32
2. From Hank to Hendrix ⋯⋯⋯⋯⋯⋯⋯⋯⋯⋯ 5:12
3. You and Me ⋯⋯⋯⋯⋯⋯⋯⋯⋯⋯⋯⋯⋯⋯⋯ 3:45
4. Harvest Moon ⋯⋯⋯⋯⋯⋯⋯⋯⋯⋯⋯⋯⋯⋯ 5:03
5. War of Man ⋯⋯⋯⋯⋯⋯⋯⋯⋯⋯⋯⋯⋯⋯⋯ 5:41
6. One of These Days ⋯⋯⋯⋯⋯⋯⋯⋯⋯⋯⋯ 4:55
7. Such a Woman ⋯⋯⋯⋯⋯⋯⋯⋯⋯⋯⋯⋯⋯ 4:36
8. Old King ⋯⋯⋯⋯⋯⋯⋯⋯⋯⋯⋯⋯⋯⋯⋯⋯ 2:57
9. Dreamin' Man ⋯⋯⋯⋯⋯⋯⋯⋯⋯⋯⋯⋯⋯ 4:36
10. Natural Beauty ⋯⋯⋯⋯⋯⋯⋯⋯⋯⋯⋯ 10.22
    (recorded live at The Civic Auditorium, Portland, Oregon, 23 January 1992)

Length: 51:39

Neil Young & Crazy Horse - Sleeps With Angels

Released 16 August 1994 (Reprise)

🎧　　🎧　　🎧

With *Harvest Moon* having continued his purple patch of outstanding mid-career albums starting with 1989's *Freedom*, Neil Young entered 1993 with his stock high, his contemporary work arguably the most lauded of any of rock's elder statesmen. His status as an influential figure for younger rock artists was further cemented when he was supported by the Black Crowes and Pearl Jam on a European tour, although his latest backing band, Booker T and the M.G.'s, very much belonged to an earlier era. Young's *MTV Unplugged* performance and subsequent album, featuring songs from across his entire career to date - some cleverly reinterpreted, such as an acoustic version of 1982's 'Transformer Man' stripped of *Trans*'s signature vocoders - was also well received.

From a place of apparent stability and contentment, it was typical that Young's next studio album, *Sleeps With Angels*, would prove to be the darkest, most unsettling record he had released since 1975's *Tonight's The Night*. A moody, murky collection of songs that are different again from the barnstorming garage rock of *Ragged Glory* and the cosily mellow *Harvest Moon*, it's one of the hardest albums to categorise in Young's entire back catalogue, but perhaps feels closest in spirit to 1974's *On The Beach*. Recorded at The Complex studio in Santa Monica with David Briggs back at the production helm following his bust up with Young during the *Ragged Glory* sessions, like its celebrated 1990 predecessor, *Sleeps With Angels* featured no musicians other than Young and Crazy Horse, although it is more varied in texture than any previous album they had made together, with straightforward guitar workouts kept to a minimum.

To prove the point, 'My Heart', the opening track of Sleeps With Angels, begins with a woozy saloon bar piano that sounds like it's straight from a Western soundtrack. With a fragile, almost childlike vocal from Young, guitarist Poncho Sampedro playing marimba, and hushed backing singing, it's a strange, slightly unsettling song, with enigmatic lyrics that seem to question the meaning of love, hinting that true fulfilment can only be found through faith in God. 'Prime of Life', for the first and last time (to date) in Young's career, sees him playing the flute (very badly) on an otherwise unremarkable mid-paced song, with more peculiar lyrics, this time about mediaeval kings and queens. The quality goes up a notch on 'Driveby', inspired by the tragic shooting of a friend of Young's daughter. With its measured, ominous pace and chanted group chorus of 'Driveby', the song succeeds in creating an atmosphere that's both tense and mournful, with details of the actual incident kept to a minimum. The way Young's voice cracks with emotion as he sings "Now she's gone/like a shooting star" is one of the record's most powerful moments.

The title track of *Sleeps With Angels* is widely believed to have been inspired by the death of Kurt Cobain, who - like many of the leading figures of the U.S. grunge scene - saw Young as an icon. Although the two men had never met, the older musician saw Cobain as a kindred spirit, and - aware of his troubles - had been trying to reach out to him to offer support via his manager Elliott Roberts during the days before Cobain took his own life. The connection was heightened further when a suicide note was found quoting a lyric from Young's 'Hey Hey, My My (Into The Black)', "It's better to burn out than to fade away." The song Young wrote in response eschews simple tribute, instead focusing on Cobain's story from both his perspective and that of partner Courtney Love. Musically, it was strikingly original, with its jagged, distorted guitars, jilting percussion and muffled, monotone singing evoking chaotic turmoil. The chorus, with its refrain of "Too late, too soon…he sleeps with angels… he's always on somebody's mind" captures the impact of the suicide on the wider public consciousness.

'Western Hero' is up next, an elegant, gently rhythmic ballad that offers a nostalgic reflection on the changing role of the conventional masculine hero in American culture, from the days of the Wild West frontier gunman to the soldier on the Normandy beaches during World War 2. The song concludes that today's technologically advanced warfare means the individual hero concept is no longer really relevant, as major conflicts between nuclear powers can only end in total annihilation.

The 14 minutes plus 'Change Your Mind', Young's longest ever studio song until topped by 2007's *Chrome Dreams II*'s 18 minute long 'Ordinary People' (and then subsequently 2012's Psychedelic Pill's 27 minute 'Driftin' Back'), is the closest *Sleeps With Angels* gets to a vintage Neil Young and Crazy Horse track. A celebration of love as the ultimate bond between two people, it has a slow burning, unhurried feel that recalls 'Down By The River' and 'Cowgirl In The Sand' right back at the very start of Young and Crazy Horse's journey together. The verses are interspersed with some quintessential Young guitar soloing, as fluid as it is unpredictable, but all the elements unify again on the strangely soothing chorus, a call and response between Young and his bandmates which exalts the ability of a partner to "change your mind" by offering emotional support and passionate companionship.

The darkly hypnotic guitar swirl of 'Blue Eden', from which disembodied fragments of lyrics from other *Sleeps With Angels* songs randomly emerge, is followed by 'Safeway Cart', an atmospheric depiction of an empty ghetto as a new day dawns. Backed by an ominous, pulsating bassline and a drumbeat like a ticking clock, Young sings in a hushed whisper, adding to the sense of uneasy quietness that he seems unwilling to disturb. 'Train of Love' is perhaps the most disappointing song on the album, with its cliched locomotive metaphors and a melody that's almost identical to 'Western Hero'. But 'Trans Am' raises the bar again, with its evocative lyrics about the decline of the American domestic car industry set to a swampy musical accompaniment that once again fizzles with restrained menace.

Even the greats occasionally come up with a song so bad it is hard to pinpoint any redeeming features, and with 'Piece of Crap' - a charmless, shouty attack on the evils of modern consumerism - Young produces a contender for his worst ever moment on record. Although clearly intended to be satirical, it sounds like Young and Crazy Horse have temporarily handed the reins to Beavis and Butthead. The album closes with 'A Dream That Can Last', which brings us back full circle to the opening 'My Heart.' The saloon bar piano is back, and the lyrics see Young enter a dreamlike state in which the subject of 'Driveby' isn't killed, the urban streets are paved with gold and "Out on the corner the angels say/There is a better life for me someday". It's as if he's found contentment, safe from the dangers of the real world, and once again, the listener is left questioning whether this idyllic state is in some way connected to religious faith.

Sleeps With Angels doesn't quite have the consistent calibre of song writing to be ranked as one of Young's very finest records. But it is one of his boldest and most original, sounding like nothing else he has ever made, an ambitious song cycle with a theme exploring violence and despair and how to escape them, backed by music that is uncharacteristically subdued yet compellingly powerful. Despite being far less commercial than his previous three releases, *Sleeps With Angels* became a Top 10 album in the U.S. and the U.K., aided by Young's anointment as the 'godfather of grunge', a status ironically enhanced further by Kurt Cobain's tragic death. But it also marked the end of a five year purple patch that began with 1989's *Freedom* - a period during which he had once again scaled artistic heights many observers thought had long since been beyond him. In the eyes of many fans, he would never quite scale those heights again.

⊙ TRACK LISTING   ⏮ ⏸ ⏭

1. My Heart ·· 2:44
2. Prime of Life ·· 4:02
3. Driveby··· 4:43
4. Sleeps with Angels ··· 2:44
5. Western Hero·· 4:00
6. Change Your Mind ·· 14:39
7. Blue Eden ·· 6:22
8. Safeway Cart ·· 6:29
9. Train of Love·· 3:57
10. Trans Am ·· 4:07
11. Piece of Crap ··· 3:15
12. A Dream That Can Last·· 5.27

Length: 62:06

Neil Young featuring Pearl Jam - Mirror Ball

Released 7 August 1995 (Reprise/Epic)

🎧　🎧　🎧

Neil Young's induction into Rock & Roll's Hall of Fame on 12 January 1995, as well as being an overdue recognition of his enormous contribution to the genre (how exactly were Rod Stewart and Elton John, for all their mass appeal, deemed worthy of inclusion a year earlier?), also marked the beginning of a new collaboration with a future Hall of Fame act: Seattle grunge legends Pearl Jam.

Only founded in 1990, the five-piece's 1991 debut album *Ten*, boosted by anthemic hit single 'Alive', became one of the cornerstone records of the grunge explosion of the early 1990s, even though their sound owed as much to classic rock as the alternative scene. Having already supported Young on his 1993 European tour, front man Eddie Vedder was among the fellow artists who paid tribute to the new inductee at the New York ceremony, and Young and Crazy Horse travelled down to Washington DC the next day to support Pearl Jam at the two day Voters for Choice benefit concert in support of pro-choice political candidates. Before the first night, Young surreptitiously visited Pearl Jam's rehearsal, and - to Crazy Horse's surprise - he joined Vedder and his bandmates on stage that evening for an encore of Young's new song 'Act of Love'. Enthused by the energy and verve of the performance, Young - never one for sentimentality - promptly fired Crazy Horse and producer David Briggs three days later and decided to make his next album with the cool kids from Washington state.

Recorded at Bad Animals studio in Seattle in the weeks following the Voters for Choice concert performance, with producer Brendan O'Brien, who had worked with many of the leading lights of the grunge scene, at the helm, *Mirror Ball* ultimately didn't sound that different to a Young and Crazy Horse record. Played live, with the sounds of studio conversations clearly audible, it's an uncomplicated, rough and ready rock album, and while Pearl Jam may be marginally more polished than the Horse, they still make one hell of a noise. Featuring ten songs written by Young - 'I Got Id' and 'Long Road', both written and sung by Vedder, were cut from the album and later released on Pearl Jam's 1995 *Merkin Ball* EP - it is essentially a Neil Young solo record rather than a true collaboration, with Vedder restricted to a supporting role alongside the rest of his group - guitarists Stone Gossard and Mike McCready, bassist Jeff Ament and drummer Jack Irons.

Mirror Ball starts strongly with the coruscating 'Song X', a striking modern sea shanty complete with a swaying chorus chant of 'hey ho, away we go' from Young and Pearl Jam. The triple guitar sound is both propulsive and layered, although there is still ample room for Young's solos to breathe. Its lyrics enter the abortion debate, with two young lovers - characterised as a modern day Romeo and Juliet - featured in scenes involving a back of a van illegal termination and a priest representing the judgment of religion.

Young continues the theme on 'Act of Love', which portrays the abortion debate as a holy war between the Christians who believe they will receive redemption by protecting life, and those who believe in the right to choose. Perhaps in order to provide balance, Young features a callous unwilling father, who offers to pay his partner to get a termination. Unfortunately, the song itself - a prosaic, plodding rocker - doesn't do justice to the complex issues the lyrics present.

The driving urgency of 'I'm The Ocean' provides a suitably dynamic backdrop to one of Young's most nakedly autobiographical songs of the 1990s. Amid the kaleidoscopic references to Native Americans, rows of lovers and sports players, Young uses various metaphors to describe his own free spirited, ever changing persona, including "I'm for rollin'/I'm for tossin' in my sleep", and "I'm an aerostar/I'm a cutlass supreme/In the wrong lane/Trying to turn against the flow/I'm the ocean/I'm the giant undertow." Perhaps most revealingly of all, the track includes the line "People my age/They don't do the things I do/They go somewhere/While I run away with you", summing up his determination to remain unpredictable and relevant when well into middle age.

'Big Green Country' is an enjoyable enough muscular guitar stomp, with more Wild West-inspired lyrics about lone riders and painted braves, as well as an oblique reference to the 'cancer cowboy', quite probably Marlboro Man David McLean, who died of lung cancer at the age 73 in 1995, with his widow suing parent company Philip Morris amid accusations that smoking packs of cigarettes on advertising shoots contributed to Mclean's death. 'Truth Be Known' is a little mellower than the previous four tracks; a reflection on faded dreams, with Vedder joining Young on vocals and a likely reference to Kurt Cobain's death towards the end of the song with the lyrics "When the fire/That once was your friend/Burns your fingers to the bone/And your song/Meets a sudden end."

We're back into a more up-tempo groove again on the good humoured boogie of 'Downtown', on which Young imagines a nightclub frequented by ageing hippies doing the Charleston, adding that "Jimi's playin' in the back room/Led Zeppelin on stage/There's a mirror ball twirlin'/And a note from Page." It's followed by Young's shortest ever song, 'What Happened Yesterday', a 45 second snapshot in which he encapsulates the impact of an unnamed event (perhaps Cobain's death) accompanying himself on pipe organ. In contrast, 'Peace and Love' clocks in at seven minutes, but still feels tight, with some of the most expressive, varied guitar work on the album, really showcasing the impact of having three players together. Vedder also has his most prominent part yet, taking the lead vocal for large parts of the song, which perhaps unsurprisingly means it sounds more like Pearl Jam than anything else on *Mirror Ball*.

'Throw Your Hatred Down', a laboured treatise on humankind's propensity for violence, and 'Scenery', which examines the treatment of heroes by the U.S. media, are both stodgy, overlong and frankly forgettable, meaning *Mirror Ball* begins to stutter towards the finishing line. At just over a minute, the closing track 'Fallen Angel', with Young back on pipe organ and the same melody as 'I'm the Ocean' has little time to halt the slide, ending the record on a rather despondent note with the lines "Fallen angel/Who's your savior tonight."

Boosted by the presence of the hugely popular Pearl Jam, *Mirror Ball* continued Young's 1990s commercial renaissance, reaching the top five of the album charts in both the U.S. and the U.K., and an 11 date tour - dubbed "Neil Jam" - followed. Despite its undoubted success and mostly warm critical reception, the erratic quality of Young's song writing, an absence of many truly memorable tunes and the somewhat samey - if impressive - musicianship means the album should be filed under the 'interesting project' rather than 'essential listen' category.

⊙ TRACK LISTING ◖◀ ❙❙ ▶◗

1. Song X ⋯⋯⋯⋯⋯⋯⋯⋯⋯⋯⋯⋯⋯⋯⋯⋯⋯⋯⋯⋯ 4:40
2. Act of Love ⋯⋯⋯⋯⋯⋯⋯⋯⋯⋯⋯⋯⋯⋯⋯⋯⋯ 4:54
3. I'm the Ocean ⋯⋯⋯⋯⋯⋯⋯⋯⋯⋯⋯⋯⋯⋯⋯ 7:05
4. Big Green Country ⋯⋯⋯⋯⋯⋯⋯⋯⋯⋯⋯⋯ 5:08
5. Truth Be Known ⋯⋯⋯⋯⋯⋯⋯⋯⋯⋯⋯⋯⋯ 4:39
6. Downtown ⋯⋯⋯⋯⋯⋯⋯⋯⋯⋯⋯⋯⋯⋯⋯⋯ 5:10
7. What Happened Yesterday ⋯⋯⋯⋯⋯⋯ 0:46
8. Peace and Love ⋯⋯⋯⋯⋯⋯⋯⋯⋯⋯⋯⋯⋯ 7:02
9. Throw Your Hatred Down ⋯⋯⋯⋯⋯⋯ 5:45
10. Scenery ⋯⋯⋯⋯⋯⋯⋯⋯⋯⋯⋯⋯⋯⋯⋯⋯⋯ 8:50
11. Fallen Angel ⋯⋯⋯⋯⋯⋯⋯⋯⋯⋯⋯⋯⋯⋯ 1.15

Length: 55:14

Neil Young - Dead Man

Released 27 February 1996 (Vapor)

Throughout his long career, Neil Young had periodically dabbled with film soundtracks. As well as his own self-directed movie projects - 1972's *Journey Through The Past,* 1979's *Rust Never Sleeps* and 1983's *Human Highway* - he also contributed several tracks to the 1980 Hunter S. Thompson biopic *Where The Buffalo Roam,* starring Bill Murray. But until *Dead Man,* he had never attempted a full film score of original material for a project not creatively led by himself.

Ohio-born Jim Jarmusch had been one of the leading figures of American art house cinema since the mid-1980s, when his 1984 debut *Stranger Than Paradise* won the Camera D'Or award (given to the best first feature that year) at the 1984 Cannes Film Festival. A long standing fan, Jarmusch had Young in mind when shooting his 1995 film *Dead Man,* his highest budget project yet starring Johnny Depp, John Hurt and Robert Mitchum. The director appeared backstage at a Crazy Horse concert in Sedona, Arizona and handed Young a copy of the script. With its loose plot featuring a man named William Blake (played by Depp) travelling across a nightmarish vision of the late 19th century American West accompanied by a Native American (Gary Farmer), the appeal to Young - who had explored similar themes in his own songs - was obvious.

Before beginning work on the score, Young watched an early cut of *Dead Man* three times over a two-day period. Shot entirely in black and white, giving the film a haunting quality, Young's sparse, ghostly, fragmented music, mostly played on electric guitar, with additional acoustic guitar, pump organ and detuned piano, effectively complements the on screen images. The extended instrumental passages are interspersed with sections of dialogue from the film, most featuring Depp, often reading the poetry of his character's namesake William Blake.

If there is a comparison to be found elsewhere in Young's catalogue, it would undoubtedly be *Arc*, the 35 minute long patchwork of feedback, guitar noise, improvisations and vocal fragments recorded during a range of Young and Crazy Horse's live shows on their 1991 U.S. tour. But the *Dead Man* soundtrack has a consistency of mood and stark yet meditative quality that is completely different to *Arc*'s more visceral assault on the senses.

Entitled 'Guitar Solos No.1 - 6', each of Young's half dozen core compositions are freeform in style, with waves of portentously sweeping, reverb-heavy guitar notes periodically giving way to shards of more delicate, defined melody. Occasionally other ambient sounds are also heard, notably waves gently lapping the shore. A brief variation is provided by one further track, the dreamy 'Organ Solo' - performed, as its name suggests, on pump organ. The excellent 'Dead Man Theme', a more lyrical, acoustic piece with some similarities to Bob Dylan's *Pat Garrett and Billy The Kid* soundtrack, was heard during the film's opening and closing credits, but was not included on the album (although it did appear on a promotional single).

The centrepiece of Young's score is 'Guitar Solo No.5', which at close to 15 minutes is almost three times as long as any of the other solos. A constantly but subtly changing sonic landscape, with Young's Old Black guitar ebbing and flowing with elemental power and grace, it mesmerizingly evokes the wide open spaces Jarmusch's film inhabits, occasionally building to passages of urgent tension before gliding back into calmer waters. It is hard to imagine any of Young's contemporaries ever attempting work as experimental as this, and his playing on *Dead Man* is further evidence that he is one of the greatest guitarists ever to plug in an amp. Years later, he would explore the limits of his instrument further on his outstanding 2010 *Le Noise* album, which shares some of the *Dead Man* soundtrack's avant garde adventurism, this time within conventional song structures.

Recorded at Mason Street studios in San Francisco in March 1995 and co-produced by Young and John Hanlon, who had worked as an engineer and mixer on several other Young records, the *Dead Man* soundtrack was released on Vapor Records, Young and manager Elliott Roberts' new label, in February 1996. After being shown at the 1995 Cannes Film Festival, the movie itself was released in May 1996, receiving a mixed critical reception and recouping only a fraction of its budget at the box office, although it is now widely regarded as one of the most ambitious and important modern Westerns.

Although clearly not an album for casual Neil Young listeners, the *Dead Man* soundtrack is far more than just an obscure curiosity. It is a fine showcase for Young's sheer versatility as a musician, demonstrating yet another string to his bow as well as being a compelling example of an effective film score in its own right.

⏵ TRACK LISTING   ⏮ ⏸ ⏭

1. Guitar Solo, No. 1 ·· 5:18
2. The Round Stones Beneath the Earth… ··························· 3:32
3. Guitar Solo, No. 2 ·· 2:03
4. Why Dost Thou Hide Thyself, Clouds… ························ 2:25
5. Organ Solo ·· 1:33
6. Do You Know How to Use This Weapon? ····················· 4:25
7. Guitar Solo, No. 3 ·· 4:31
8. Nobody's Story ·· 6:36
9. Guitar Solo, No. 4 ·· 4:22
10. Stupid White Men… ··· 8:46
11. Guitar Solo, No. 5 ·· 14:41
12. Time for You to Leave, William Blake… ······················· 0:51
13. Guitar Solo, No. 6 ·· 3:22

Length: 62:24

Neil Young & Crazy Horse - Broken Arrow

Released 2 July 1996 (Reprise)

🎧 🎧 🎧

On 26 November 1995, Young lost one of his closest collaborators when producer David Briggs - who had worked with him on almost 20 albums since his 1968 debut - passed away from lung cancer at the age of just 51. Shortly before his old friend died, Young asked him frankly for any advice on his career moving forward, and was told to keep things simple and focused, with as much of his own singing and playing as possible, because "no-one gives a shit about anything else."[1]

Young's response was to return once again to Crazy Horse following their latest spell out in the cold while he consummated his new relationship with Pearl Jam. Seeking to recapture the spirit of a similar tour 20 years before, when the band were at their *Zuma*-era peak, Young booked a series of low key dates with Poncho Sampedro, Billy Talbot and Ralph Molina at the 150-capacity Old Princeton Landing bar, close to Young's ranch in northern California, during March and April 1996. Loving the spontaneity and energy of the performances, he then took the decision to get Crazy Horse into the studio as soon as possible, in the hope of capturing their reinvigorated live sound on record.

The resulting album, recorded at Plywood Digital studios in Woodside, near San Francisco, was predictably undercooked. Recorded almost straight after the live dates over a period of less than a month, it is hampered by Young's most uninspiring collection of songs for a decade, playing that is brutally raw even by the Horse's standards, and Young's own sludgy production. It's the beginning of a trend in Young's records with Crazy Horse that has continued on and off to this day - a tendency to value groove and vibe over song writing craft, which leads to

---

1 Neil Young, *Waging Heavy Peace*, p. 473

Neil Young - After The Gold Rush album cover, 1970. (Alamy)

Neil Young, 1971. (Alamy)

Neil Young in concert at Austin's Municipal auditorium, November 9, 1976.
(Photo: Mark Estabrook)

Billboard promoting Neil Young's *Zuma* album on the Sunset Strip in 1976. (Alamy)

Farm Aid founders Neil Young (L) and Willie Nelson speak to farmers at a rally outside the New World Music Theatre in Tinley Park, prior to the start of Farm Aid 1997. (Alamy)

Stephen Stills and Neil Young performing during a 2006 tour as part of Crosby, Stills, Nash, and Young. (Photo: Matthew Harris) - (Wikimedia Creative Commons)

Young with his band at Massey Hall, Toronto, 27 November 2007 - from left to right: Rick Rosas, Anthony Crawford, Pegi Young, Neil, Ralph Molina and Ben Keith. (Photo: 3rdparty!)

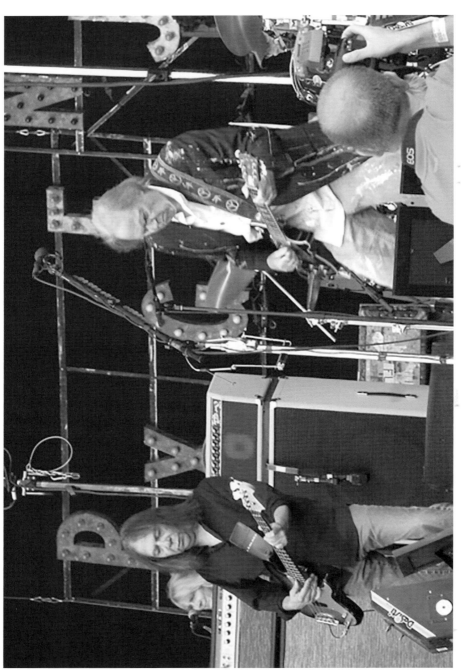

Neil Young, 2008 (with Rick Rosas). (Photo: snikwas)

Neil and Pegi Young at the Trent FM Arena in Nottingham, England, 2009. (Photo: Andy Roo)

Neil Young at the Trent FM Arena, with Ben Keith (left) and Rick Rosas (behind Young) (Photo: Andy Roo). (Wikimedia Creative Commons)

Young at the premiere of the concert film *Neil Young Journeys*, 2011. (Photo: Ross Belot)

Neil Young, 2012. (Photo: By Man Alive!)

Neil Young and Crazy Horse, 2012: Ralph Molina (drums), Billy Talbot (bass), Neil Young (guitar). Guitarist Frank "Poncho" Sampedro is seen only partially. (Photo: Shane Hirschman)

Young playing with Promise of the Real at the main stage of Stavernfestivalen, Norway, 7 July 2016. (Photo: Tore Sætre)

Neil Young at the music festival Desert Trip in California, where he performed
with Paul McCartney, October 18, 2016. (Photo: Raph_PH)

Neil Young performs at the Wayhome Music & Arts Festival in Oro-Medonte, Canada. (Alamy)

many tracks becoming little more than shapeless extended jams, with little in the way of melody or lyrical sophistication.

Broken Arrow doesn't open too badly with the spirited, nostalgia-tinged 'Big Time', in which Young seems to be looking back to his now legendary arrival in California from Canada 30 years earlier with Bruce Palmer, driving a Pontiac hearse: "Gettin' in an old black car/Gonna take a ride so far/To the land of suntan lotion." But the near-ten minute long 'Loose Change', after a promising start built around some typically crunchy guitar chords and a squalling harmonica break, soon deteriorates into the kind of directionless noodling that plagues much of the album, with Young's voice so deep in the mix it's almost suffocating - not that the lyrics, a tired blend of cliches and uninspired imagery, have much interesting to say.

'Slip Away' is stronger, with a world-weary, melancholy guitar sound framing Young's enigmatic lyrics about a woman who finds freedom from the challenges of her life when music starts playing. Young's guitar solo here is one of his most underrated, bringing the song to a hypnotic, graceful conclusion. But 'Changing Highways' is a throwaway chug, so sluggish it almost feels like the record's speed has been deliberately slowed down. 'Scattered (Let's Think About Livin')' isn't much better: despite having perhaps the most engaging guitar riff on the album, it's once again let down by ponderous playing and poor mixing. Completing a triumvirate of weak mid-album filler is 'This Town', another plodding, middle of the road affair, with flimsy, tossed off lyrics about urban dysfunction.

The gentle acoustic guitar ballad 'Music Arcade', sang by Young in a gravelly whisper, has echoes of *Nebraska*-era Bruce Springsteen, and while a little out of place among the sprawling garage rock of most of *Broken Arrow*, it's the most thoughtful song on the album. The lyrics focus on the ups and downs of life and how we all perceive ourselves differently depending on what we're experiencing, with Young concluding "There's a comet in the sky tonight/Makes me feel like I'm alright/I'm movin' pretty fast/For my size." It would have been a nice way to end the record, but mercurial as ever, Young tags on a fuzzy live version of Jimmy Reed's 1959 blues classic 'Baby What You Want Me to Do' from one of the recent Old Princeton Landing gigs. Recorded using a single microphone hanging from the ceiling, the sound is barely bootleg quality, with the crowd noise as prominent as the musicians. The vinyl edition of Broken Arrow also included an excellent outtake from the *Ragged Glory* sessions, the elegantly dreamy, softly strummed 'Interstate', completely unlike its parent album with guitar figures that have a distinctive classical feel.

Young seemed resigned to the fact that *Broken Arrow* would be poorly received, telling Jimmy McDonough, "They'll shit on this one. I've given them a moving target... it's purposefully vulnerable and unfinished. I wanted to get one under my belt without David."[2] In the end, the album sold respectably enough, reaching the top 20 in the U.K. charts and 31 in the U.S., but compared to the stellar Briggs-produced Young and Crazy Horse records, it feels a minor work, with a few decent songs struggling to break through the prevailing mediocrity.

What followed was Young's longest ever gap between albums, with four years passing before he re-emerged with 2000's *Silver and Gold*. *Broken Arrow* wasn't the way Young fans would have liked him to sign off for the millennium, but as always, there would be plenty more twists and turns to come as he entered the 21st century.

⊙ TRACK LISTING ⏮ ⏸ ⏭

1. Big Time ⸱⸱⸱ 7:24
2. Loose Change ⸱⸱⸱ 9:49
3. Slip Away ⸱⸱⸱ 8:36
4. Changing Highways ⸱⸱⸱ 2:28
5. Scattered (Let's Think About Livin') ⸱⸱⸱⸱⸱⸱⸱⸱⸱⸱⸱⸱⸱⸱⸱⸱⸱⸱⸱⸱⸱⸱⸱⸱ 4:13
6. This Town ⸱⸱ 2:59
7. Music Arcade ⸱⸱ 3:59
8. Baby What You Want Me to Do   8:08
   (Jimmy Reed, live at the Old Princeton Landing)

Length: 47:02

---

2 McDonough, p.728

Neil Young - Silver and Gold

Released 25 April 2000 (Reprise)

🎧   🎧   🎧

By his own formidably energetic standards, the late 1990s was perhaps the lowest key period of Neil Young's career. 1997 had seen the release of the *Year of the Horse* double CD live album, culled from the previous year's *Broken Arrow* album tour with Crazy Horse, followed by a movie of the same name directed by Young's friend Jim Jarmusch and focusing on the singer's unique relationship with his most enduring musical collaborators. During the next three years, although he continued to perform regularly, including a 1999 U.S. solo tour, the only new Young material appeared on the latest CSN&Y revival later that year. Unfortunately, the album *Looking Forward* did the opposite of its title, being another pale imitation of the super group's halcyon days three decades before. But Young's three songs on the record - warm, acoustic and reflective - did give a hint of the direction his now long-awaited next solo release would take.

While *Broken Arrow* and *Mirror Ball* had both been written and recorded in a matter of a few weeks, *Silver and Gold* gestated gradually over several years before finally appearing in 2000, with a couple of songs dating back to the 1980s. Originally envisaged as an entire album of performances by Young only, a small but stellar cast of backing musicians ended up joining him for the ride: backing singers Linda Ronstadt and Emmylou Harris, Booker T. & the M.G. 's bassist Donald "Duck" Dunn, revered session drummer Jim Keltner, Spooner Oldham on piano/organ and - inevitably - Ben Keith on pedal steel, who also co-produced with Young. The end result is perhaps the quietest, gentlest record in Young's entire discography, with similar, country-influenced feel to 1992's *Harvest Moon,* but sparser in texture and more intimate.

Opening track 'Good To See You' sets the tone for the album. An amiable tribute to the simple joys of domestic stability, this is Young in his rocking chair rather than the elemental force of nature of many of his earlier works. There is rarely heard contentment in his voice as he sings "I've been down on the endless highway/I passed on the solid line/Now at last I'm home to you/I feel like making up for lost time." It's followed by the title track, which has a similar theme around the stability of a strong relationship. Even though Young had apparently been striving to perfect it for nearly 20 years, it's no more than a pleasant, rather bland acoustic strum.

The next two songs maintain the same cosy vibe, but teeter into tweeness. 'Daddy Went Walkin'' sees a son affectionately depicting his elderly farmer parents, with an excessively chirpy harmonica and some cloying lyrics - "Brown leather boots and an old straw hat/Daddy's getting wood with the barnyard cat". 'Buffalo Springfield Again' sees Young reminiscing fondly about the band where he first made his name, making clear their breakup shouldn't be a blame game - "I'm not saying who was right or wrong" - and even adding "Like to see those guys again/ And give it a shot." However, the song is let down by its gratingly jaunty tune and musicianship.

Thankfully, *Silver and Gold* recovers its footing quickly with 'The Great Divide'. A plaintive, world weary ballad, sung by Young in his most vulnerable, high register, the song again sees him seeking comfort and certainty among the world's challenges and features some beautifully understated harmonium and pedal steel work from Oldham and Keith respectively. 'Horseshoe Man', the tale of a mythical figure who repairs broken hearts, is another gem, built on cascades of elegant rolling piano, softly shuffling percussion and once again, Keith's haunting pedal steel. The album reaches its peak with 'Red Sun', another paean to the enduring power of love. With its gorgeous melody and stunning harmony vocals from Harris and Ronstadt on the blissful, sighing chorus, it's one of Young's most underrated songs.

'Distant Camera' provides more of the same - nostalgic, dreamy lyrics about the timeless nature of a lifelong relationship as all around you is changing, wistfully sang by Young with an impeccably arranged and played accompaniment from his supporting cast of seasoned veterans. 'Razor Love' - the second song on the album that can trace its roots back to the 1980s - is a serene, graceful meditation on love, family and the transience of the touring musician's life, with Young singing "Make a living like a rolling stone/On the road/There's no place like home." It meanders unhurriedly for over six minutes, but delightfully so. *Silver and Gold* ends with the melancholy, hypnotic 'Without Rings', perhaps the most enigmatic song on the album, with lyrics that seem to picture a man struggling to adjust to having lost connection with a partner.

Admittedly, there's little variation in pace or mood on *Silver and Gold,* and there's some justification in perceptions of the album as Young on autopilot, sleepwalking his way through songs that flicker prettily without ever properly catching fire. But for those willing to cut the man some slack and allow him the occasional untaxing stroll rather than expecting him to push the boundaries every time he makes a record, for the most part it's an effortlessly engaging, lovingly crafted work from an artist unafraid to slow down, sit contentedly on his porch and let his listeners bask in an autumnal glow of calm introspection. The album made the top 10 in the U.K. charts (number 22 in the U.S.) and there's a strong case for categorising it as the last flowering of his 1990s creative rebirth.

⊙ TRACK LISTING   ⏮ ❚❚ ⏭

1. Good to See You ·· 2:48
2. Silver & Gold ··· 3:17
3. Daddy Went Walkin' ·· 4:02
4. Buffalo Springfield Again ·· 3:21
5. The Great Divide ·· 4:32
6. Horseshoe Man ·· 3:59
7. Red Sun ·· 2:46
8. Distant Camera ·· 4:06
9. Razor Love ··· 6:29
10. Without Rings ·· 3:42

Length: 39:02

Timeline - Rebirth (1989 - 2000)

🎧　🎧　🎧

1989

11 January - 23 February: U.S. tour with The Restless.

5 April - 5 May: Tour of Japan, Australia and New Zealand, with The Restless now known as The Lost Dogs.

17 April: Release of the *Eldorado* EP in Japan and Australia only.

14 June: The live acoustic version of 'Rockin' In The Free World' used as the opening track on Young's *Freedom* album is recorded at the Jones Beach Theater in Wantagh, New York. The remaining tracks for the album are finalised over the summer of 1989.

28 July: Release of *The Bridge: A Tribute to Neil Young*, featuring covers of Young's songs by alternative rock musicians including Nick Cave and Sonic Youth.

30 September: Young makes his memorable appearance on Saturday Night Live performing 'Rockin' In The Free World'.

2 October: *Freedom* album released.

1990

16 April: Young performs at the Nelson Mandela tribute concert at Wembley stadium in London.

24-30 April: Records *Ragged Glory* with Crazy Horse.

9 September: *Ragged Glory* is released.

15 October: Young's mother Rassy dies of cancer.

1991

22 January - 27 April: 'Smell the Horse' tour of the U.S. and Canada with Crazy Horse.

September - February 1992: Recording of Harvest Moon with the reformed Stray Gators at Redwood Digital studios in Woodside, California.

23 October: Release of two-disc live album *Weld*, recorded on the 'Smell The Horse' tour.

1992

20 January - 24 March: First of four U.S. solo tours of 1992.

17 May - 11 July: Second U.S. solo tour.

11 - 27 September: Third U.S. solo tour.

16 October: Plays with Booker T. & the M.G.s at a Madison Square Garden, New York concert to celebrate Bob Dylan's 30 years as a recording artist.

2 November: Release of *Harvest Moon*.

14-22 November: Fourth U.S. solo tour.

1993

6 January: Release of *Lucky Thirteen*, a compilation of Young's music during his period at Geffen.

7 February: Appears on *MTV Unplugged* show.

8 June: *Unplugged* album released.

26 June - 19 September: Young tours the U.S. and Europe with Booker T. & the M.G.s.

November - April 1994: Recording of *Sleeps with Angels* album with Crazy Horse.

1994

February: Young receives an Oscar nomination for Best Original Song for 'Philadelphia', the closing song of Jonathan Demme's movie of the same name. Bruce Springsteen's 'Streets of Philadelphia' from the same film wins the award the following month.

5 April: Nirvana frontman Kurt Cobain, widely believed to have inspired the title track of Young's Sleeps with Angels album.

2 August: Release of *Borrowed Tunes: A Tribute to Neil Young*, featuring contributions by a variety of Canadian musicians covering songs written by Young.

16 August: *Sleeps with Angels* released.

1995

12 January: Young is inducted into the Rock and Roll Hall of Fame in a ceremony at New York's Waldorf Astoria hotel.

January - February: Records *Mirror Ball* with Pearl Jam.

27 March: Records soundtrack for Jim Jarmusch's film *Dead Man*.

27 June: Release of *Mirror Ball*.

12 - 27 August: Tour of Europe backed by Pearl Jam.

26 November: Young's long standing producer David Briggs dies of lung cancer.

1996

27 February: Dead Man soundtrack album released.

March - April: Recording of *Broken Arrow* album with Crazy Horse at Plywood Digital, Woodside, California.

18 March - 9 June: Tour of California clubs with Crazy Horse under the name of The Echoes.

June 20 - July 22: Broken Arrow European tour with Crazy Horse.

July 2: Release of *Broken Arrow*.

9 August - 17 November: Broken Arrow tour of the U.S. with Crazy Horse.

1997

9 May: Release of *Year of the Horse*, Jim Jarmusch's concert film of Young and Crazy Horse's Broken Arrow tour.

17 June: *Year of the Horse* live album released, also featuring recordings from the Broken Arrow tour.

11 July - 24 August: Headlines the 1997 HORDE festival tour, performing alongside Beck and Ben Folds Five among others.

18 November: Release of The Bridge School Concerts Volume 1, featuring a range of performances from the concert's first decade from artists including Young, Willie Nelson and R.E.M.

1998

An uncharacteristically quiet year for Young, with his only live performances being his usual Farm Aid and Bridge School Benefit Concert appearances on 3 and 17/18 October respectively.

1999

2 March - 2 June: *An Evening with Neil Young* solo tour of the U.S. and Canada.

26 October: Release of CSN&Y's Looking Forward album, recorded between 1996 and 1999.

2000

24 January - 19 April: CSNY2K North American tour by CSN&Y.

25 April: Release of *Silver and Gold* album, which Young had worked on intermittently between August 1997 and May 1999.

8 August - 1 October: *Music in Head* tour of the U.S., backed by Friends and Relatives, a band including 'Duck' Dunn, Spooner Oldham, Jim Keltner, wife Pegi and half-sister Astrid.

5 December: Release of *Road Rock Vol 1: Friends and Relatives*, recorded during the Music in Head tour.

PART 5

21st century maverick (2001-2023)

Neil Young & Crazy Horse - Toast

Released 8 July 2022 (Reprise)

🎧　　🎧　　🎧

Neil Young's collaboration with the legendary Booker T. & the M.G.'s on 2002's *Are You Passionate?* is often (perhaps a little unfairly) cited by critics and fans alike as one of his least successful genre experiments. Dominated by polite, bland soul and R&B pastiches, the inclusion of one Crazy Horse collaboration - 'Goin' Home', a gloriously messy, driving guitar epic completely unlike the rest of the record - gave a tantalising glimpse of another of Young's fabled lost albums: *Toast*, recorded with Crazy Horse at the San Francisco studios of the same name during 2001.

Recorded at a time when Young was experiencing serious marital tensions with his wife Pegi, the music on *Toast* is portentous and bleak, although the R&B and jazz grooves that he went on to nail with Booker T. & the M.G.'s are already present here in a less polished form, with Crazy Horse's very creditable playing belying their reputation as limited sluggers. As Young put it: "I played my guitar like an old horn, with a big fat sad sound. Ralphie, Billy and Poncho gave it the old funky feel."[1]

However, Young was dissatisfied with the record, and after a break away from the studio playing concerts in South America, followed by a further set of San Francisco sessions, he decided enough was enough. "Eventually I gave up and abandoned the album," Young wrote in his second volume of autobiography, 2014's *Special Deluxe*. "I was not happy with it, or maybe I was just generally unhappy. I don't know. It was a very desolate album, very sad and unanswered."[2] Four of *Toast*'s seven songs went on to appear on *Are You Passionate?* either as re-recorded versions or reworked with new titles.

---

1 Neil Young, Special Deluxe (2014), p.305
2 Neil Young, Special Deluxe, p.305

The laid back, reflective mood of opener 'Quit' is not dissimilar to the version released on *Are You Passionate*? with Young and Poncho Sampedro's lithe, languid guitar playing providing a soulful vibe that's anchored by the usual thudding Ralph Molina beat. "I know I treated you bad/But I'm doin' the best I can", Young protests, with the backing vocals ironically provided by wife Pegi and stepsister Astrid. 'Standing In The Light Of Love', the first of *Toast*'s three unreleased tracks, is Crazy Horse at their loudest and rockiest, similar in feel to 1996's *Broken Arrow*. The guitar chords sizzle and crunch and Young wears his wounded heart on his sleeve as he once again addresses the state of his marriage: "I don't wanna get personal/Or have you put me on the spot? /Don't know how you feel/But for me it's getting hard."

After the aforementioned 'Goin' Home', which is the same cut, or near identical, to the one included on *Are You Passionate*? we get the second of the unreleased tracks, 'Timberline', which tells the story of a troubled logger whose struggles have caused him to lose faith in God. Combining Young's environmental concerns with a deeply personal crisis, it's a thoughtful yet furious stomp of a song, with the chanted chorus adding to the sense of barely controlled panic. The trio of new songs is completed by 'Gateway of Love', a sprawling, tormented 10 minutes of Young wrestling with his inability to confront his relationship issues: "Try to find the perfect time/To say something to you/Filled with need and filled with truth/But I'm just a drifting soul/With nothing much to say." Featuring the album's most varied, intricate guitar work, the song is underpinned by a shimmying bossa nova rhythm likely to have been inspired by Young and Crazy Horse's recent visit to Latin America.

'How Ya Doin', which reappeared as 'Mr Disappointment' on *Are You Passionate*? is another maudlin study of fading love. It's more effective here than on the slicker, emptier M.G.'s cut, with the funereal beat and Crazy Horse's sighing backing vocals ably supporting Young's sad, elegant guitar playing. The final track 'Boom Boom Boom' also featured on *Are You Passionate?,* reduced down from 13 minutes to a mere nine and renamed 'She's A Healer'. The decision to cull a third of the length can now be seen as some small relief, as the original version proves just as shapeless and plodding, with Crazy Horse's usual glorious chaos firmly tethered, but is even more interminable.

Toast isn't a vintage later Young and Crazy Horse record like *Ragged Glory* or *Sleeps With Angels*, but it absolutely warrants inclusion in any retrospective of their work together. The emerging R&B influences Young was to hone further with Booker T. & the M.G 's on *Are You Passionate*? gives the music here an intriguingly different feel to anything else in Young and Crazy Horse's canon, while there are still some more typical guitar workouts like 'Goin' Home' and 'Timberline' to keep the purists satisfied. *Toast* is also one of Young's most lyrically direct collections of songs, and while the stark depictions of emotional turmoil don't always sit comfortably with the musical accompaniment, it's still a superior album to the largely unmemorable and over-produced *Are You Passionate?* released in its stead.

⊙ TRACK LISTING   ◄◄ ❙❙ ►►❙

1. Quit ··· 5:24
2. Standing In The Light Of Love ·· 4:19
3. Goin' Home ··· 7:53
4. Timberline ·· 4:10
5. Gateway Of Love ··· 10:11
6. How Ya Doin ·· 7:00
7. Boom Boom Boom ·· 13:06

Length: 51.23

Neil Young - Are You Passionate?

Released 9 April 2002 (Reprise)

Neil Young's unlikely association with legendary R&B instrumental group Booker T. & the M.G.'s began in October 1992, when the band's surviving members - Booker T. Jones (keyboards), Steve Cropper (guitar) and Donald "Duck" Dunn (bass) - backed him at Bob Dylan's thirtieth anniversary concert at Madison Square Garden in New York. The band went on to support Young on his world tour the following year, with Dunn also playing on 2000's *Silver and Gold* album.

It therefore shouldn't have come as a major surprise when Young decided to make an entire record with Jones, Dunn and drummer Steve Potts (who joined the M.G.'s in 1999), even though this represented a shift back to the kind of unpredictable genre hopping that had seemed to have ended with 1988's *This Note's For You* album. Recorded between March and June 2001 at The Site studio in Marin County, California, *Are You Passionate?* also featured Poncho Sampedro on guitars and Young's wife Pegi and his half-sister Astrid - the daughter of his father Scott - on backing vocals. The remaining members of Crazy Horse, Billy Talbot and Ralph Molina also appeared on one track - 'Goin' Home' - which was culled from the then unreleased 2001 *Toast* sessions at the studio of the same name in San Francisco.

Derided by some critics and fans as a self-indulgent failure, *Are You Passionate?* does have its moments. But at over an hour long, it significantly outstays its welcome, with many of the tracks so similar they seem to blend into one. Although he strives gamely, Young is no Wilson Pickett or Otis Redding, with a voice too thin and reedy to front an M.G.'s sound that propelled so many classic Stax Records soul recordings of the 1960s.

The ghost of The Temptations' timeless 'My Girl' looms large on *Are You Passionate?'s* opening track, 'You're My Girl' which gets the record off to a promising start. The combination of Jones's signature organ, the effortlessly funky rhythm section and Young and Sampedro's restrained guitars works well, and Young sings sweetly about saying goodbye to his daughter Amber, who had just gone away to college. 'Mr. Disappointment', a sad tale of fading love, sung by Young in a gravelly low murmur, sees the M.G.' s more muted, with Young's mournful electric guitar taking the lead.

But by the end of tracks three and four - 'Differently' and 'Quit (Don't Say You Love Me) - both polished and pleasant but utterly forgettable - this incarnation of Young as a wide eyed soul boy is already beginning to wear a little thin. Thankfully, he shows he still has some fire in his belly with the ominous, edgy 'Let's Roll', with lyrics adapted from the passenger phone calls and black box recordings of United Airlines' Flight 93, one of the planes hijacked as part of the 9/11 terrorist attacks. However, the song's dated style, which brings to mind the overblown Pink Floyd albums of the 1980s such as *The Final Cut*, together with some gung-ho lyrics from Young - "Let's roll for freedom/Let's roll for love/We're going after Satan/On the wings of a dove" - mean 'Let's Roll' feels decidedly unsubtle, even though Young explained years later that the song was about the reaction of a would be hero on the aeroplane itself, not the U.S. government's response to the attacks.

The theme of 9/11 and its impact continues on the album's title track, which focuses on the role of the U.S. soldier in the resulting "War on Terror." Much more effectively realised than on the song that preceded it, it depicts the soldier as both combatant and captive, the latter referring to the parading of prisoners of war on TV by the Taliban in Afghanistan. Young cleverly shows the range of emotions the pilot may have experienced, from excitement and fear to disgust, and the musical accompaniment is patient and emotive, with swathes of organ interplaying with stabs of guitar and a tinkling piano.

The incongruous inclusion of 'Goin' Home', a quintessential Young and Crazy Horse sprawling epic recorded completely separately from the rest of *Are You Passionate?* is a typically leftfield decision by Young. Musically, it's from a completely different planet to the slick, tight craftsmanship of Booker T. & the M.G.'s, with primitive drumming, searing guitars and lyrics that see a present day woman bizarrely drive to the scene of General Custer's last stand and reconnecting with the earth: "Battle drums were pounding/All around her car/She saw her clothes were changing/Into sky and stars." It's the best track on the album, but belongs on another one.

After this brief disturbance of the peace, the album settles back seamlessly into its polite default groove, and the next three tracks - 'When I Hold You in My Arms', 'Be With You' and 'Two Old Friends' - barely register, seemingly content to slip by unobtrusively in bland middle of the road anonymity. The final track, 'She's A Healer' leaves more of an impression, but unfortunately for the wrong reasons. Nine minutes of aimless, tuneless jazz funk noodling, with Young proclaiming

"The touch of my woman/can soothe my soul", most listeners will be left praying for the record to end long before it eventually does.

Despite being very different to his 1990s output, *Are You Passionate?* still sold surprisingly well, reaching the Top 10 of the U.S. albums charts. It's by no means a terrible record - with the exception of the gruelling last track, it's mostly an agreeable enough collection of tasteful, flawlessly performed mid-tempo soul and R&B songs, with the title track and Crazy Horse collaboration 'Goin' Home' providing a brief mid-album purple patch. But do we really want Neil Young to be tasteful and mid-tempo?

⊙ TRACK LISTING   ◄◄ ❚❚ ►►

1. You're My Girl··4:43
2. Mr. Disappointment···5:24
3. Differently ··6:03
4. Quit (Don't Say You Love Me)··6:03
5. Let's Roll··5:53
6. Are You Passionate?···5:11
7. Goin' Home ···8:47
8. When I Hold You in My Arms ··4:43
9. Be With You ··3:34
10. Two Old Friends···6:15
11. She's a Healer···9:10

Length: 65:46

Neil Young & Crazy Horse - Greendale

Released 19 August 2003 (Reprise)

🎧　🎧　🎧

O ne of the most consistent themes in Neil Young's 21st century music is his increasing focus on environmental activism, anti-war protest and other social issues. Young had been no stranger to these kind of subjects periodically during his earlier career - for example, 'Ohio's condemnation of the state's National Guard shooting dead four students at an anti-Vietnam war demonstration, *Ragged Glory* track 'Mother Earth (Natural Anthem)''s warning not to over-exploit nature's resources, and his role setting up and supporting the annual Farm Aid benefit concert for U.S. farmers. But it wasn't until 2003's *Greendale* that Young embarked on an entire project dedicated to exploring his views on the challenges facing the U.S. in an uncertain post-9/11 world.

Greendale began as a series of Young songs featuring the same characters, which gradually mushroomed into arguably the most ambitious artistic undertaking he has ever attempted. Telling the story of a fictional Californian town through the voices of a cast of interconnected characters, Young ultimately presented the work through a range of different channels. As well as the core, near-80 minute long album, *Greendale* also yielded a DVD film, with actors mouthing the words as Young and Crazy Horse's songs are played, a multi-media stage show with a cast of 50, and (in 2010) a graphic novel by Josh Dysart and Cliff Chiang. The album's front cover was a meticulously designed map of the town of Greendale, with the sleeve notes providing detailed narratives explaining each song in more detail.

In contrast to its wide conceptual scope, the music at the heart of *Greendale* is remarkably simple and unpolished. Based around a trio of Young, bass player Billy Talbot and drummer Ralph Molina, with guitarist Poncho Sampedro absent for the first time since his debut on 1975's *Zuma*, this is Young's music at its rawest and most unadorned, with only the backing vocals from a quartet dubbed The Mountainettes (including Young's wife Pegi) added to the garage rock minimalism.

The album's story, told over a mostly lengthy 10 tracks (only one clocking in at under five minutes), revolves around the Green family, who run the town's Double E inn. Two of the central characters - gnarled patriarch Grandpa Green and his environmental campaigner teenage daughter Sun - seem to respectively represent traditional and future America. Opening track 'Falling From Above' sets the scene for what's to come. Grandpa Green bemoans a world in which homespun values have been overtaken by consumerism before the song goes on to attack the futility of religious wars - a clear reference to the Iraq and Afghanistan conflicts in which the U.S. was embroiled. As ever, the spirit of Young himself inhabits the lyrics he writes, with Grandpa listening to the radio and saying: "I won't retire/ But I might retread/Seems like that guy singing this song/Been doing it for a long time." Musically, it's gritty but rambling, with no tune to speak of.

'Double E' continues in a similar vein, a plodding two chord boogie which introduces the wider Green family in more detail, including the Double E bar owners Earl and Edith, parents of Sun. But the album goes up a notch with 'Devil's Sidewalk', on which the band finally hit their stride with a hypnotic, raga like guitar riff from Young and lyrics which imagine the town of Greendale is stalked by Beelzebub - perhaps a harbinger of what's to come next.

'Leave The Driving" is another monotonous bluesy jam but is central to *Greendale*'s narrative. Young tells the fateful story of drug dealing Jed Green's panicked shooting of a policeman when stopped for minor traffic offences, which leads to a media frenzy in the town. It's followed by a powerful switch in perspective on 'Carmichael', which paints a movingly human picture of the cop killed. As well as tributes from colleagues - "It's like we got a big hole in our side/Where he fit" - we hear Carmichael's devastated wife recounting some of the happy times they spent together: "That was a great vacation/Maybe the best of all/But goddamnit Carmichael you're dead now/And I'm talking to the wall."

The woozily mellow 'Bandit' provides a welcome change of pace, although Young sounds half asleep as he murmurs the lyrics, according to the sleeve notes about Earl Green's unsuccessful painting career, although they could just as easily be Jed's life spinning out of control. 'Grandpa's Interview', while once again hamstrung by the relentless, uncompromising musical accompaniment and over-extended to 13 minutes, is a great piece of writing by Young, examining the angry reaction of Grandpa to the unwelcome media intrusion directed towards Jed's family, with tragic consequences as the old warhorse keels over from a heart attack. There's little doubt Young is making a broader point in the penultimate verse, "Grandpa died like a hero/Fighting for freedom of silence/Trying to stop the media/Trying to be anonymous."

'Bringin' Down Dinner' adopts a more reflective tone, with Young's sonorous organ and a steady drumbeat giving it an almost funereal atmosphere, in keeping with the sad lyrics about a devoted relative bringing the now deceased Grandpa his meal, only to be confronted by a host of TV vans. The last two tracks of the album complete the story by focusing on Sun Green, the youngest member of the Green family, who reacts to her beloved Grandpa's death by devoting herself to activism against corruption and greed in the corridors of power. On 'Sun Green', "She chained herself to a statue of an eagle/In the lobby of Powerco/And started yelling through a megaphone/"There's corruption on the highest floor!" By the time we get to the anthemic closer 'Be The Rain', she's taken her fight beyond smalltown Greendale to the farthest flung corners of America: "We got to get there/Alaska/We got to be there/Before the big machines/We got a job to do/We got to/Save Mother Earth." On both songs, Young shouts his lyrics through a megaphone to project the campaigning messages, and on 'Be The Rain' in particular, he and Crazy Horse go through the gears with impressive energy.

While it would be harsh to write off *Greendale* quite as emphatically as some critics did - David Segal of the Washington Post dismissed it as "a vanity project gone stupefyingly wrong"[1] - there is no doubt it is bloated, lacks quality control and sharpness in much of its song writing, and feels musically repetitive. This absence of light and shade, and of immediately accessible melodies, means the album requires perseverance in order for the idiosyncratic charm and narrative cohesion it does possess to be fully appreciated. Greendale failed to break the top 20 in either the U.K. or the U.S., and it would be over two years before Young's next album, by which time he would have faced some of the most challenging experiences of his life.

⊙ TRACK LISTING   ⏮ ⏸ ⏭

1. Falling from Above ⋯⋯⋯⋯⋯⋯⋯⋯⋯⋯⋯⋯⋯⋯⋯⋯⋯ 7:27
2. Double E ⋯⋯⋯⋯⋯⋯⋯⋯⋯⋯⋯⋯⋯⋯⋯⋯⋯⋯⋯⋯⋯ 5:18
3. Devil's Sidewalk ⋯⋯⋯⋯⋯⋯⋯⋯⋯⋯⋯⋯⋯⋯⋯⋯⋯ 5:18
4. Leave the Driving ⋯⋯⋯⋯⋯⋯⋯⋯⋯⋯⋯⋯⋯⋯⋯⋯ 7:14
5. Carmichael ⋯⋯⋯⋯⋯⋯⋯⋯⋯⋯⋯⋯⋯⋯⋯⋯⋯⋯ 10:20
6. Bandit ⋯⋯⋯⋯⋯⋯⋯⋯⋯⋯⋯⋯⋯⋯⋯⋯⋯⋯⋯⋯⋯ 5:13
7. Grandpa's Interview ⋯⋯⋯⋯⋯⋯⋯⋯⋯⋯⋯⋯⋯ 12:57
8. Bringin' Down Dinner ⋯⋯⋯⋯⋯⋯⋯⋯⋯⋯⋯⋯ 3:16
9. Sun Green ⋯⋯⋯⋯⋯⋯⋯⋯⋯⋯⋯⋯⋯⋯⋯⋯⋯⋯ 12:03
10. Be the Rain ⋯⋯⋯⋯⋯⋯⋯⋯⋯⋯⋯⋯⋯⋯⋯⋯⋯⋯ 9:13

Length: 78:19

---

1   David Segal, The Washington Post, 20 August 2003

Neil Young - Prairie Wind

Released 27 September 2005 (Reprise)

🎧   🎧   🎧

For 18 months after the release of *Greendale*, unsure of what direction he wanted to take his music in next, Neil Young stopped writing songs entirely. He was in the early stages of working on a new album in March 2005 when a routine medical procedure led to the discovery of a potentially life-threatening brain aneurysm. Successful surgery swiftly followed, but this brush with mortality, together with his father Scott's rapidly worsening dementia (he would die in June of that year, just weeks before *Prairie Wind*'s release), were integral influences on a record that would be one of the most personal and reflective of his career.

Recorded at Master-Link studios in Nashville and featuring a number of familiar Young stalwarts including Ben Keith, Spooner Oldham, Emmylou Harris, drummer Karl T.Himmel and bass player Rick Rosas, *Prairie Wind* is often seen as the third instalment of a trilogy of gentle, melodic and accessible country rock albums that began with *Harvest* in 1972 and continued with 1992's *Harvest Moon*. While there are certainly many stylistic and thematic similarities, especially with the more mature, nostalgic *Harvest Moon*, *Prairie Wind* also has its fair share of more up-tempo songs, as well as lyrics that ruminate on the impact of 9/11 - a topic he had previously explored on *Are You Passionate?* and *Greendale* and would soon dedicate a whole project to on 2006's *Living With War* - and the meaning of life itself.

The album opens with 'The Painter', a textbook Young plaintive acoustic ballad with all the hallmarks that had served him so well ever since *Harvest* - a relaxed, swaying rhythm, mournful twangs of pedal steel guitar and a chorus on which Young's high, yearning tenor is joined by soaring female vocals, in this case from Emmylou Harris. The first of several family-focused tracks on the album, it focuses on Young's daughter Amber leaving home, with her father musing on his own life while simultaneously offering some words of warning: "It's a long road behind me/ It's a long road ahead/If you follow every dream/You might get lost."

'No Wonder' is more urgent, simmering with anger about the decline of America since Young's youth (spent, lest we forget, in Canada), when the prairies were teeming with birds and people led simpler, more wholesome lives. He also references the U.S. response to 9/11, mentioning the patriotic song 'America The Beautiful' sang by Willie Nelson after the attacks, and comedian Chris Rock, who was one of many celebrities to be involved in benefit concerts. Young returns to more personal subject matter on the touching, vulnerable 'Falling Off the Face of the Earth', on which Young sings - perhaps to his ailing father - "I just want to thank you/For all of the things you've done/I been thinking about you/I just want to send my love."

Young continues to reminisce fondly on the rootsy 'Far From Home', recalling ""When I was a growing boy rockin' on my daddy's knee/ Daddy took an old guitar and sang 'Bury me on the lone prairie.'" backed by a squalling harmonica and a parping brass section. By this stage, the images of idyllic rolling rural landscapes populated by herds of roaming buffalo are starting to wear slightly thin, but Young handles the wistful nostalgia less tritely on 'It's A Dream', picturing a small boy fishing in the river running through his hometown, just as he had done in Omemee, Ontario decades before. Unfortunately, the syrupy, overblown strings Young had deployed occasionally throughout his career make an unwelcome reappearance, making the song feel excessively sentimental.

Prairie Wind's seven minute title track is the centrepiece of the album, bringing together many of the elements that feature elsewhere on the record. The lyrics directly tackle Scott Young's advancing Alzheimer's "Tryin' to remember what my Daddy said/Before too much time took away his head" and goes on to describe "a place on the prairie where evil and goodness play." Once again, some of the content feel slightly hackneyed, but the intricate, folksy guitar playing and rich horn and backing vocal textures give the song gravitas. Meanwhile, 'Here For You' is a pretty but slight little tune, returning to the theme of daughter Amber Young leaving home, that sags under the weight of another unnecessary string arrangement halfway through.

'This Old Guitar', so mellow and laid back it's practically asleep, lazily repurposes the sublime guitar riff from *Harvest Moon*'s title track, suggesting that Young is beginning to run out of ideas. 'He Was The King' provides little evidence to the contrary with its throwaway tribute to Elvis, although at least the Young and his band sound like they're enjoying themselves. But closing track 'When God Made Me' is an altogether different proposition, which sees Young question the intentions of a higher being who sees fit to allow war, intolerance and dogma to proliferate in his name. The combination of a stately piano and gospel-tinged choral section give the song an aptly hymnal quality, and it seems fitting that Young, who has spent much of the album looking back at his own life following critical brain surgery, ends it by contemplating whether or not human beings are subject to a divine power in all that we do.

Overall, *Prairie Wind* is more notable for the themes it explores than the quality of its songs, which is patchy and often feels like more of the same from an artist now sixty years of age and onto his 26th studio album. But as an insight into a man of late middle age compelled to question his own place in the world by the inevitable consequences of ageing on both him and those close to him, it has an important place in Young's discography.

⊙ TRACK LISTING   ⏮ ⏸ ⏭

1. The Painter ·· 4:36
2. No Wonder ·· 5:45
3. Falling Off the Face of the Earth ····································· 3:35
4. Far From Home ··· 3:47
5. It's a Dream ··· 6:31
6. Prairie Wind ··· 7:34
7. Here for You ·· 4:32
8. This Old Guitar ·· 5:32
9. He Was the King ·· 6:08
10. When God Made Me ·· 4:05

Length: 52:05

Neil Young - Living With War

Released 8 May 2006 (Reprise)

🎧 🎧 🎧

During the late 1990s and early 2000s, Neil Young's previously prolific rate of writing, recording and releasing albums had noticeably slowed, with only three new studio albums emerging between 1996's *Broken Arrow* and 2005's *Prairie Wind*. *Living With War*, which arrived in May 2006 just eight months after *Prairie Wind*, showed the world that Young could still deliver fresh new work with impressive speed and spontaneity.

After spending much of the 1980s flirting with Republicanism and praising Ronald Reagan, by the early 2000s Young had become a staunch opponent of the U.S. government, and in particular President George W. Bush, the Republican in office from 2001-2009. Bush oversaw the country's response to the 9/11 terrorist attacks, including the U.S.-led military action in Afghanistan and Iraq under the banner of 'the War On Terror.' While 9/11 and its impact had featured in Young's songs on his previous three albums - notably 'Let's Roll' on 2002's *Are You Passionate?* - it was the relentless media coverage of the Iraq war that prompted the veteran Canadian to go for the jugular.

Shocked and upset by newspaper coverage of wounded soldiers, Young launched into the kind of sudden burst of phenomenal creative energy he had been capable of summoning up periodically throughout his career, writing half of the songs on *Living With War* in a single day, with the entire album recorded in just nine days between 29 March and 6 April 2006. A core band of Young on guitar and harmonica, Rick Rosas on bass and Chad Cromwell on drums were joined on the recording sessions at Redwood Digital and Capitol Studio A in California by trumpet player Tommy Bray and the 100 Voices choir. Knowing that the immediacy of his message was key, Young rush released *Living With War* only a month later, first via an internet download on 2 May (as one unbroken whole, rather than individual tracks) before arriving in record stores six days later.

Despite - or maybe because of - the rapid turnaround in writing and recording *Living With War*, it is one of his most focused, instantly accessible records of the 21st century. While he can sometimes be guilty of releasing material that feels sketchy and undercooked (especially on Crazy Horse albums like *Broken Arrow* and *Greendale*) here Young's songs mostly succeed in projecting the instinctive, raw energy and anger he intended, while still feeling fully formed and structured.

Opening track 'After The Garden' kicks off with the primitive snarl of Young's inimitable Old Black guitar and shifts through the gears impressively, with Rosas and Cromwell every bit as gloriously noisy as Crazy Horse's rhythm section. Young's lyrics home in on the big picture, pointing out that warfare can ultimately only bring about the environmental destruction of the planet - depicted here as 'the garden' as he sings "Won't need no shadow man/runnin' the government/won't need no stinkin' war... After the garden is gone."

There's no such subtle imagery on the title track, which hammers home a simple message: war is very bad, and the American people are having to live with it every day on their TV screens. While admittedly lacking sophistication, Young's pleas for peace are delivered with real passion, aided by the massed voices of the choir joining later in the song, although the guitar and trumpet directly tracking the melody in tandem sounds a tad clunky. Next, Young switches targets to the evils of big business and advertising on the ferocious 'The Restless Consumer' - "Don't need no TV ad/ telling me how sick I am/don't want to know how many people are like me" - before going on to lambast the cost of war when the money spent on it could be spent on addressing global poverty "A hundred voices from a hundred lands/Need someone to listen/People are dying here and there/They don't see the world the way you do."

'Shock and Awe' is an absolute belter, a jet propelled rock anthem in a similar vein to 1989's Young classic 'Rockin' In The Free World' with some scintillating guitar and percussion work and lyrics that spit with fury about the impact of the conflict "Thousands of children scarred for life/Millions of tears for a soldier's wife/ Both sides are losing now, Heaven takes them in." It's followed by 'Families', the first song he wrote for the album, which is narrated from the perspective of a soldier killed in action, who pleads "When you write your songs about us/won't you try to do us justice/because we want to be just like you/and your families." The ironic 'Flags of Freedom', meanwhile, is a clear dig at the flag-waving patriotism that accompanies soldiers being sent off to war, with Young referencing Bob Dylan's anti-war songs during the early stages of the U.S.'s involvement in Vietnam 40 years earlier to make the point that the lessons of history haven't been learnt.

The next two songs focus firmly on the political situation in America. 'Let's Impeach The President' outraged right wing commentators across the nation with its no holds barred attack on President Bush, who Young accuses of lying, illegal surveillance of citizens, creating racial divisions and misappropriating Christianity, accompanied by snippets from Bush's speeches and chants of "flip flop." The less incendiary but equally impactful 'Lookin' For A Leader' calls for the country to find a new commander in chief "to bring our country home/reunite the red white and blue/before it turns to stone", also suggesting that a woman or a black man could be the solution, even name checking Barack Obama before adding "But he thinks that he's too young." Obama would go on to be elected president just two years later.

'Roger And Out' sees *Living With War* briefly slow to a more reflective pace, with the guitar more muted and the choir providing a soft, hymnal backing as Young remembers an old friend from his Sixties youth who died in service: "Trippin' down that old Hippie Highway/Got to thinkin' 'bout you are again/Wonderin' how it really was for you/And how it happened in the end." The album closes with a choral rendition of the early 20th century American patriotic song 'America The Beautiful", serving as a final reminder of Young's view that his adopted country had now abandoned the values that once made it great.

Living With War made the top 20 album charts in both the U.S. and the U.K. and was praised by critics as a return to form for Young following a run of indifferently received releases. A stripped down version of the album, *Living with War - In the Beginning,* without the backing instrumentation and choral accompaniment present on the original release, followed in December.

For the first time in years, Young was seen as a relevant artist with something new and powerful to say, although not everyone agreed with the sentiments, as was shown by the booing and walkouts from Bush-supporting fans when material from *Living With War* was played on CSN&Y's reunion tour later that year. As an overall work, it feels very much a snapshot in time, a protest record always intended to hit out hard in the moment rather than aim for a lasting legacy, but it nevertheless provided fizzing evidence that there was plenty of life left in Young yet.

⊙ TRACK LISTING ⏮ ⏸ ⏭

1. After the Garden ⋯⋯⋯⋯⋯⋯⋯⋯⋯⋯⋯⋯⋯⋯⋯⋯⋯⋯⋯⋯⋯⋯⋯⋯⋯ 3:23
2. Living with War ⋯⋯⋯⋯⋯⋯⋯⋯⋯⋯⋯⋯⋯⋯⋯⋯⋯⋯⋯⋯⋯⋯⋯ 5:04
3. The Restless Consumer ⋯⋯⋯⋯⋯⋯⋯⋯⋯⋯⋯⋯⋯⋯⋯⋯⋯⋯ 5:47
4. Shock and Awe ⋯⋯⋯⋯⋯⋯⋯⋯⋯⋯⋯⋯⋯⋯⋯⋯⋯⋯⋯⋯⋯⋯ 4:53
5. Families ⋯⋯⋯⋯⋯⋯⋯⋯⋯⋯⋯⋯⋯⋯⋯⋯⋯⋯⋯⋯⋯⋯⋯⋯⋯⋯ 2:25
6. Flags of Freedom ⋯⋯⋯⋯⋯⋯⋯⋯⋯⋯⋯⋯⋯⋯⋯⋯⋯⋯⋯⋯⋯ 3:42
7. Let's Impeach the President ⋯⋯⋯⋯⋯⋯⋯⋯⋯⋯⋯⋯⋯ 5:10
8. Lookin' for a Leader ⋯⋯⋯⋯⋯⋯⋯⋯⋯⋯⋯⋯⋯⋯⋯⋯⋯⋯ 4:03
9. Roger and Out ⋯⋯⋯⋯⋯⋯⋯⋯⋯⋯⋯⋯⋯⋯⋯⋯⋯⋯⋯⋯⋯⋯ 4:25
10. America the Beautiful (Katharine Lee Bates, Samuel Augustus Ward) ⋯⋯ 2:57

Length: 41:49

Neil Young - Chrome Dreams II

Released 23 October 2007 (Reprise)

🎧 🎧 🎧

Originally planned for release in 1977 before belatedly emerging in 2023, Neil Young's legendary *Chrome Dreams* album, believed (correctly) during the intervening years to have included a number of classic songs later to appear on other Young records,was long considered one of the great lost albums of the period.

Quite why Young chose to release a sequel to a then unreleased album three decades later is anybody's guess. Perhaps the most likely explanation is that he was capriciously marking the 30th anniversary of the original record's planned release by putting out a new collection of songs he felt replicated its style and spirit. Certainly, the mix of acoustic and electric material on *Chrome Dreams II* is consistent with what Young is said to have planned for *Chrome Dreams*, the track listing of which is understood to have encompassed everything from the solo troubadour strum of 'Pocahontas' to the elemental adrenalin rush of 'Like A Hurricane.' Thematically, the new album explored the search for security and contentment, although as always with Young, one or two songs erred well off course into completely different territory.

Mostly recorded at Young's Broken Arrow ranch between May and July 2007, *Chrome Dreams II* was a combination of newly written songs and revivals of abandoned 1980s tracks. A new band line up composed of Rick Rosas on bass, Crazy Horse drummer Ralph Molina and Ben Keith on pedal steel (as well as various other instruments) joined Young for the sessions, along with several different combinations of backing singers (each credited separately as The Wyatt Earps, The Jane Wyatts and The Dirty Old Men).

The album gets off to a rather underwhelming start with 'Beautiful Bluebird', a twee, sickly country ballad which failed to make the cut for Young's less than stellar 1985 *Old Ways* album. 'Boxcar' - first recorded as part of another unreleased album project, 1988's *Times Square* - is better, with a lilting banjo and the sonorous, chant-like backing vocals giving the song the feel of a Western soundtrack as Young tells the tale of a chameleon-like drifter, perhaps referring to his own idiosyncratic career when he sings "I don't care if I ever get back to/Where I'd already been around."

However, *Chrome Dreams II* is dominated by the extraordinary, 18 minute long 'Ordinary People', an outtake from the *Freedom* sessions included here in its original 1988 version. Similar in style to other tracks from the same period such as 'Crime In The City (Sixty to Zero Part I)', with an edgy, ominous mood and a prominent horn section, it's sheer length and relentlessness makes it a challenging listen at times, but there's no denying its power or lyrical ambition, which draw obvious comparisons with Dylan's mid-60s epics, although it's no 'Desolation Row'. A kaleidoscopic array of characters - out of work models, a game but defeated boxer, an illicit gun seller masquerading as an antiques dealer - are used to depict a society gone rotten due to the exploitation of good honest Americans by corrupt, greedy forces. The 'ordinary people' then begin to fight back, taking to the streets as vigilantes to fight crime and finally restoring America's ruined industrial economy in what sounds like a modern socialist utopia. It's heady stuff, delivered with customary gusto and drama by Young, but it feels out of place among the far more understated content of the rest of the album, begging the question why Young didn't include it on the much more bold and swaggering *Freedom*.

The hymnal 'Shining Light', the first of the new songs that make up the rest of *Chrome Dreams II*, is a quasi-religious plea for guidance, with its softly cooing backing vocals and gently soulful swing not dissimilar to some of the gospel-tinged rock ballads perfected by The Rolling Stones in the early 1970s. 'The Believer', a quirky, homely little ditty about continuing to believe in your dreams, doesn't live long in the memory; in contrast, the fiery garage rock of 'Spirit Road', on which Young urges a friend wrestling with demons to get back on the straight and narrow, features the album's best guitar work and some soaring group vocals on the driving chorus.

'Dirty Old Man' is Young at his most ramshackle and grungy. With a guitar riff scraped off the floor of a basement dive bar and Molina's customary thuggish drumming, Young sounds like he's having a ball as he recounts the disreputable deeds of an ageing drunk, gleefully recounting "I like to get hammered/on Friday night/sometimes I can't wait/so Monday's alright." Unfortunately, the energy levels then drop precipitously on the dreary, somnambulant 'Ever After' which plods nowhere for three and a half pointless minutes.

The daunting stature of 'Ordinary People' rather overshadows the other very lengthy track on *Chrome Dreams II*, the sprawling 'No Hidden Path', which ebbs and flows pretty uneventfully for nearly a quarter of an hour, with its loose, funky rhythm and sinuous guitar unable to compensate for the song's lack of basic direction. Young finishes up with 'The Way', one of the oddest entries in his entire catalogue: a duet with a children's choir, the Young People's Chorus of New York City. Set to a simple piano melody, its wide eyed call to follow a road towards inner peace is simultaneously both charming in its innocence and cloying in its sentimentality.

Chrome Dreams II continued Young's mid-2000s run of steady album sales, hovering just outside the top 10 of the U.S. and U.K. charts. The record can be viewed overall in two ways - either as a moderately successful synthesis of Young's range of musical styles on one record, or as an uneven collection of 80s leftovers and new songs that varied in quality from good to insipid. This writer would err towards the latter perspective.

⊙ TRACK LISTING   ◄◄ ❚❚ ►►|

1. Beautiful Bluebird ⋯⋯⋯⋯⋯⋯⋯⋯⋯⋯⋯⋯⋯⋯⋯⋯⋯⋯ 4:27
2. Boxcar ⋯⋯⋯⋯⋯⋯⋯⋯⋯⋯⋯⋯⋯⋯⋯⋯⋯⋯⋯⋯⋯⋯ 2:44
3. Ordinary People ⋯⋯⋯⋯⋯⋯⋯⋯⋯⋯⋯⋯⋯⋯⋯⋯⋯ 18:13
4. Shining Light ⋯⋯⋯⋯⋯⋯⋯⋯⋯⋯⋯⋯⋯⋯⋯⋯⋯⋯ 4:43
5. The Believer ⋯⋯⋯⋯⋯⋯⋯⋯⋯⋯⋯⋯⋯⋯⋯⋯⋯⋯ 2:39
6. Spirit Road ⋯⋯⋯⋯⋯⋯⋯⋯⋯⋯⋯⋯⋯⋯⋯⋯⋯⋯⋯ 6:32
7. Dirty Old Man ⋯⋯⋯⋯⋯⋯⋯⋯⋯⋯⋯⋯⋯⋯⋯⋯⋯ 3:17
8. Ever After ⋯⋯⋯⋯⋯⋯⋯⋯⋯⋯⋯⋯⋯⋯⋯⋯⋯⋯⋯ 3:32
9. No Hidden Path ⋯⋯⋯⋯⋯⋯⋯⋯⋯⋯⋯⋯⋯⋯⋯⋯ 14:31
10. The Way ⋯⋯⋯⋯⋯⋯⋯⋯⋯⋯⋯⋯⋯⋯⋯⋯⋯⋯⋯ 5:15

Length: 65:53

Neil Young - Fork in the Road

Released 7 April 2009 (Reprise)

🎧　🎧　🎧

O f all Neil Young's vast range of musical projects over the past six decades, his decision to write an entire concept album about a 1959 Mark IV Lincoln Continental he converted to run on eco-friendly fuels is arguably the most esoteric and leftfield of all. Young has always been a big fan of vintage cars, going right back to the legendary 1953 Pontiac hearse in which he first entered the U.S. back in 1966, and he even entitled his second volume of autobiography *Special Deluxe: A Memoir of Life and Cars*. But until 2009's *Fork in the Road*, their presence in his music had been relatively unobtrusive.

The previous year, Young began working with motorcar engineer Jonathan Goodwin on the Linc Volt eco car initiative, which aimed to develop a viable electric power system with zero emissions, using Young's own Lincoln Continental as a prototype. Neil being Neil, he became utterly absorbed with the work, and began writing, performing and recording songs inspired by it with a touring band which included Ben Keith on pedal steel, Rick Rosas on bass, Chad Cromwell on drums and multi-instrumentalist Anthony Crawford.

Opening track 'When Worlds Collide' sets the tone with its meaty garage guitar riff and Young announcing we'll be "taking a trip across the U.S.A/Gonna meet a lot of people along the way." It's simple, no frills stuff, similar in sound to Young's later work with Crazy Horse, with groove and mood taking precedence over melody. The jarring cacophony of 'Fuel Line' introduces us to the Linc Volt project, with spectacularly banal lyrics that are essentially advertising slogans as Young eulogises "the awesome power of electricity/Stored for you in a massive battery/She don't use much though, that's smart for a car" before a chorus that consists of chanting "fill her up".

'Just Singing A Song' is way better, with Young's guitar suddenly transformed from scratchy jamming to the vast, elemental beast of *Zuma* and *Ragged Glory,* with some soaring, CSN&Y-style harmonies on the chorus, which makes the valid point that "just singing a song won't change the world" because actual action is needed. It's a tantalising glimpse of how great Young can still be when he puts his mind to it. 'Johnny Magic' - a tribute to Linc Volt partner Goodwin - has some clever lyrics, for example, capturing the essence of an electric car as "she burst from the garage in a blaze of silence", but musically it feels slight and tossed off.

'Cough Up The Bucks' sees Young park the Lincoln temporarily to launch an attack on the 2008 financial crisis, singing "Where did all the money go/Where did all the cash flow?" over a jagged guitar riff, before adding "It's all about my car... and my girl... it's all about my world" to emphasise the impact economic issues have at an individual level. The execrable clump of 'Get Behind The Wheel', meanwhile, feels so retro it could be an outtake from 1983's *Everybody's Rockin'*, Young's infamous middle finger salute to Geffen Records, but performed by REO Speedwagon.

The tempo slows right down on the languorous 'Off The Road', given a weary end of day mood by a floating organ and some gently sighing backing vocals, and lyrics that warn motorists to remain vigilant when driving long distances and late at night. But we're soon back at full throttle with the now increasingly familiar, uninspiring chug of 'Hit The Road' (three of the last four tracks on the album have 'road' in the title, further evidence of the project's off the cuff nature). However, 'Light a Candle' sees Young again veer off in an unexpected direction, this time coming up with an eerie, timeless folk ballad, elegantly tinged with Ben Keith's inimitable pedal steel, which wouldn't sound out of place on his very best albums. Perhaps reflecting again on the financial crisis, Young strikes a note of optimism as he counsels "Instead of cursing the darkness/Light a candle for where we're going/There's something ahead, worth fighting for."

Fork in the Road reaches the end of its journey with the rollicking title track, which boogies along amiably for nearly six not unenjoyable minutes as Young delivers a wide ranging state of the nation stream of consciousness that covers everything from American military action overseas "We salute the troops/They're all still there/In a fucking war/It's no good" and (again) the financial crisis "There's a bailout coming but it's not for me/It's for all those creeps watching tickers on TV" to the evils of music downloads and social media "Download this/Sounds like shit/ Keep on blogging/Until the power goes out."

With the exception of a couple of standout tracks - 'Just Singing A Song' and 'Light a Candle' - overall *Fork in the Road* is one of a number of 21st century Young albums where more thought has been given to the subject matter than the song writing and execution, which mostly feels hasty and undercooked. It reached number 22 in the U.K. album charts and 19 in the U.S., but left many critics unimpressed, with The Observer's Miranda Sawyer describing the record as "the sound of a massive talent revving on the spot without ever getting out of first gear."[1]

Young's LincVolt plans had a major setback 18 months later, when a wall charging point fault led to a warehouse fire that damaged the Lincoln Continental (as well as a range of rare Neil Young memorabilia stored there) but the car was subsequently rebuilt and continues to be driven to this day.

⊙ TRACK LISTING   ⏮ ⏸ ⏭

1. When Worlds Collide ··· 4:14
2. Fuel Line ··· 3:11
3. Just Singing a Song ··· 3:31
4. Johnny Magic ··· 4:18
5. Cough Up the Bucks ·· 4:38
6. Get Behind the Wheel ·· 3:08
7. Off the Road ··· 3:22
8. Hit the Road ··· 3:36
9. Light a Candle ·· 3:01
10. Fork in the Road ··· 5:47

Length: 38:46

---

1 The Observer, 5 April 2009.

Neil Young - Le Noise

Released 28 September 2010 (Reprise)

🎧 🎧 🎧

Now in his mid-sixties, Neil Young showed no signs of slowing down as he entered his sixth decade in the music business. After spending the summer of 2009 headlining the Glastonbury, Isle of Wight and Hyde Park festivals in the U.K., followed by the release of his gargantuan, 128 track *Archives Volume 1; 1963 - 1972*, he began 2010 by being awarded the Musicares Person of the Year award, which recognises the philanthropic efforts of musicians, performing at the closing ceremony of the Vancouver Winter Olympic Games, and helping Beach Boy Al Jardine with his first solo album. In the meantime, he was also working on an intriguing new album of his own.

During the previous 25 years, Young's fellow countryman Daniel Lanois had built a reputation as one of the most innovative and in demand producers around, working with stellar names including U2, Bob Dylan, Willie Nelson and Peter Gabriel. Impressed after watching Lanois' videos of his Black Dub collective, a heady brew of soul, dub, blues and soul, Young got in touch and asked the Quebecois to produce what he was envisaging as a sparse, solo acoustic record. However, what emerged over the coming months was a remarkable sound that remains unlike anything else he ever came up with in his long and varied career.

Le Noise (a pun on the producer's name) was recorded over four months at a series of sessions at Lanois' home in Silverlake, Los Angeles, with engineer Mark Howard setting up the studio equipment in different rooms in order to achieve different acoustics. Lanois and Howard recorded Young singing and playing his Gretsch Falcon guitar live, applying a series of sonic manipulations to the notes and encouraging the musician to respond to them in real time. This technique suited Young's instinctive, raw style and transformed what was already a promising batch of songs into what would turn out to be perhaps his best record of the 21st century.

Sparks fly from the start on opening track 'Walk With Me', which sounds vast, like it was recorded in a cathedral. Molten shards of guitar chords and feedback

161

echo and vibrate from the speakers as Young - his voice piercing through the swirling fog like a beam of light - eulogises the power of enduring love, one of the key topics of his later work. The song ends with Young singing "I lost some people I was traveling with", perhaps a reference to film director Larry Johnson, a long-time collaborator and friend who died in January 2010, before fading away into a ripple of oscillating ambient noise.

If you listen carefully, the riff from Young's 1969 classic 'Cinnamon Girl' can be heard amid the distortion on 'Sign of Love', while 'Someone's Gonna Rescue You', another paean to the value of a strong relationship, contrasts Young's sweet vocal with guitar notes that echo so much they practically bounce. But it's on the fourth track 'Love And War' that *Le Noise* peaks. One of two acoustic tracks on the album, it is simultaneously luminously beautiful, angry and sad, with lyrics that see Young admitting that even after a lifetime of writing about the song title's two subjects, which he sees as fundamental to human existence, he still struggles to understand them. Wisely, Lanois keeps the effects here to a minimum, allowing the graceful, Spanish-guitar tinged melody and Young's plaintive vocal to maximise their impact.

'Angry World' merges dizzy fragments of Young's disembodied voice with a tectonic plate of a riff, and also features the record's most memorable lyric as the singer observes that "Some see life as hope eternal/Some see life as a business plan." Young then treats us to a long-forgotten treasure from his vaults. First written as far back as 1974 and included on his at that stage unreleased 1976 acoustic album of the same name, the version of 'Hitchhiker' included here has been updated so the lyrics reflect the decades that have passed since. It was revisiting this song that prompted Young to shift his plan for *Le Noise* to become a predominantly electric rather than an acoustic record, and the wall of sound guitars on 'Hitchhiker' undoubtedly add drama and heft to his confessions of epic drug consumption.

The second acoustic track, 'Peaceful Valley Boulevard', is another standout. Young recalls the frontier days of the American West and uses examples of environmental destruction from that time alongside modern day images to warn us that we continue to make the same mistakes. This song sees Young at his poetic best, as he laments the savagery inflicted by late 19th century American 'rail hunters' on the buffalo population: "One day shots rang across the peaceful valley/God was crying tears that fell like rain/Before the railroad came from Kansas City/And the bullets hit the bison from the train" before going on to express frustration at today's inaction on climate change: "A polar bear was drifting on an ice floe/Sun beating down from the sky/Politicians gathered for a summit/And came away with nothing to decide." Once again, Lanois leaves the song relatively stripped back, allowing the lilting, melancholy tune space to breathe over seven atmospheric minutes.

Le Noise ends with the murky, subterranean 'Rumblin', which often sounds like it's been recorded underwater, with Young's voice periodically emerging through layers of overdubbed guitars and processed noise, uncertain and self-critical as he asks himself "When will I learn how to listen? When will I learn how to feel?" It's a suitable way to end for an album where Young openly reflects on his failings, which even sixty-five years of life experience have left him unable to fully conquer.

Another solid but unspectacular showing in the album charts - top 20 in both the U.S. and the U.K. - was scant reward for what was Young's most fresh and original release in many years. Listening slightly enviously from the side lines was Crazy Horse's Poncho Sampedro, who told Uncut magazine in January 2012" that was our record" as he and his bandmates had played several of *Le Noise*'s songs with Young before he took off with Lanois.[1] But Young would soon be back in the saddle with the Horse for two very different albums that would make 2012 one of his most productive years yet.

⊙ TRACK LISTING   ◄◄ ❙❙ ►►

1. Walk with Me ·· 4:25
2. Sign of Love ·· 3:58
3. Someone's Gonna Rescue You ·· 3:29
4. Love and War ··· 5:37
5. Angry World ··· 4:11
6. Hitchhiker ··· 5:32
7. Peaceful Valley Boulevard ·· 7:10
8. Rumblin ··· 3:39

Length: 37:59

---

1 Uncut magazine, January 2012

Neil Young & Crazy Horse - Americana

Released 5 June 2012 (Reprise)

🎧   🎧   🎧

Neil Young's decision to record an album of cover versions taken from the Great American Songbook was hardly a ground-breaking one. Artists like Dylan, Johnny Cash and Rod Stewart have all shown that this kind of late career path can be both reinvigorating and lucrative, and it was not a surprise that Young, long steeped in the traditional music of his adopted country, chose to pursue a similar direction. But as ever, Young's approach to the material on *Americana* was wildly different to his more conservative contemporaries. Rather than opting for polished crooning or folksy prettiness, he instead called up Crazy Horse and allowed their inimitable brand of pounding garage rock to give the songs a thorough going over.

After the longest ever gap between his collaborations with Crazy Horse (since 2003's *Greendale*, which Poncho Sampedro sat out), Young brough the band back into his Broken Arrow studio in late 2011 to begin work on a new record. At this stage, he didn't have any new songs, so the band began doing live recordings of classic American standards, some rearranged by Young, and - as he warmed to the project - it ended up mushrooming into an entire album. Although perceived by most observers as a covers album, Young was keen to refute this categorisation, telling Uncut magazine in January 2012: "Those songs have been done by so many people that we're not covering anybody. Everyone owns them. They belong to everyone."[1]

Young also delved back deep into his own past when making *Americana*. As a teenager, Young's first band The Squires had regularly played folk songs in their sets in Ontario clubs, and he even credits the group on a couple of the arrangements here. The first track on the record, the mid-19th century minstrel song 'Oh Susannah' also uses an arrangement from this period, by the now largely forgotten

---

1 Uncut magazine, January 2012

1960s folk-rock singer Tim Rose, rather than the better known traditional melody popularised by The Byrds on their 1965 *Turn! Turn! Turn!* Album. But in the hands of Young and Crazy Horse, it becomes a loose-limbed, often discordant romp, with the first minute essentially the band tuning up before the chanted backing vocals and Young's raggedly off key singing enter the fray. It's simultaneously slipshod and enthralling as the band join together on the chorus to sing "I come from Alabama with my b-a-n-j-o on my knee" before ending with some good natured studio chatter as a clearly pleased Young concludes the song "gets into a good groove", adding to the impression that this may have been the first time they'd ever played it before.

'Clementine', another 19th century ballad, is given a complete makeover, transformed by Young's arrangement from a gentle singalong to a brooding, seething epic, complete with the reinstatement of a controversial 'lost' verse in which the grieving narrator consoles himself by making a pass at his dead bride's younger sister. Young also puts his own stamp on 'Tom Dula' (often better known as 'Tom Dooley'), made popular by grizzled folkies like The Kingston Trio, by slowing down the melody and replacing the usual twanging banjos with jagged guitar riffs.

But what starts off as a fresh, bold take on some very familiar songs soon starts to flag. A plodding 'Gallows Pole' pales in comparison to Led Zeppelin's version, while the doo wop of The Silhouettes' 1957 hit 'Get A Job' brings back unwelcome memories of Young's Shocking Pinks and their insipid 50s pastiche *Everybody's Rockin'*. Their lumber through 'Travel On', a 1958 country single by Billy Grammer, is agreeable enough, but completely forgettable.

Things improve again with 'High Flyin' Bird', Billy Edd Wheeler's slice of early 1960s country that is put through the Young and Crazy Horse blender and comes out the other end sounding like an outtake from *Ragged Glory* with its cascades of squalling guitar and soaring harmonies. It's followed by 'Jesus' Chariot (She'll Be Coming Round the Mountain)', is a tune so ubiquitous it's hard to imagine anyone making it sound different and interesting, but to their credit, Young and Crazy Horse do just that, successfully retaining the song's joyous energy but with the added heft of a garage rock band in full flow.

It's perhaps inevitable that Woody Guthrie's 'This Land Is Your Land', practically an alternative U.S. national anthem, is included, and perhaps because the original is the closest in style and spirit to Young's own work of all the songs on *Americana*, the version is a no frills rendition rather than a radical reworking. 'Wayfarin' Stranger', the sole acoustic track on the album, is another 19th century folk song recorded by everyone from Paul Robeson to Emmylou Harris. Young's version is a stripped back and haunting, its sparse arrangement providing a by now welcome contrast to what's an otherwise unapologetically loud record.

Mischievous and unpredictable as ever, Young ends the album with a chaotic version of 'God Save The Queen' - not the Sex Pistols, but the actual British national anthem. As well as being a nod to the U. S.'s pre-independence history, it's also worth noting that as a Canadian, Young would have grown up with the late Queen Elizabeth II as his Head of State, as Canada is a member of the British Commonwealth, and heard the anthem played regularly at school. It's perhaps with these memories in mind that Young adds a children's choir to his version, which, once the novelty value has worn off, is almost unlistenable.

Americana is one of the most difficult of Neil Young's albums to evaluate, as it features none of his own songs and is instead all about his interpretations of some of his adopted nation's rich musical heritage. The results differ considerably from track to track, from inspired and intriguing to dull and outright bad. But what's consistent throughout, as one would expect from Young, is a fiercely uncompromising approach to doing things his way. Perhaps unsurprisingly given its material, the album did much better in the U.S. than the U.K, peaking at number 4 in the charts. For those for whom Young and Crazy Horse's foray into the Great American Songbook was not to their taste, they did not have long to wait for the next course.

⊙ TRACK LISTING   ◄◄ ‖ ►►|

1. Oh Susannah (Stephen Collins Foster; arrangement: Tim Rose) ·········· 5:03
2. Clementine (Traditional; arrangement: Young) ································· 5:42
3. Tom Dula - (Traditional; arrangement: Young)································ 8:13
4. Gallows Pole (Traditional; arrangement: Odetta Felious Gordon) ········ 4:15
5. Get a Job (Richard Lewis, Earl Beal, Raymond Edwards, William Horton) ·· 3:01
6. Travel On··· 6:47
    (Traditional; arrangement: Paul Clayton, Larry Ehrlich,
    David Lazar, Tom Six)
7. High Flyin' Bird (Billy Edd Wheeler)·· 5:30
8. Jesus' Chariot ·· 5:38
    (She'll Be Coming Round the Mountain)
    (Traditional; arrangement: Young)
9. This Land Is Your Land (Woody Guthrie) ··· 5:26
10. Wayfarin' Stranger (Traditional; arrangement: Burl Ives) ···················· 3:07
11. God Save the Queen·· 4:08
    (Thomas Augustine Arne; medley arrangement: Young)

Length: 56:50

Neil Young & Crazy Horse - Psychedelic Pill

Released 30 October 2012 (Reprise)

After nearly a decade apart from his most enduring musical soulmates Crazy Horse, 2012 saw Neil Young energetically revive the relationship by releasing not one but two new albums in what would prove to be the last hurrah for the band's long standing line up of Poncho Sampedro, Billy Talbot and Ralph Molina. While *Americana* was an idiosyncratic take on a range of iconic songs from U.S. history, the collection that followed barely six months later was quintessential Young and Crazy Horse at their most raucous, sprawling and free spirited.

Once again recorded at Young's Broken Arrow ranch, at 87 minutes in length *Psychedelic Pill* is his longest ever album, spanning two CDs and three vinyl records. Many of the songs on the album came out of extended jam sessions with Crazy Horse while recording *Americana,* a genesis reflected by three of the tracks clocking in at more than 15 minutes in length.

2012 also saw the release of Young's autobiography, *Waging Heavy Peace*. Unlike many rock memoirs, it was entirely self-written, with a freeform, off the cuff anecdotal style that saw the narrative switch back and forth between different times and topics with little sense of conventional structure. The process of writing the book clearly influenced the songs on *Psychedelic Pill*, which often reflect on his childhood and early career.

Few artists would have the levels of chutzpah required to begin an album with a track 27 and a half minutes long, but 'Driftin' Back' is an absolute tour de force of guitar dynamics and stream of consciousness lyrics that never flags over its close to half hour duration. It begins with just a gentle solo acoustic strum and Young's voice, briefly joined by the sighing harmonies of Crazy Horse, before the full band sound emerges triumphantly from the speakers and takes centre stage.

The jagged yet graceful guitar shapes ebb and flow unhurriedly, anchored as ever by Talbot and Molina's indomitable rhythm section and interspersed with Young's scattergun observations on everything from the evils of downloaded music "Don't want my mp3" to the commercialisation of Picasso's art "I used to dig Picasso/ Then the big tech giant came along/And turned him into wallpaper" to his religious beliefs "Finding my religion/I might be a pagan." At one point, he even announces bizarrely "going to get me a hip hop haircut" - perhaps a wry observation on the challenges of an elder statesman like himself staying relevant to a modern audience.

After such an epic opener, the album's title track, clocking in at a mere three and a half minutes, is something of an anti-climax. A decent, gutsy rock riff is let down by a somewhat laboured tune and the decision to process Young's vocals with *Le Noise*-style distortion, which unfortunately sounds rather like he's singing in a wind tunnel. Thankfully, it's only a brief misstep and Young is soon back on top of his game on the fantastic, near 17 minutes long *Ramada Inn*. A poignant tale of an ageing couple whose relationship is threatened by the effects of alcoholism, its emotive subject matter is complemented by Young's searing, mournful guitar playing and world weary vocals. It's one of his finest stories in a song, beginning by setting the scene "So many years now together?/All those good times, ups and downs/So many joys raising up those kids/Well they've moved on now, out of town" before starkly describing the impact of the husband's self-destructive boozing "A few drinks now and she hardly knows him/He just looks away and he checks out." The refrain of "Every morning comes the sun/And they both rise to the day/Holding on to what they've done" movingly encapsulates the mindset of two people who believe being united by the bond of their shared past will help them to overcome the challenges of the present.

Young delves deep into his own past on 'Born in Ontario', a scratchy, jaunty boogie in which Young reflects that the Canadian province of his youth was "where I learned most of what I know/Because you don't learn much/When you start to get old." He also recalls his childhood trips to Florida with writer father Scott and his decision to leave home at a young age to pursue his musical ambitions, as well as offering perhaps his most neatly expressed summary yet of his habitual song writing restlessness with the delicious "I still like to sing a happy song/Once in a while and things go wrong/I pick up a pen, scribble on a page/Try to make sense of my inner rage."

'Twisted Road' is another wistful nostalgia trip, this time eulogising Young's musical influences, including The Grateful Dead, Roy Orbison and Bob Dylan, recalling that the "first time I heard "Like A Rolling Stone"/I felt that magic and took it home." 'She's Always Dancin'', meanwhile, is a rather cliched depiction of a free spirited woman that bears some musical similarities to the immortal *Like A Hurricane,* with Young's guitar at its most coruscating and some soaring harmonies. 'For the Love of Man' had been performed live since 1981 and is revived here as a slightly schmaltzy ballad that stands apart stylistically from the rest of the album. It was originally written shortly after Young's son Ben was born with severe cerebral palsy, a life changing event reflected in the heartfelt lyric "When a child is born to live/But not like you or I."

Psychedelic Pill's third titanic track, 'Walk like a Giant', may even be its best. Young and Crazy Horse summon up a 16 minute maelstrom of frothing, surging majesty, yet above it all, the defiant melody is never lost, sometimes accompanied by some strangely ominous whistling from the Horse. Young returns to his now familiar theme of the impact of ageing, beginning with the memorable image "I used to walk like a giant on the land/Now I feel like a leaf floating in a stream" before lamenting his generation's failure to deliver the changes they hoped for and expressing frustration at the powerlessness of his older self. The song ends with a cacophony of feedback and clanging noise, sometimes extended for up to 10 minutes on live performances. It's a shame the album doesn't end there, but in a typical act of contrariness, Young signs off with another cut of the underwhelming title track, which is admittedly improved by the removal of the bizarre treatment of Young's vocals on the earlier version.

Psychedelic Pill falls short of being consistently great, with its shorter songs varying in quality, but the three long songs here are undoubtedly Young and Crazy Horse's finest moments of the 21st century, and arguably the closest they came to recapturing the very particular slow burning groove of *Everybody Knows This Is Nowhere* over four decades before. The album was another U.S. Top 10 hit for Young and is a highlight of an often unheralded late purple patch in his discography - from 2010's *Le Noise* to 2014's *Storytone* - that showed yet again he remained a vital, ever-unpredictable force of nature when most of his contemporaries had long since let the fires go out.

⊙ TRACK LISTING   ◄◄ ❚❚ ►►|

1. Driftin' Back ·· 27:36
2. Psychedelic Pill ·· 3:26
3. Ramada Inn ··· 16:49
4. Born in Ontario ·· 3:49
5. Twisted Road ··· 3:28
6. She's Always Dancing ·· 8:33
7. For the Love of Man ·· 4:13
8. Walk like a Giant ··· 16:27
9. Psychedelic Pill (Alternate Mix) ·· 3:12

Length: 87:41

Neil Young - A Letter Home

Released 19 April 2014 (Reprise)

🎧　🎧　🎧

Shortly after bemoaning the quality of modern digital music in his 2012 autobiography *Waging Heavy Peace,* Neil Young decided to do something about it personally. Never one to do things by halves, he founded the company PonoMusic with Silicon Valley entrepreneur John Hamm, with the aim of developing a portable digital media player and music download service for high-resolution audio of studio recording quality. An impressive crowdfunding campaign on Kickstarter reached the initial funding target figure in a single day, and PonoPlayers were rolling off the production line by late 2014.

It was therefore rather ironic that at the same time as he was working on achieving the ultimate in cutting edge modern sound quality, Young was also making a new album in a vintage 1947 Voice-O-Graph recording booth. The booth was owned by Jack White of The White Stripes, who also co-produced the record, and featured Young solo acoustic performances of a range of fellow singer-songwriters whose careers overlapped with or influenced his own, making the album an intriguing combination of *Le Noise*'s stripped back aesthetics and *Americana*'s mining of America's musical traditions.

With the booth installed at White's Third Man studios in Nashville, Young began the album with a sweetly rambling personal message to his deceased mother Rassy, now presumably ensconced in heaven, in which he talks about the weather and climate change and encourages her to speak to ex-husband, Neil's father Scott, with the audible crackling in the background adding atmosphere and authenticity.

The first track proper is protest singer Phil Ochs' 'Changes', recorded and first released by Young's fellow Canadian Gordon Lightfoot in 1966, two of whose own songs appear later on *A Letter Home*. With its gracefully poetic lyrics about ageing and death, it's a poignant opening selection, and no doubt Young was thinking of his parents and others he had recently lost - notably long-term collaborator Ben

Keith, who had died in 2010 - as he sang "Green leaves of summer turn red in the fall/To brown and to yellow, they fade/And then they have to die."

Young stays with the folk movement of the early 1960s with a faithful cover of Bob Dylan's ageless 'Girl From The North Country', even adopting the great man's distinctive muffled drawl. It sounds great in a weathered, world weary kind of way, but the choice of song, covered by everyone from Rod Stewart and Sting to Eels and George Ezra (plus of course, Dylan's later reworking with Johnny Cash) is hardly ground-breaking.

The same could be said of the next track, which crosses the Atlantic to take on revered Scottish folk/blues guitarist Bert Jansch's best known song, the gorgeous but harrowing 'Needle of Death'. But the subject matter is so personal to Young with his own experience of losing people close to him to heroin addiction that it works beautifully, feeling like a later life companion piece to Young's self-penned classic 'The Needle and the Damage Done.'

Four of the remaining songs are written by either Gordon Lightfoot or country legend Willie Nelson. Lightfoot's earnestly pretty acoustic folk-rock is a cosy fit for Young, hardly a stranger to similar material himself, and both 'Early Morning Rain' and 'If You Could Read My Mind' are vintage Lightfoot compositions that are in safe hands here. The two Nelson covers - 'Crazy' and 'On The Road Again' fare a little less well, being both extremely familiar to the point of cliche and unsuited to Young's yearning, reedy voice and the ramshackle arrangements.

Elsewhere, Tim Hardin's 'Reason to Believe' follows on from another short Young monologue to Rassy, and features a piano set up in the studio outside the Voice-O-Graph booth with the door left open. The resultant echoes further diminish the track's sound quality, which, combined with White's saloon bar playing style, makes the song feel like a visitation from 1865 rather than 1965. 'Since I Met You Baby', by the relatively obscure 1950s R&B singer songwriter Ivory Joe Hunter, is gentle and charming if slight, while the inclusion of Bruce Springsteen's quietly anthemic 'My Home Town', which only dates back to 1985, feels just a little too contemporary, with the urgency of Springsteen's original largely lost beneath the layers of static.

A Letter Home ends with Young and White duetting on The Everly Brothers' '
I Wonder If I Care as Much'. The softly undulating guitar and the duo's harmony vocals sound strangely sinister, as if emerging at night from the deep, dark woods after decades of isolation from the modern world. Here, as at other times on the record, the sound is less like the work of a 21st century artist and more akin to something unearthed by the *Anthology of American Folk Music*, a seminal collection of early traditional recordings compiled by filmmaker Harry Smith in 1952.

Like many of Neil Young's more experimental albums, *A Letter Home* is too niche and unconventional a listen to rank as one of his essential works, and some of the song choices are undeniably better than others. But it's still a record quite literally crackling with atmosphere, mostly striking the right balance between gimmicky weirdness and a very personal, back to basics snapshot of America's acoustic songwriting past. A Top 20 hit in both the U.S. and the U.K., it once again showed the durability of Young's appeal, even when releasing albums that were stubbornly uncommercial.

As for Pono, its promising start was sadly short lived. Bedevilled by lukewarm sales as an expensive option in a crowded download market and lacking sustainable funding, in April 2017 Young announced the PonoMusic store was being discontinued. Pledges of an evolution to become a streaming service remain unfulfilled, and it seems likely that Pono - which means 'proper' in the Hawaiian language - is destined to be remembered as a failed Young passion project rather than the revolution in digital music he had hoped for.

⊙ TRACK LISTING   ⏮ ⏸ ⏭

1. A Letter Home Intro ·· 2:16
2. Changes ································· (Phil Ochs) - 3:56
3. Girl from the North Country (Bob Dylan) ········· 3:32
4. Needle of Death (Bert Jansch) ···················· 4:57
5. Early Morning Rain (Gordon Lightfoot)·········· 4:24
6. Crazy (Willie Nelson) ···························· 2:16
7. Reason to Believe (Tim Hardin) ················· 2:47
8. On the Road Again (Willie Nelson) ·············· 2:23
9. If You Could Read My Mind (Gordon Lightfoot)···· 4:04
10. Since I Met You Baby (Ivory Joe Hunter)········· 2:13
11. My Hometown (Bruce Springsteen) ··············· 4:08
12. I Wonder If I Care as Much (The Everly Brothers) ···· 2:29

Length: 39:25

Neil Young - Storytone

Released 4 November 2014 (Reprise)

After 36 years of marriage, it came as a surprise to many when Neil and Pegi Young announced their divorce in 2014. By this stage, Young was in a new relationship with the Hollywood actress and environmental activist Darryl Hannah, and it is the contrasting emotions Young experienced during this period of personal upheaval that formed the core of his second album of 2014, the lushly orchestrated *Storytone*.

Young had toyed for some time with the idea of recording a record with a full orchestra, and the sessions were a real labour of love, as the now 68 year old explained on his official website: "First, I recorded the songs at Capitol Records with my old friends Niko Bolas and Al Schmitt. I sang them alone with only the instruments I desired to use. There was no over dubbing or enhancing. The resulting music is from my heart, directly to you. Then, I entered the hallowed MGM soundstage where The Wizard of Oz soundtrack was recorded. Surrounded by the finest musicians in Hollywood, with arrangements and orchestrations by Christ Walden and Michael Bearden, I sang seven of the *Storytone* songs live for the second time. I sang into Barbra Streisand's microphone, a perfectly cared-for antique with a wonderful tone that I loved. I also went to Sunset Boulevard to record the remaining three songs with a big band in an old Hollywood studio rebuilt and now known as East West. All the performances are live with no added effects or recording. I just stood singing into the microphone with occasional harmonica notes blown in between verses, while the musicians played."[1]

Opening track 'Plastic Flowers' instantly sets the template for what is probably Young's most unashamedly romantic album. Accompanied by gorgeous, gliding strings and elegant piano, Young high, frail voice tells the tale of his first meeting with Hannah and how they bonded over a shared passion for environmental issues:

---

1   Neil Young Times, Neil Young Archives, 10 November 2014

"In the summertime we met to see a threat/That came to harm something we both loved." Although brimming with the first flush of love, there is sometimes doubt in Young's words too as he sings "I got my promises made but before the timeless father/I showed plastic flowers to mother nature's daughter."

Fears of an impending ecological catastrophe dominate 'Who's Going To Stand Up', with Young pulling no punches as he outlines his manifesto for urgent change: "Ban fossil fuel, draw the line/Before we build one more pipeline/End fracking now, let's save the water/And build a life for our sons and daughters." While the sentiments are laudable, the song feels overwrought and preachy at times, with the overblown orchestration evoking unwelcome memories of previous missteps such as Harvest's bloated folly 'There's A World.' In what seems a bizarrely contradictory move, Young follows 'Who's Going To Stand Up' with 'I Want To Drive My Car', a swaggering big band ode to the joys of the automobile.

Things get a bit too saccharine to stomach on the excessively gloopy 'Glimmer', with Young sounding uncannily similar to Kermit the Frog as he proclaims "Tough love can leave you almost alone/But new love brings back everything to you" while a sickly sweep of strings washes over him. 'Say Hello to Chicago", meanwhile, is an empty Rat Pack pastiche with the big band horns jostling uncomfortably with occasional squalls of Young's guitar. 'Tumbleweed' has a beautiful lilting melody but is pure cheese, with Young sounding like the old hippy he'd always vowed never to become as he croons "Animal/Care for your kind, in the way you always do/When the flower moon is shining" while harps shimmer and flutes flutter. 'Like You Used to Do', the final big band arrangement on the album, is the most acerbic track here, with Young sounding decidedly bitter as - presumably addressing ex-wife Pegi - he sings "I got my problems/But they mostly show up with you/ Someday you'll see me, like you used to do."

Storytone only really hits the right balance consistently on its final three tracks. 'I'm Glad I Found You', another paean to Young's burgeoning romance with Hannah, still feels a little too ornate, but its heartfelt lyrics and Young's passionate delivery give it emotional heft. Young also reflects on the impact of fame on how he is perceived as he declares "So many people don't understand/What it's like to be like me/But I'm not different from anyone else." Penultimate track 'When I Watch You Sleeping' is the closest the album comes to a straightforward Young acoustic song, with its twangs of pedal steel, folksy harmonica and more restrained strings not unlike his late 1970s *Comes A Time* sound. *Storytone* signs off with 'All Those Dreams', a gentle ballad with a cosy, wintery feel. Even after a full album of similarly sentimental fare, it still feels slightly weird hearing an artist as uncompromising as Young warbling unashamedly twee lines like "Out by the car our snowman's melting/Nothing can bring him back now/His smile a twig and his nose a cucumber/His eyes two pine cones looking out." Yet somehow it works here in a goofily charming way.

Storytone was also released as a deluxe edition which includes stripped-back recordings of the songs, some of which - notably 'Tumbleweed' - benefit from the quiet intimacy the removal of the orchestration allows. The album's sales performance was underwhelming, reaching 20 in the U.K. and 33 in the U.S., and its critical reception was similarly unenthusiastic. But for those fans willing to go along with Young's latest reincarnation as a schmaltzy, syrupy crooner, there are some very lovely songs here, brimming with warmth and sweet melodies, that make it a record well worth the occasional spin.

⊙ TRACK LISTING   ◄◄ ❚❚ ►►|

1. Plastic Flowers ··· 4:06
2. Who's Gonna Stand Up? ································· 4:23
3. I Want to Drive My Car ······························· 3:08
4. Glimmer ·· 4:59
5. Say Hello to Chicago ·································· 4:57
6. Tumbleweed ·· 3:37
7. Like You Used to Do ································· 2:39
8. I'm Glad I Found You ································ 3:39
9. When I Watch You Sleeping ····················· 5:30
10. All Those Dreams ····································· 4:25

Length: 41:32

Neil Young & Promise of the Real - The Monsanto Years

Released 29 June 2015 (Reprise)

Although he had always collaborated with other groups of musicians on his records, ranging from established acts such as Pearl Jam and Booker T. and the M.G.'s to purpose-built collectives of stellar individuals like The Stray Gators, for many years Crazy Horse were the only backing band to be a regularly recurring presence in Neil Young's career. But as the decades passed and the ravages of life took their toll, it was inevitable that some of his contemporaries would gradually fade from the picture, as the deaths of Tim Drummond and Rick Rosas in 2014 sadly proved. Recognising the importance of introducing fresh blood to his sound, Young began performing regularly with Willie Nelson's sons Lukas and Micah. These gigs laid the foundation for Young's new studio band, Promise of the Real, a five piece fronted by Lukas and also featuring Anthony LoGerfo, Corey McCormick and Logan Metz.

Promise of the Real had already recorded two albums together before entering Daniel Lanois's Teatro Studios in California to record *The Monsanto Years* with Young in early 2015. The album saw Young returning to the theme of ecological awareness that had characterised several of his 21st century records, but with a specific focus on the American biotechnology corporation Monsanto, who are frequently referenced throughout as the embodiment of big business's threat to the environment, farming and food production. Musically, the earthy, hard edged country rock on *The Monsanto Years* is not dissimilar to a slightly more polished Crazy Horse.

The album kicks off with the surging, anthemic rock of 'A New Day for Love', built around a chorus that offers optimism for the future "It's a new day for the planet/It's a new day for the sun/To shine down on what we're doing/It's a new day for love." But elsewhere in the song, Young warns us that this state can only be achieved if we all play our part in fighting what he sees as the enemies of the planet, singing "It's a bad day to do nothing/With so many people needing our help." In contrast to the muscular guitar riffs of 'A New Day for Love', 'Wolf Moon' is a gentle acoustic shuffle that wouldn't sound out of place on *Harvest Moon*, with Young's quivering vocal backed by flecks of pedal steel. The lyrics celebrate the resilience of nature in the face of relentless exploitation by humans: "Less fish swimming in your ocean/Old ice floating in your sea/Still you hold against the constant plundering."

'People Want to Hear About Love' is perhaps the most immediate song on the album. Recalling the ragged, woozy sound of Young's *Time Fades Away* era, its pounding drums, squalls of guitar and chanted group vocals spark with energy as Young bemoans what he sees as a lack of engagement from his fellow musicians on the key issues of our time. You can sense his frustration as he sarcastically belts out the words "Don't talk about the corporations hijacking all your rights/People want to hear about love/Don't mention world poverty, talk about global love/People want to hear about love." The momentum is maintained on the pulsating eight minute-long 'Big Box', a good old fashioned Young guitar epic that lambasts big corporations as "Too big to fail /Too rich for jail."

Coffee behemoth Starbucks is next in line for Young's ire on the less than subtly titled 'A Rock Star Bucks a Coffee Shop', which also focuses on industrial food companies challenging legislation requiring the labelling of genetically modified food products in the U.S. state of Vermont. "Mon-san-to (and Starbucks)/Mothers want to know/What they feed their children," Young growls, although the decision to augment an already jaunty tune with *Snow White and the Seven Dwarves*-style whistling unfortunately dampens the song's impact somewhat.

The rest of *The Monsanto Years* largely fails to live up to the standard of the first few tracks. After the forgettable garage stomp of 'Workin' Man', which tells the tale of Vernon Bowman, an Indiana farmer accused of infringing Monsanto's patent for genetically modified soya beans, we get the insipid 'Rules of Change', with its drippy lyrics proclaiming, "No one owns the sacred seed/No man's law can change that." The title track plods unconvincingly, with the guitars sounding sloppy and the lyrics a sledgehammer assault on Monsanto, which by this stage is starting to wear a little thin. It's only on the elegant, maudlin 'If I Don't Know' that Young and Promise of the Real hit their stride again. Featuring the best guitar playing on the album, the song expresses despair at how the decisions of humankind are ravaging the planet: "If I don't know what I'm doin'/And all my big ideas fail/Like building a dam against the water so the river dies/The veins, Earth's blood."

The Monsanto Years failed to break into the top 20 album charts in either the U.S. or the U.K., with critics' reviews mostly tepid (with the exception of The

Guardian's Jon Dennis, who described it as Young 'on-form and on-song.')[1]. Overall, it's fairly typical of Young's late period records - song writing of variable quality, with ideas and messages often taking precedence over structure and melody. The subject matter and angry denunciation of the titular corporation do feel stretched and eventually wearying over an entire album, while the partnership with Promise of the Real shows flashes of real potential without ever scaling the heights of Young's Crazy Horse peaks.

⏵ TRACK LISTING ⏮ ⏸ ⏭

1. A New Day for Love ⋯⋯⋯⋯⋯⋯⋯⋯⋯⋯⋯⋯⋯⋯⋯⋯⋯⋯ 5:52
2. Wolf Moon ⋯⋯⋯⋯⋯⋯⋯⋯⋯⋯⋯⋯⋯⋯⋯⋯⋯⋯⋯⋯⋯⋯ 3:52
3. People Want to Hear About Love ⋯⋯⋯⋯⋯⋯⋯⋯⋯⋯ 6:19
4. Big Box ⋯⋯⋯⋯⋯⋯⋯⋯⋯⋯⋯⋯⋯⋯⋯⋯⋯⋯⋯⋯⋯⋯⋯⋯ 8:17
5. A Rock Star Bucks a Coffee Shop ⋯⋯⋯⋯⋯⋯⋯⋯⋯ 5:00
6. Workin' Man ⋯⋯⋯⋯⋯⋯⋯⋯⋯⋯⋯⋯⋯⋯⋯⋯⋯⋯⋯⋯⋯ 4:43
7. Rules of Change ⋯⋯⋯⋯⋯⋯⋯⋯⋯⋯⋯⋯⋯⋯⋯⋯⋯⋯⋯ 4:39
8. Monsanto Years ⋯⋯⋯⋯⋯⋯⋯⋯⋯⋯⋯⋯⋯⋯⋯⋯⋯⋯⋯ 7:46
9. If I Don't Know ⋯⋯⋯⋯⋯⋯⋯⋯⋯⋯⋯⋯⋯⋯⋯⋯⋯⋯⋯ 4:26

Length: 50:54

1 The Guardian, 25 June 2015

Neil Young - Peace Trail

Released 9 December 2016 (Reprise)

🎧 🎧 🎧

The recording of *The Monsanto Years* with youthful new backing band Promise of the Real seemed to revitalise Neil Young. He spent much of 2015 and 2016 playing with the band, fronted by Willie Nelson's sons Lukas and Micah, including his Rebel Content tour of North America and Europe. A live album documenting the tour- *Earth* - emerged in June 2016, featuring live performances bizarrely overdubbed to include a range of animal sounds, providing further evidence that the older he got, the more ferocious an environmental activist Young was becoming.

But rather than cementing his burgeoning relationship with Promise of the Real by recording another studio album with them, in time-honoured fashion, Young decided to take a completely different path. *Peace Trail*'s sessions at Shangri-La Studios in Malibu during September 2016 took place with just Young himself and two additional musicians - bass player Paul Bushnell and legendary drummer Jim Keltner. A low key but likeable collection of mostly acoustic songs, commenting on a range of social and ecological issues of the time and recorded in a mere four days, the quality of the musicianship on *Peace Trail* means it manages to simultaneously sound both off the cuff and accomplished.

The opening title track is a quietly propulsive reflection by Young on what he sees as an increasingly confusing, threatening world. "The world is full of changes/Sometimes all these changes make me sad/ (But I keep planting seeds/'Til something new is growing)", he sings defiantly, as Old Black makes what's a rare appearance on this record, scattering molten fragments of melody across the otherwise unobtrusive musical backdrop. More questionable is Young's use of Auto-Tune, which he rediscovered while working on the *Earth* album project. Deployed here to multi-track his voice, it gives the song a starkly artificial feel at odds with the prevailing organic, ramshackle vibe.

Next up is the scruffy bluesy shuffle of 'Can't Stop Workin'', which provides a wry insight into Young's always prolific creative output. "Well I can't stop working/'Cause I like to work

When nothing else is going on," he informs us, before concluding "It's bad for the body/But it's good for the soul." Brash squalls of harmonica occasionally interrupt what's a predominantly gentle outing. 'Indian Givers' has a similarly mellow mood, but lyrically it's much more urgent, addressing the encroachment of oil pipelines on sacred Native American lands. Keltner's percussion is particularly prominent on this track, interplaying expertly with Young's plaintive vocals.

The songs on *Peace Trail* are often loose and slight, but, as evidenced by the delightfully Spanish guitar influenced riff and loping rhythms on 'Show Me', sometimes all you need is a good honest groove. But this approach doesn't always work: 'Texas Rangers' is a monotonous, tune-free dirge that fails to provide a worthy platform for its important subject matter - the often brutal treatment of Latin American migrants at the U.S. border. 'Terrorist Suicide Handgliders', which focuses on smalltown America's reaction to Islamic fundamentalist terrorism, is better, with Young perceptively capturing the domestic xenophobia the attacks generate: "I think I know who to blame/It's all those people with funny names/Moving in to our neighborhood/How can I tell if they're bad or good?"

Young's environmental agenda returns to the fore on 'John Oaks', which tells the story of an eco-activist shot dead by police while protesting about major farming companies' illegal irrigation pipelines. It's by far the most substantial song on the album lyrically, similar in style to the protest folk of the early 1960s, although the amiable, rootsy and rambling delivery by Young and his sidemen does deprive the song of some of its anger. It's followed by 'My Pledge', the latest in a long line of Young's surreal, time-hopping fantasies in which the passengers of the Mayflower rub shoulders with references to Jimi Hendrix and Marvin Gaye. Auto-Tune also makes a reappearance, providing a ghostly counterpoint to Young's Dylanesque, near-spoken word narrative. 'Glass Accident', with its echoes of the tune from *Rust Never Sleeps'* 'Sail Away', is a melancholy, world-weary track that uses shattered glass as a metaphor for the plethora of issues affecting U.S. society.

Peace Trail ends with 'My New Robot', in which a lonely man, we presume recently separated from his partner, seeks solace from the delivery of an electronic companion from Amazon, who had recently released their Alexa voice assistant. The song ends with a flurry of mechanical instructions asking for a range of personal details including PIN numbers and your mother's maiden name before cutting out unexpectedly, perhaps reflecting Young's concerns with both the development of artificial intelligence and sharing information online. The use of vocoders also brings back memories of the much-maligned *Trans*, now unbelievably more than 30 years old.

Although only a footnote in a discography as formidable as Young's, *Peace Trail*'s relaxed, unfussy approach to tackling a diverse selection of subject matter makes it one of his more interesting records of recent years. Unfortunately, not many people were listening, and the album's feeble chart performance saw Young hit his lowest commercial ebb since the mid-1980s. But as he entered his eighth decade still as buoyant, restless and full of ideas as ever, it's doubtful Young himself was losing any sleep about it.

⊙ TRACK LISTING   ◄◄ ❚❚ ►►❘

1. Peace Trail ··· 5:32
2. Can't Stop Workin' ··· 2:45
3. Indian Givers ··· 5:41
4. Show Me ··· 4:02
5. Texas Rangers ··· 2:29
6. Terrorist Suicide Hang Gliders ··· 3:17
7. John Oaks ··· 5:12
8. My Pledge ··· 3:54
9. Glass Accident ··· 2:53
10. My New Robot ··· 2:35

Length: 38:20

Neil Young & Promise of the Real - The Visitor

Released 1 December 2017 (Reprise)

🎧 🎧 🎧

After choosing to go it alone again on the largely acoustic *Peace Trail*, it wasn't long before Neil Young was back in the studio with Promise of the Real, the Lukas and Micah Nelson-fronted band who he had spent much of 2015 and 2016 playing and recording with. Their collaboration on 2015's *The Monsanto Years* saw Young relentlessly attacking the destructive impact of large corporations upon the environment, and on *The Visitor*, he fixed his sights on one particularly high profile former businessman who was now a hugely divisive figure in another arena - new U.S. President Donald Trump, who was elected to office in 2016 following a campaign built around right wing populism and a disregard for any established political etiquette.

While *The Monsanto Years* was essentially a no frills garage rock album, with Promise of the Real very much taking on the Crazy Horse role, *The Visitor* is a more varied collection, featuring everything from country folk ballads to orchestral epics. The combination of contrasting arrangements and politically focused anger is in some ways reminiscent of *Freedom* almost 30 years before, although its song writing limitations means it doesn't have the impact of Young's triumphant late 1980s comeback.

Trump's flagship slogan "Make America Great Again" gave Young the inspiration for *The Visitor*'s tremendous first track 'Already Great.' A direct riposte to the Republican's depiction of a U.S. that has lost its identity and preeminent place in the world, Young begins by singing "I'm Canadian by the way/And I love the U.S.A/I love this way of life, the freedom to act/And the freedom to say" before attacking the new president's anti-immigration policies, which included building a wall on the Mexican border and banning people from six Muslim-majority countries from entering the U.S.A, declaring: "No wall, no ban/No fascist U.S.A."

Add in a soaring, hymnal chorus and 'Already Great' is probably Young's best album opener of the 21st century.

'Fly By Night Deal' is an abrasive, percussion-heavy assault on the careless destruction of the environment by construction projects, in which a foreman seems to question the righteousness of his actions. In contrast, 'Almost Always' is a gentle, acoustic tune, which shamelessly repurposes 1992's *Harvest Moon*'s classic 'Unknown Legend', right down to the mournful guitar and harmonica chords. It's not the first time Young had pulled this trick in his later years, and it's indicative of the steady loss of his ability to conjure up the kind of fresh, gorgeous melodies that seemed to flow from him effortlessly earlier in his career. Lyrically, Young continues his withering portrayal of Trump, describing the former star of *The Apprentice* as "a gameshow host who has to brag and has to boast/About tearing down the things that I hold dear."

The strident 'Stand Tall' returns to Young's familiar ecological themes, this time denouncing the climate change sceptics in the Trump administration with the scathing broadside "The boy king don't believe in science/It goes against the big money truth/His playpen is full of deniers/They'll flush our future down the tubes." 'Change of Heart', meanwhile, is a breezy, mandolin-led shuffle not dissimilar to Bob Dylan's 'I Want You', with Young suggesting that in time the people of the U.S. will realise love conquers hate and then reject Trump's toxic politics. In common with several other songs on his recent records, the song also features whistling, which only really worked on 2012's *Psychedelic Pill*'s towering 'Walk Like A Giant'.

The second half of *The Visitor* kicks off with 'Carnival', one of the strangest songs in Young's entire canon. A painfully over-extended pastiche of Mexican mariachi telling the tale of a daredevil circus performer, it's sung by Young in a comically melodramatic voice laced with occasional bouts of maniacal laughter. This bizarre misstep is followed by the thankfully far briefer 'Diggin' A Hole', an unconvincing, laboured attempt at vintage blues. A triumvirate of genre experiments is completed with the marginally more successful 'Children of Destiny', which sees Young return to the lush, showtune-influenced orchestral indulgences of 2014's *Storytone*. Backed by histrionic horns, Young urges the American people to rise up against Trumpism, exhorting them to "Stand up for what you believe/Resist the powers that be/Preserve the land and save the seas for the children of destiny." He then goes a step further on the tubthumping, shouty 'When Bad Got Good', chanting "He lies, you lie/Lock him up/Lock him up/No belief in the liar in chief."

After the cacophony of the previous few tracks, it's something of a relief when Young opts to close *The Visitor* with the peaceful, elegant 'Forever', which lilts and meanders blissfully for over 10 minutes. The song's wispy prettiness belies a rather sad series of reflections in which Young argues humankind has abandoned the planet - which he describes memorably as 'like a church without a preacher'.

As he approached the end of his sixth decade as a recording artist, Young showed no signs of running out of things to write about, or causes to energetically champion, and it was perhaps inevitable that such a cantankerous yet fearless elder statesman would be among the first to take aim at the polarising figure of Trump. But musically, *The Visitor* continued the pattern of uneven song writing quality that had characterised all Young's recent records, with the flurry of stylistic shifts only accentuating the problem and Promise of the Real's role little more than efficient session men. It sank without trace among the record buying public, but nevertheless has flashes of quality well worth seeking out for Young completists.

⊙ TRACK LISTING   ◄◄ II ►►

1. Already Great ·· 5:47
2. Fly by Night Deal ··· 2:37
3. Almost Always ·· 4:50
4. Stand Tall ··· 5:13
5. Change of Heart ·· 5:54
6. Carnival ··· 8:21
7. Diggin' a Hole ··· 2:33
8. Children of Destiny ·· 3:24
9. When Bad Got Good ··· 2:00
10. Forever ··· 10:32

Length: 51:11

Neil Young & Promise of the Real - Paradox OST

Released 23 March 2018 (Reprise)

🎧 🎧 🎧

After a period as one of the world's most famous film stars in the 1980s, including her most iconic role as the mermaid in *Splash* opposite Tom Hanks, by the time she began dating Neil Young in 2014 Daryl Hannah was focusing as much on her work as a political activist and film director as on her acting career - two areas in which she shared a common interest with her new partner. She and Young had already jointly supported the Cowboy and Indian Alliance, a group of ranchers, farmers and indigenous leaders who joined forces to protest against the construction of the Keystone XL pipeline, intended to bring oil from Canada's Western tar sands to U.S. refiners. With Young's own long track record of dabbling with film making and soundtracks since the early 1970s, it was always likely to just be a matter of time before the two collaborated on a movie project together.

Paradox, released in 2018, was written and directed by Hannah, with Young and his now semi-permanent backing band Promise of the Real starring in the film and providing the soundtrack. A strange, nigh on impossible to follow visual ramble through the American West by a ramshackle group of musicians led by Young's enigmatic Man in the Black Hat, *Paradox* is set in an imagined near future where men and women are separated until a full moon unites them, with mostly improvised dialogue. It was almost universally panned by the critics, but the soundtrack, classed as part of Young's Special Release Archives series, is a mildly diverting selection of moody instrumental fragments, quite similar in feel to Young's 1996 score for Jim Jarmusch's *Dead Man*, off the cuff performances by the ensemble of characters of songs by artists including Willie Nelson and Lead Belly, and a few of Young's own songs.

The instrumental tracks include a loose collection of snapshots entitled 'Paradox Passage', numbered 1 to 6, alongside other individually titled compositions, mostly short and either languid acoustic tune ups or more urgent flurries of electric guitar, harmonica and drums. Snippets of dialogue and familiar Young melodies occasionally shimmer into view, for example 'Show Me' from his recent *Peace Trail* album and 'Love and Only Love' from 1991's *Ragged Glory* (a separate track entitled 'Hey' here). By far the best of these is the coruscating, 10 minute long 'Cowgirl Jam', which reworks elements of Young's classic 'Cowgirl in the Sand' into evocative new shapes through some surging, dynamic electric guitar work.

Of the covers, the standout is a sleepy rendition of Willie Nelson's 'Angel Flying Too Close to the Ground', sung with an easy grace by his son, Promise of the Real's Lukas Nelson. In contrast, a serviceable version of Lead Belly's 'How Long' segues into a brief, impromptu singalong of The Turtles' 'Happy Together' which sounds like a group of drunks around a campfire, quickly descending into uproarious laughter. Jimmy Reed's 'Baby What You Want Me to Do?' flickers briefly before ebbing away again.

Paradox features one new Young original song, co-written with Lukas and Micah Nelson, the shambling, bluesy 'Diggin' In The Dirt', as well as versions of *Peace Trail's* title track and 'Tumbleweed', the sweet ukulele ballad from 2014's *Storytone* which plays over the film's closing credits. The most interesting inclusion is a stately live performance of the mighty 'Pocahontas', dating from 2014, on which Young accompanies himself on pipe organ. It does, however, sound completely incongruous on a soundtrack that is otherwise deliberately mercurial in mood and scrappy in delivery.

Fractured and dreamlike, 'Paradox' is effective in capturing the essence of the film it scores, but as an album in its own right it is little more than an intriguing curiosity, lacking the ambition and cohesion that made Young's 'Dead Man' soundtrack so compelling. Perhaps surprisingly, it also marked the end (to date at least) of his recording relationship with Promise of the Real, who he had worked with consistently for the past few years. Even well into his seventies, the irresistible lure of Crazy Horse remained as strong as ever for Young, and the time had arrived for them to ride out together once again.

⊙ TRACK LISTING   ⏮ ⏸ ⏭

1. Many Moons Ago in the Future ··· 0:30
2. Show Me ·· 1:46
3. Paradox Passage ·· 2:16
4. Hey ··· 3:18
5. Paradox Passage ·· 1:23

Length: 53:00

Neil Young & Crazy Horse - Colorado

Released 25 October 2019 (Reprise)

🎧　🎧　🎧

Although the development of his PonoMusic portable digital media player and music download service had ground to a halt by 2019, Neil Young's crusade against the inferior sound quality of streamed and downloaded music remained as passionate as ever. He outlined his manifesto for change in a 250-page book, T*o Feel The Music: A Songwriter's Mission to Save High-Quality Audio,* written jointly with Pono Music hardware developer Phil Baker, which was published in September 2019. In the meantime, he was also back in the studio with Crazy Horse, working on what was his rootsiest, most quintessentially Neil Young-sounding album for years.

Recorded at the Studio in the Clouds in the Rocky Mountains of Colorado (which also inspired the album's name), *Colorado* saw Young reunited with Billy Talbot and Ralph Molina on bass and drums, as well as guitarist and multi-instrumentalist Nils Lofgren, who had featured on several other Young albums but last played with Crazy Horse back in 1971, here replacing the now retired Poncho Sampedro. With the exception of the 13 minute plus 'She Showed Me Love', the songs are relatively tight, earthy country-rock, continuing Young's now inevitable strong focus on political and environmental issues and infused with a palpable, wistful sadness likely to have been generated by the deaths of former wife Pegi and long-time manager Elliot Roberts (to whom the album is dedicated) during 2019.

Opening track 'Think of Me' starts off *Colorado* promisingly: a woozy harmonica intro ushers in the trademark thud of Crazy Horse's rhythm section and a rolling saloon bar piano before the group's always underrated harmonies coalesce sweetly on the song's gently uplifting chorus." When you see those geese in the sky, think of me," Young croons, painting a picture of a man with the confidence and freedom of spirit to do whatever he wants, without regrets. Next up is the sprawling 'She Showed Me Love', clearly written about Young's now wife Daryl Hannah (they tied the knot in August 2018) and how she has inspired his activism.

Young acknowledges he may be seen by some as "an old white guy" and "a few bricks short of a load" before praising the younger generation's commitment to environmental causes "I saw young folks fighting to save mother nature (where I've been)/I saw them standing (where I've been)." Musically however it's a bit of a weary trudge, over long at the best part of a quarter of an hour and failing to ignite in the same way as earlier Young and Crazy Horse guitar epics.

The tender, nostalgic 'Olden Days' is one of *Colorado*'s highlights. A pretty melody is lent additional emotional heft by Crazy Horse's world weary grind, while Young sings movingly about the friends he has made and lost through his now long life: "Where did all the people go?/Why did they fade away from me?/They meant so much to me and now I know/That they're here to stay in my heart." Things get altogether fierier on the angry, scabrous garage rock of 'Help Me Lose My Mind', on which Young rails against consumer obsession with the latest new technology "I gotta find a new television/Got to find a new display system/To make the sky look like the Earth is flattened." But he switches back into maudlin mode again on the gently devastating 'Green Is Blue', lamenting the impact of climate change with stark images of animals in distress: "We saw the pod of whales lay bloated/On the shore where they baked, but we missed that sign/We saw the polar bear, she floated/On a piece of ice from another time."

Young addresses the environmental crisis more aggressively on 'Shut It Down', a relentless, tune-free guitar barrage accompanied by bellows of "have to shut the whole system down". Thankfully the bar is soon raised again on 'Milky Way', which harks back to the classic Crazy Horse slow burning sound of 'Down By The River' or 'Dangerbird' with its smouldering guitars and Young's fragile, bruised voice. 'Eternity', meanwhile, is the sweetest, softest song on the album, with a gorgeous piano recalling Young's *Harvest* period and some delightful, doo-wop influenced backing vocals. The 73 year old sounds blissfully content as he sings: "Woke up this morning in a house of love/The birds were singing in the sky above/ The dogs were barking and the deer were free/And we were living in a house of love." In contrast, Young had made no secret of his loathing of Donald Trump and his right wing politics on 2017's *The Visitor*, so it's hardly a surprise that he gives the incumbent president another lambasting on 'Rainbow of Colors', championing the U.S.'s long history as a melting pot of ethnicities: "There's a rainbow of colors/ In the old U.S.A/No one's gonna whitewash/Those colors away."

Colorado closes with the hushed, acoustic reflections of 'I Do', on which Young seems to acknowledge the inimitable, unbreakable bond he has with Crazy Horse as he murmurs "Thanks for making all this happen again/We're gonna do it just like we did back then." It's an apt way to close an album which, while no *Everybody Knows This Is Nowhere* or *Zuma,* showed that Young and Crazy Horse still had a unique connection an astonishing half a century after their first record together.

An accompanying documentary directed by Hannah, *Mountaintop*, gave an insight into the creative process as the record was made.

Colorado was hailed by critics as Young's most consistent collection in years, hitting the U.K. top 20 and demonstrating that for all his artistic wanderings, the great man still knew when it was time to come home.

⊙ TRACK LISTING ◄◄ ‖ ►►

1. Think of Me··3:02
2. She Showed Me Love ···13:36
3. Olden Days··4:04
4. Help Me Lose My Mind···4:14
5. Green Is Blue···3:48
6. Shut It Down ··3:43
7. Milky Way··5:59
8. Eternity···2:43
9. Rainbow of Colors ···3:35
10. I Do··5:37

Length: 50:21

Neil Young & Crazy Horse - Barn

Released 10 December 2021 (Reprise)

After reuniting with Crazy Horse for his most cohesive, enjoyable record in years on 2019's *Colorado*, one could be forgiven for expecting Neil Young to do what he always does - promptly head off in a completely different musical direction for his next project. In fact, Young did exactly the opposite - recording another very similar album in a converted 19th century barn in his new home in Colorado, with Crazy Horse kept on board and the emphasis very much on recreating the classic rock template of their peak years. As with its predecessor, an accompanying documentary - *A Band A Brotherhood A Barn,* again directed by Daryl Hannah - was also released.

Young had remained very much in the headlines during 2020 with his vociferous opposition to President Donald Trump, who was bidding to be re-elected for a second term in the White House. Young issued a lawsuit against the Republican in August of that year for his use of his songs 'Rockin' in the Free World' and 'Devil's Sidewalk' at a campaign rally in Tulsa, claiming copyright infringement, with the complaint stating that the songwriter "cannot allow his music to be used as a 'theme song' for a divisive, un-American campaign of ignorance and hate". The lawsuit was dropped by Young a few months later, but the affair only enhanced his status as a fearless speaker of truth to power. The songs on *Barn*, however, are often less explicitly political than most of Young's recent releases, predominantly focusing on warm, occasionally bittersweet nostalgia. It's a more relaxed, melodic and homely record than *Colorado*, although a little less immediate, needing a few listens for its not inconsiderable merits to shine through.

The opening track, 'Song of the Seasons', gets things off to a gentle start, with rickety acoustic guitar chords and a mournful accordion providing the backdrop for Young's wistful lyrics, which celebrate the power of nature, including a reference to the impact of the ongoing COVID-19 pandemic upon human society, describing a city where "Masked people are walkin' everywhere/It's humanity in my sights." The volume is cranked up on the punchy "Heading West', which has a touch of Springsteen about it as Young sings about "the good old days" of his childhood in small town Ontario, accompanied by sparky guitars and a swaggering piano. It's one of several examples of the fluent musicality Nils Lofgren brings to this latest incarnation of Crazy Horse, adding some complementary virtuosity to the earthier talents of Billy Talbot and Ralph Molina's rhythm section.

'Change Ain't Never Gonna' is a bluesy, harmonica-heavy stomp that returns to the familiar Young topic of the evils of big corporations harming the environment, highlighting the impact they have on the livelihoods of those who oppose their actions. Young then explores his own dual nationality in the fiery 'Canerican', reminding us that although "I was born in Canada, came south to join a band," he cares deeply about his adopted country, expressing concern about the changes he saw coming (no doubt in the form of Trump and his politics) and stating proudly "I am all colors, all colors is what I am/Stand beside my brother for freedom in this land." It's followed by the disappointing 'Shape of You', a rambling tribute to Young's new spouse Hannah featuring some of his clumsiest lyrics, with the couplet "You changed my life for the better/Wore my love like your favorite sweater" perhaps the worst offender.

The evocative 'They Might Be Lost' is suffused with both nostalgia and unease, as the narrator waits for unnamed figures from his past to arrive, smoking a joint as he muses ominously "Well, the jury is out on the old days, you know/ The judgement is soon comin' down." In contrast, the surging 'Human Race' focuses on the future - albeit an apocalyptic one after the planet is ravaged by climate change. "Who's gonna tell/The children of destiny/That we didn't try to save the world for them?" Young asks, as his guitar squalls with electrifying urgency. 'Tumblin' Through The Years' is hokey and slight, with more vapid lyrics about the most recent Mrs Young built around an annoying, tinkling piano part.

Barn features one bona fide Young and Crazy Horse epic - penultimate track 'Welcome Back', which shows that Young is still capable of wringing notes of devastating emotional resonance from his trusty Old Black guitar. Its eight and half minutes of sprawling, languid yet expertly controlled dynamics standout from the rest of *Barn* as a piece of work that would not sound out of place on his finest albums, with Young's whispered, surreal lyrics adding to the sense of quiet drama. Sweet final song 'Don't Forget Love' provides a charming close to the record with its delightful coo of a chorus, the calm after the storm of 'Welcome Back', just like Young did by following the monumental 'Cortez the Killer' with the comedown of 'Through My Sails' on *Zuma* 46 years before.

Like so many of Young's later albums, *Barn* doesn't have the consistent song writing strength of his Seventies pomp, with the septuagenarian long since having prioritised feel and mood over pure craft. But even with its sometimes raw, dashed off feel, it's still far better than one has any right to expect from any artist releasing his 46th studio album.

⊙ TRACK LISTING ⏮ ⏸ ⏭

1. Song of the Seasons ··· 6:04
2. Heading West ·· 3:22
3. Change Ain't Never Gonna ··· 2:53
4. Canerican ·· 3:12
5. Shape of You ·· 2:55
6. They Might Be Lost ··· 4:32
7. Human Race ··· 4:14
8. Tumblin' Thru the Years·· 3:19
9. Welcome Back ·· 8:28
10. Don't Forget Love ·· 3:48

Length: 42:47

Neil Young & Crazy Horse - World Record

Released 18 November 2022 (Reprise)

🎧　🎧　🎧

Appearing less than a week after Neil Young's 77th birthday, *World Record* followed hot on the heels of December 2021's *Barn*, indicating that even well into his eight decade, the grand old man remains as capable as ever of sudden bursts of prolific recording activity.

Once again featuring his redoubtable backing band Crazy Horse, with Nils Lofgren now firmly established as the group's third member alongside the evergreen Ralph Molina and Billy Talbot, *World Record* also saw Young teaming up with legendary producer Rick Rubin, whose stellar career had seen him work alongside everyone from the Beastie Boys and The Red Hot Chilli Peppers to Mick Jagger and Johnny Cash. Relocating from their recent base in the Colorado mountains to the warmer climes of Rubin's Shangri-La studio in Malibu, Young and Crazy Horse laid down ten new tracks, written by Young using phone recordings of melodies that came into his head while on walks in the Rockies around his converted barn home. Many of the songs feature the ecological themes prominent in so much of Young's later work, and the sound is mostly wistful and world weary, although some of the guitar playing is as ragged and raw as ever.

World Record begins with 'Love Earth', a gentle paean to the importance of treating nature with respect. Backed by a languid, rolling piano and a delightful slide guitar, Young sings "Love Earth/And your love comes back to you/Love Earth/It's such an easy thing to do," a simple message that is central to the album. 'Overhead' ups the pace a little, but it's bluesy swagger is still Young and Crazy Horse in relatively avuncular mood, with Young cooing contentedly about being in love "Overhead in the skies of blue/Not a thing between me and you/All the love in the world there too."

'I Walk with You (Earth Ringtone)' kicks off with a rumbling, distorted guitar riff that recalls Young's scintillating 2010 *Le Noise* album, but ends up being a rather plodding dirge, which is a shame as the lyrics see Young at his most poetic as he reflects on reaching old age: "I saw the change rolling by out the window of my life/I'm so grateful to have lived all these years/From the falling leaves to the snow in the trees/And the spring to the summertime we knew." But next track 'This Old Planet (Changing Days)' is a treat; a sweetly lilting ballad with a classic plaintive Young vocal complemented delightfully by a wistful accordion.

The volume then cranks up again on the stomping garage rock of 'The World (Is in Trouble Now)', with Molina pounding the drums like a man half his age and Young growling defiantly tracked by an urgent, spiky pump organ. 'Break the Chain' is even heavier, a sprawling, clanging, messy blast that makes up with sheer energy for what it lacks in structure and melody, although it's not completely clear what the chain Young wants to break actually is. The mood then shifts back effortlessly to another acoustic song, the rather whimsical waltz of 'The Day Before'.

'Walkin' on the Road (To the Future)' is one of the album's high points, delicately blending pump organ, harmonica and some classic Crazy Horse harmonies on the heartfelt chorus. The lyrics aren't exactly subtle: "Walkin' with me now to the future of all mankind/One step right in front of the other...We've got to do it now, though some may say it's too late." But then Young has never been one to shy away from a direct message.

There's a brief sense of things running out of steam on the forgettable 'The Wonder Won't Wait', but Young and Crazy Horse go out with a bang on closing track 'Chevrolet', which sees Young returning to another of his favourite subjects - cars.

At 15 minutes long, it's the kind of driving, elemental epic they've made their stock in trade for half a century now, and while it's no 'Cortez The Killer' (or even a 'Walk Like A Giant') it still showcases the line-up's hypnotic groove and weaving, soaring guitar patterns to often thrilling effect. Although Young himself describes the song as a completely separate piece to the rest of *World Record*, there is still a similar sense of looking back through the decades to a way of life that no longer exists: "Gone is the crowded highway, lost are the roads we left behind/Found in the place they live inside me." If *World Record* turns out to be Young and Crazy Horse's last album together (although despite their advancing ages, you wouldn't bet on that) then 'Chevrolet' is a pretty good way to go out.

There's still time for a brief reprise of 'This Old Planet' which closes the record by reminding us that there's still hope of averting environmental catastrophe "You're not alone on this old planet/It's still all yours to do as you may". Sung in a hushed, frail whisper by Young accompanying himself on electric piano, it's a quietly powerful ending to an album that is by turns nostalgic, forward-looking, angry and joyful.

⊙ TRACK LISTING ◀◀ ❚❚ ▶▶

1. Love Earth ·· 4:03
2. Overhead ·· 3:40
3. I Walk with You (Earth Ringtone) ·················· 3:57
4. This Old Planet (Changing Days) ·················· 2:30
5. The World (Is in Trouble Now) ···················· 3:15
6. Break the Chain ·· 4:07
7. The Long Day Before ·································· 2:18
8. Walkin' on the Road (To the Future) ·············· 2:57
9. The Wonder Won't Wait ······························ 3:17
10. Chevrolet ·· 15:15
11. This Old Planet (Reprise) ·························· 1:19

Length: 46:38

Neil Young - Before and After

Released 8 December 2023 (Reprise)

🎧 🎧 🎧

A few weeks after celebrating his 78th birthday, at the end of a year which had seen him return to live performance for the first time since before the COVID-19 pandemic with a tour of the U.S West Coast, Neil Young released what was - judged by the criteria of this book at least - his 50th studio album. Perhaps fittingly when hitting his half-century landmark, *Before and After* is essentially a retrospective of Young's six decade career, but it's a far more interesting record than a simple rehash of well-trodden greatest hits.

Recorded entirely solo with the exception of some unobtrusive piano and vibraphone playing by Los Angeles session musician Bob Rice and co-produced by the veteran Lou Adler, *Before and After* sees Young revisit some of the less celebrated songs from his back catalogue, ranging from his Buffalo Springfield youth to 2021's *Barn*. Intended to be consumed as one seamless, flowing piece of music similar to a live performance, the album feels meticulously crafted - not a phrase often associated with Young's late period output which has frequently had an off the cuff, raw style - with songs segueing expertly into one another throughout. This may be partly explained by the presence of Adler, who produced Carole King's golden era of highly polished albums, including the revered *Tapestry*.

Before and After opens with 'I'm The Ocean', one of the best tracks from Young's middling collaboration with Pearl Jam on 1995's *Mirror Ball*. With the relentless guitar assault stripped back to just the singer with his acoustic guitar and harmonica, the song's lyrical themes of restlessness and ageing come to the fore, without losing the driving urgency of the original. It's followed by 'Homefires', an obscure 1974 track which first surfaced as part of the *Neil Young Archives Volume II: 1972 - 1976* box set, which while admittedly a minor entry in his stellar 70s back catalogue, has an easy rustic charm that fits well here.

Equally surprising is a version of Buffalo Springfield's 'Burned', originally sang by Young back in 1966 but lent a completely different perspective by the intervening 57 years that the vocalist has experienced since with lyrics like "No time left and I know I'm losin'/Burned and with both feet on the ground/I've learned that it's painful comin' down."

After another Buffalo Springfield refresh, 1968's 'On The Way Home', which opened the band's final album *Last Time Around*, Young treats us to the one unreleased track on *Before and After* - 'You Got Love', which dates from the *Trans* sessions of 1982. It's a gentle if largely forgettable and lyrically banal song which offers little in itself, although it fits the prevailing reflective mood of the record. The reworkings of 'My Heart' and 'A Dream That Can Last', the bookend tracks from 1995's *Sleeps With Angels*, one of Young's bleakest, edgiest records, are once again perfect selections with their pretty rolling piano lines and Young's achingly vulnerable vocal, although they don't differ greatly from the originals.

Fitting neatly between them in a mid-album piano led section is 'Birds', from the superlative *After The Goldrush,* sparser and sadder here than when Young first recorded it back in 1970. 'When I Hold You In My Arms', meanwhile, is perhaps the most pleasant surprise on the whole album, rehabilitating the listless R&B of the *Are You Passionate?* original into an elegant ballad, modestly seasoned with some delightfully understated electric guitar playing.

The later songs of *Before and After* include a couple of more familiar favourites - Buffalo Springfield's 'Mr Soul', similar in style here to Young's 1993 *MTV Unplugged* version, and a wonderful performance of 1978's *Comes A Time's* title track, which retains the joyousness of the original while simultaneously adding greater tenderness. Unfortunately, 'Mother Earth' - the weakest track on 1991's otherwise superb *Ragged Glory* album - will never be a great Young song even when shorn of much of its bombast as it is here. But 'Don't Forget Love', from 2021's *Barn,* is one of his strongest recent songs and rounds off the album on just the right note as Young sings "When the storm comes and the lights go out, don't forget love."

Intimate and hopeful without falling into the trap of being cosy or bland, *Before and After* sees Young subtly dipping into his vast vault of material to offer us something that feels fresh and interesting, performed in a style that casts new light on many of the songs and showcases a unique voice that remains as expressive and idiosyncratic as ever, even as he approaches his 80th year.

⏵ TRACK LISTING ⏮ ⏸ ⏭

1. I'm the Ocean ··· 6:44
2. Homefires ·· 2:04
3. Burned ·· 2:06
4. On the Way Home ·· 3:14
5. If You Got Love ·· 3:32
6. A Dream That Can Last ·· 4:32
7. Birds ·· 2:47
8. My Heart ·· 3:01
9. When I Hold You in My Arms ·· 5:23
10. Mother Earth ·· 3:43
11. Mr. Soul ·· 3:42
12. Comes a Time ··· 3:20
13. Don't Forget Love ·· 3.41

Length: 47:49

Timeline - 21st century maverick (2001-2023)

🎧   🎧   🎧

2001

18-20 January: Young plays his first ever gigs in South America, two festivals in Buenos Aires and Rio de Janeiro with Crazy Horse.

Spring: Young takes the decision to abandon the Toast album he has been working on in San Francisco with Crazy Horse.

9 June - 24 July: Eurotour '01 with Crazy Horse.

21 September: Young performs at *America: A Tribute to Heroes* televised benefit show in response to the 9/11 attacks.

2002

6 February - 29 April: Tours U.S. and Canada with CSN&Y.

9 April: Release of *Are You Passionate?* album, recorded with Booker T. & the M.G.'s.

18-21 May: Plays a handful of concerts in the U.K. and Germany with the M.G.'s and Poncho Sampedro of Crazy Horse.

July - November: Recording of *Greendale album* with Crazy Horse, at Plywood Analog studios, Redwood City, California. The 'rock opera' format also spawned a movie, book and graphic novel.

2003

22 April - 24 May: Young undertakes a solo tour of Europe.

8 June - 20 September: Greendale tour of the U.S. with Crazy Horse.

19 August: Release of *Greendale* album.

9 October: Release of *Greendale* movie, directed by Young and featuring actors mouthing Young's lyrics as the album's songs play.

6-22 November: *Greendale* tour of Japan, Hong Kong and Australia with Crazy Horse.

2004

19 February - 21 March: *Greendale* tour of the U.S. and Canada with Crazy Horse.

2-6 October: Joins the Vote for Change tour of the U.S. in support of John Kerry's presidential campaign, alongside other musicians including Bruce Springsteen and Pearl Jam.

16 November: Release of *Greatest Hits* one disc compilation.

2005

March: Recording of *Prairie Wind* album in Nashville.

29 March: Young undergoes surgery at the New York-Presbyterian-Weill Cornell Medical Center for a potentially fatal brain aneurysm.

12 June: Young's father Scott dies at the age of 87.

2 July: Young performs at the Live 8 concert in Barrie, Ontario, one of a series of concerts globally which supported the aims of the *Make Poverty History* campaign and the *Global Call to Action Against Poverty* and were held to coincide with the G8 nations conference in Scotland.

18-19 August: Young premieres Prairie Wind in two concerts at the Ryman Auditorium, Nashville.

27 September: Release of *Prairie Wind* album.

2006

10 February: Release of Jonathan Demme's film *Neil Young Heart of Gold*, featuring the Ryman auditorium *Prairie Wind* concerts.

29 March - 6 April: Recording of *Living with War* album at Redwood Digital and Capitol Studio A studios in California.

8 May: Release of *Living with War* album.

6 July - 10 September: Freedom of Speech tour of the U.S. and Canada with CSN&Y.

14 November: *Live at the Fillimore East 1970,* a concert with Crazy Horse, is released as Volume 02 of the Archives Performance Series, the first album of the *Neil Young Archives* series of releases.

19 December: Release of *Living with War - In the Beginning*, a stripped-down version of original recordings of the main album release in May.

2007

13 March: Release of *Live At Massey Hall 1971*, a solo Young concert, as Volume 03 of the Archives Performance Series.

May - July: Recording of *Chrome Dreams II* album at Broken Arrow Ranch.

18 October - 19 December: Chrome Dreams Continental tour of the U.S. and Canada.

23 October: Release of *Chrome Dreams II* album.

6 November: Release of *Borrowed Tunes II: A Tribute to Neil Young*, a follow up to 1994's first volume.

2008

11 February - 15 March: Chrome Dreams Continental Tour of Europe.

22 June - 20 September: Further Continental Tour of Europe.

14 October - 16 December: Continental Tour of the U.S. and Canada.

Autumn 2008 - Spring 2009: Recording of the *Fork in the Road* album at Legacy Studios, New York and RAK Studios, London.

2 December: Release of *Sugar Mountain: Live at Canterbury House 1968*, Volume 00 of the Archives Performance Series.

2009

16 January - 1 February: The Continental Tour moves on to Australia and New Zealand.

6 April - 3 May: The Continental Tour returns to the U.S. and Canada.

7 April: Release of the *Fork in the Road* album.

30 May - 27 June: The Continental Tour concludes with a final tour of Europe, including headline appearances at the U.K.'s Glastonbury and Isle of Wight festivals.

2 June: Release of the *Neil Young Archives Volume 1: 1963-1972* box set.

8 December: Release of *Dreamin' Man Live '92*, featuring performances from Young's *Harvest Moon* album, as Volume 12 of the Archives Performance Series.

2010

29 January: Receives the MusiCares Person of the Year Award, in recognition of his philanthropic activities.

19-20 February: *The Neil Young Project*, two tribute concerts to Young, take place in Vancouver, featuring artists including Lou Reed and Ron Sexsmith.

28 February: Performs at the closing ceremony of the Vancouver Winter Olympics.

19 March: Release of *Neil Young: Trunk Show*, a documentary and concert film by Jonathan Demme.

March - July: Recording of *Le Noise* album at the home of producer Daniel Lanois in Silverlake, Los Angeles.

18 May - 28 September: Twisted Road solo tour of the U.S. and Canada.

15 June: *Neil Young's Greendale*, a graphic novel by Josh Dysart, Cliff Chiang and Dave Stewart, is published.

28 September: *Le Noise* album released.

2 October: Farm Aid 25th anniversary concert.

23-24 October: Buffalo Springfield reform to play at the annual Bridge School Benefit concert.

9 November: A fire starts in the charging system of Young's LincVolt eco car while it was recharging at a warehouse belonging to Young, damaging the car as well as a range of rare memorabilia stored there.

2011

13 February: Wins a Grammy Award (Best Rock Song) for *Le Noise*'s 'Angry World'.

15 April - 11 May: Further dates on the Twisted Road tour of the U.S. and Canada.

1 - 11 June: Buffalo Springfield reunion tour.

11 June: Release of *A Treasure*, a live album featuring performances by Young's International Harvesters band during 1984-85, as Volume 09 of the Archives Performance Series.

September: Jonathan Demme documentary *Neil Young Journeys* premieres at the Toronto Film Festival.

October - December: Recording of *Americana* album with Crazy Horse at Young's Broken Arrow ranch.

2012

January: *Psychedelic Pill* album recorded with Crazy Horse at Broken Arrow.

10 February: Young and Crazy Horse play at the Paul McCartney tribute gala at the Los Angeles Convention Center.

5 June: *Americana* album released.

3 August - 6 December: Alchemy tour of the U.S. and Canada with Crazy Horse.

25 September: Young's autobiography *Waging Heavy Peace* is published by Blue Rider Press.

30 October: Release of *Psychedelic Pill* album.

2013

2-21 March: Alchemy tour of Australia and New Zealand with Crazy Horse.

2 June - 7 August: Alchemy tour of Europe with Crazy Horse.

September: Young supports opposition to the proposed Keystone XL oil pipeline in Fort Mcmurray, Alberta, where he meets actress and activist Daryl Hannah.

September: Recording of *A Letter Home* album at Jack White's Third Man Records in Nashville, using a 1947 Voice-O-Graph vinyl recording booth.

10 December: Release of *Live at the Cellar Door*, taken from six Young concerts in Washington D.C during late 1970, as Volume 2.5 of the Archives Performance Series.

2014

6-10 January: Young plays four solo concerts at Carnegie Hall in New York.

12-19 January: Honour of the Treaties solo tour of Canada to raise money for anti-oil sand deposit organisations and raise awareness of issues affecting indigenous communities.

March: Launch of Young's high resolution digital download service, Pono, is announced.

29 March - 22 April: Solo tour of the U.S.

14 April: *A Letter Home* is released.

June - September: Recording of *Storytone* album (solo and orchestral/big band versions).

7 July - 8 August: Tours Europe with Crazy Horse.

29 July: After 36 years of marriage, Young files for divorce from wife Pegi.

5-9 October: Solo tour of the U.S.

14 October: Publication of *Special Deluxe: A Memoir of Life and Cars*, Young's second volume of autobiography.

4 November: *Storytone* album released.

2015

January: The Pono music player is officially launched.

January - February: Records *The Monsanto Years* album at Teatro Studios, Oxnard, California with new band Promise of the Real.

25 April: Performs at the Light Up The Blues concert in aid of autism research, alongside Stephen Stills.

30 June: *The Monsanto Years* released.

2-24 July & 1-17 October: Rebel Content tour of the U.S. and Canada with Promise of the Real.

13 November: *Bluenote Cafe* live album released as Volume 11 of the Archives Performance Series, featuring performances from Young's 1987–88 American tours with the Bluenotes.

2016

26 April - 1 May: Further Rebel Content tour dates in the U.S.

5 June - 23 July: Rebel Content tour of Europe with Promise of the Real.

24 June: *Earth* live album released, featuring performances by Young and Promise of the Real.

9-12 September: *Peace Trail* album sessions at Shangri La studios, Malibu.

18 September - 15 October: Further Rebel Content tour dates in the U.S.

November 2016 - August 2017: Sessions for *The Visitor* album with Promise of the Real, at Shangri La studios and Capitol studios in Hollywood.

9 December: *Peace Trail* album released.

2017

17 September: The *Hitchhiker* album, originally recorded in 1976, is released as Volume 05 of the Neil Young Archives Special Release Series.

1 December: *The Visitor* album released.

1 December: Young plays a solo concert in his hometown of Omemee, Ontario.

2018

23 March: Release of the Original Soundtrack from *Paradox* by Young and Promise of the Real as Volume 10 of the Archives Special Release Series. The movie, released by Netflix on the same day, was directed by Daryl Hannah with Young in an acting role.

24 April: Volume 05 of the Archives Performance Series, *Roxy: Tonight's the Night Live*, featuring recordings made at the Roxy Theatre in Los Angeles in 1973 by Young and the Santa Monica Flyers, is released.

1-6 May: Young plays five California dates with Crazy Horse.

19 June - 27 September: Plays a range of U.S. venues with Promise of the Real.

28 June - 1 October: U.S. Solo Theater Tour takes place alongside Promise of the Real performances.

25 August: Young marries Daryl Hannah in a ceremony held in Atascadero, California.

14 December: Release of *Songs for Judy*, a series of solo acoustic performances on Young's 1976 North American tour, as Volume 07 of the Archives Performance Series.

2019

23 January - 18 May: Solo Theater Tour of U.S. venues.

3 - 4 February: Plays two tours in Winnipeg with Crazy Horse.

20-25 May: U.S. shows with Promise of the Real.

29 June - 14 July: European tour with Promise of the Real.

7 June: Release of *Tuscaloosa*, Volume 04 of the Archives Performance Series, featuring recordings from Young's 1973 tour with The Stray Gators.

21 June: Elliot Roberts, Young's manager since 1967, dies aged 76.

10 September: Release of *To Feel The Music: A Songwriter's Mission to Save High-Quality Audio*, a book written jointly with Pono Music hardware developer Phil Baker.

25 October: Release of *Colorado* album with Crazy Horse, recorded earlier in that year at the Studio in the Clouds, Colorado with Nils Lofgren replacing the retired Poncho Sampedro on guitar. The album is accompanied by the Young-directed documentary *Mountaintop*.

2020

22 January: After being a resident of California since 1966, Young finally becomes a U.S. citizen.

19 March - 3 July: Young streams Fireside Sessions on the Neil Young Archives website from his home in Telluride, Colorado during the COVID-19 pandemic.

19 June: The *Homegrown* album, originally recorded in 1974/75, is released as Volume 02 of the Archives Special Release Series.

6 November: Release of *Return to Greendale*, Volume 16 of the Archives Performance Series, taken from the 2003 Greendale tour.

20 November: Release of the *Neil Young Archives Volume 2* (1972-76) box set.

2021

26 February: Release of *Way Down In The Rust Bucket*, a 1990 concert with Crazy Horse, as Volume 11.5 of the Archives Performance Series.

26 March: Release of *Young Shakespeare*, Volume 0.35 of the Archives Performance Series, a solo concert by Young from 22 January, 1971.

Spring-Summer: Recording of *Barn* album with Crazy Horse at the Barn studio in the Rocky Mountains.

1 October: The first of Young's Official Bootleg Series, *Carnegie Hall*, a solo concert from December 1970, is released.

10 December: Release of *Barn* album, with an accompanying documentary directed by Daryl Hannah, *A Band A Brotherhood A Barn*.

2022

26 January: Spotify removes Neil Young's music from their service after he challenges them to stop streaming the podcast The Joe Rogan Experience, which he believes is spreading misinformation about COVID-19 vaccines.

6 May: Release of three further Official Bootleg Series performances - *Royce Hall* and *I'm happy that y'all came down* (dating from early 1971) and *Citizen Kane Jr Blues 1974*.

8 July: Volume 09 of the Archives Special Release Series, *Toast*, a Young and Crazy Horse album dating from 2001, is released.

5 August: Release of *Noise & Flowers* live album, featuring performances from Young and Promise of the Real's 2019 European tour.

23 September: 1973's *Time Fades Away* album released as a standalone CD.

18 November: *World Record* album released.

2023

14 April: Two more releases from Young's Official Bootleg Series, *Somewhere Under The Rainbow* with the Santa Monica Flyers (dating from 1973) and *High Flyin'* with The Ducks (1977).

30 June - 24 July: Coastal Tour of U.S. West Coast venues, Young's first since 2019.

11 August: *Chrome Dreams* album, originally dating from 1977, released as Volume 06 of Young's Special Release series.

1 September: Vinyl-only release of *Odeon Budokan* live album, recorded in 1976.

8 December: *Before and After* album released

PART 6

Off the Beaten Track -
live albums, compilations
and archives

Neil Young's career has always been incredibly prolific. As well as his remarkably frequent studio albums, a large number of live albums - some mainstream releases, others part of Young's *Archives* series or shared as official bootlegs - offer a comprehensive overview of his unforgettable on-stage presence. Furthermore, those seeking either an introduction to his work or alternatively keen to explore the full, dauntingly vast range of his music are well served by Young's compilations and the *Archives* series respectively. It should be noted that some of the *Archives* series have a somewhat haphazard approach to catalogue numbering and chronological release dates, no doubt in part due to the overseeing influence of the great man himself.

The first few years of Young's solo career offers the widest selection of live albums to explore. The earliest disc is Volume 00 of the Neil Young Archive Performance Series; *Sugar Mountain - Live at Canterbury House 1968*. A rather tentative Young, clearly a little unsure of himself in his infancy as a solo artist, sings a range of Buffalo Springfield and early album tracks, including a gorgeous, embryonic rendition of 'Birds' from *After The Goldrush*. Volume 01 of the Archive Performance Series, *Live at the Riverboat 1969*, is broadly similar in content and quality, although Young is noticeably more confident in his audience interaction.

Live At Fillmore East 1970, Volume 02 of the Archive Performance Series, is a different kettle of fish entirely. Featuring the first incarnation of Crazy Horse at the peak of their powers, with Danny Whitten a compelling vocal and guitar counterpoint to Young, it includes coruscating performances of some of their *Everybody Knows This Nowhere* classics. Interestingly, the first half of this concert, featuring Young solo, was not released. *Live at the Cellar Door* and *Live At Massey Hall and Young Shakespeare* (volumes 0.25, 03 and 3.5 of the Archive Performance Series respectively) date from late 1970 and 1971 and showcase Young at his singer-songwriter best. In particular, the Massey Hall concert, which sees Young playing to his adoring home fanbase in Toronto, is a magnificent selection of songs from *After The Goldrush* and *Harvest*, delivered with spine-tingling brilliance on acoustic guitar and piano.

Young's dislike of the *Time Fades Away* album is well documented, but for the many fans who beg to differ, *Tuscaloosa*, dating from 1973 and released as Volume 04 of the Archive Performance Series, is a compelling further example of the woozy, bar brawl rock of the Stray Gators, with an intriguing blend of *Harvest* and *Time Fades Away* material. Also dating from 1973 is *Roxy*, a live performance of *Tonight's The Night* songs in California with The Santa Monica Flyers, which, with the song order mixed up, feels less powerful than the studio album. Young's *Zuma* period is represented by *Odeon Budokan* (Archive Performance Series Volume 06), culled from two concerts in London and Tokyo during 1976. It's another strong blend of Young acoustic tracks and performances with the new incarnation of Crazy Horse, with the recently released *Zuma* material like 'Don't Cry No Tears' sounding particularly good.

A few months later, he was touring solo around small, intimate U.S. venues, captured on *Songs for Judy* (Archive Performance Series Volume 08), a compilation of performances that illustrate the plethora of top-quality songs flowing from him at that time. Future Young archivist Joel Bernstein, who recorded the shows, and teenage rock journalist Cameron Crowe compiled a 20-plus-track mix that, when leaked and bootlegged, was known for years as The Bernstein Tapes, although its late name was inspired by Young claiming to have seen Judy Garland in the audience. Highlights are many but include flawless renditions of several late 60s and early 70s favourites, a delightful bluegrass version of *Tonight's the Night*'s 'Mellow my Mind' and a number of then-unreleased songs taken from his shelved *Homegrown* and *Hitchhiker* albums. Young is in his element throughout, with his on-stage banter avuncular and assured.

Perhaps the most iconic of Young's live albums is *Live Rust*, documenting the *Rust Never Sleeps* tour of late 1978 and released the following year. It's essentially a live greatest hits collection, featuring some of Young's best loved songs from his stellar previous decade, with a mixture of solo acoustic performances and Crazy Horse rock outs. The quality is consistently high, with highlights including a rousing take of 'Cinnamon Girl' and a truly epic 'Like A Hurricane', although Young's bizarre attempt to sing in a Caribbean accent on 'Cortez The Killer' is cringeworthy.

The 1980s isn't a fertile ground for Young live albums, but one that has emerged in recent years as part of the Archives series is *A Treasure* (Volume 09 of the Archive Performance Series), which showcases the International Harvesters, the highly accomplished band of Nashville session musicians who collaborated with Young on 1985's *Old Ways* album and toured around rodeos and other country music venues with him during 1984/85. The material here isn't vintage Young, but the quality of the musicianship, including 70s sidekick Rufus Thibodeaux on Cajun fiddle, makes *A Treasure* worth investigating. Later that decade, *Bluenote Cafe* (Archive Performance Series Volume 11), taken from the Bluenotes Club Tour of 1987-88, is Young in his big band phase, with a swinging horn section that featured on the *This Note's For You* and *Freedom* albums. Like *A Treasure*, it's an intriguing snapshot of a very specific period in Young's career, finishing with a funky, bluesy reinvention of 'Tonight's The Night'.

Rivalling *Live Rust* as Young's most acclaimed live outing is 1991's *Weld*, a double album taken from the 1991 'Smell the Horse' tour with Crazy Horse. With its mix of cuts from 1990's *Ragged Glory* - for many the pick of Young's post 1970s albums - and perennial favourites from his earlier career, it's undoubtedly a very strong collection. The gigantic guitar sound and scabrous squalls of feedback make this a particularly compelling choice for fans of Young and Crazy Horse at their loudest and most abrasive, but it does lack a little light and shade with its sheer relentlessness. A triple album - *Arc Weld* - was released as a limited edition, with *Arc*, a 35-minute-long sound collage taken from a range of tour performances, included alongside the double live album. Comprising a mish mash of guitar tune ups, crashing drums, distorted feedback and fragments of Young singing 'Like a Hurricane' and 'Love and Only Love', it's hard to imagine most of his contemporaries ever releasing anything as bold and experimental as *Arc*. Even so, to describe it as anything other than a deeply challenging listen would be misleading. Dating from the same period is *Way Down In The Rust Bucket* (Archive Performance Series volume 11.5), a late 1990 complete show from Santa Cruz, California which has a set list taking in tracks from *Ragged Glory*, *Zuma* and - less welcomely - *Re.ac.tor*.

Those who love Young at his most mellow and stripped back will find much to enjoy on *Dreamin' Man Live '92* (Archive Performance Series Volume 12), a series of solo performances previewing the release of *Harvest Moon*. It's a world away from *Weld* only a year before, but Young is in excellent form. During the 1990s, the MTV Unplugged series featured many of the world's greatest rock artists and it was no surprise that Young took part in 1993, with his celebrated acoustic singer-songwriter background making him ideally suited to the format. His *Unplugged* session, backed on some tracks by the Stray Gators, is predictably excellent, ranging from faithful renditions of the evergreen 'Pocahontas' and 'The Needle and the Damage Done' to a reworking of *Trans*'s 'Transformer Man' and the unreleased 'Stringman', dating from 1976.

1997's *Year of the Horse*, recorded on the road the previous year, is a middling collection of tracks from 1996's disappointing *Broken Arrow* and old favourites, including an electric version of 'Pocahontas' and a sweepingly dramatic 'Danger Bird.' 2000's *Road Rock Volume 1: Friends and Relatives* suffers from a combination of poor sound quality and some questionable song choices, including one of Young's career lows in 'Motorcycle Mama'. His furious guitar work on a vigorous cover of 'All Along The Watchtower' - also featuring Chrissie Hynde - is well worth hearing, however.

While a steady stream of Archive Performance Series live albums from earlier stages of Young's career emerged during the 2000s, new live collections were thin on the ground. *Return to Greendale* (Archive Performance Series Volume 16), recorded on Young and Crazy Horse's 2003 tour of the *Greendale* album, is essentially a run through of the studio version. It has a little more urgency live, but the fact most of the songs are rather rambling to start with and hardly crowd pleasers means it's one for diehard fans only.

The most notable recent addition is *Earth* (2016) a live album with a strong focus on ecological subject matter. Recorded on his 2015 tour of the U.S. and Canada, new backing band Promise of the Real are a tight unit who back Young manfully, although they lack the raw, elemental energy of Crazy Horse. Other than 'After The Goldrush' - which fits the prevailing theme - most of the songs here are less well known, several from *The Monsanto Years*, his latest release, which excoriated the major U.S. biotechnology corporation. But the most memorable element of *Earth* is the cacophony of bird, monkey and insect noises that have been added to the mix throughout, sometimes appearing in the middle of songs woven into the music. An attempt by Young to hammer home his already fairly direct messaging around impending environmental catastrophe, it's frankly rather bizarre. 2019's *Noise and Flowers*, meanwhile, recorded on Young and Promise of the Real's 2019 European tour, shows what an energetic performer the veteran remained even well into his seventies, although his voice is unsurprisingly now a little shakier than in his youth. A pulsating 'Rockin' In The Free World' is probably the pick of a very solid selection.

During 2021, a series of releases classified as 'Official Bootlegs' began to appear: recordings of full concerts during the early 1970s with a crackly, intimate sound quality. *Carnegie Hall,* Royce *Hall* and *I'm happy that y'all came down* all date from December 1970 - February 1971 and don't really offer anything much different to the superior Young solo Archive Performance Series albums from the same period. In contrast, while *Under the Rainbow, November 5th, 1973* (featuring the Santa Monica Flyers),has similar material from the *Tonight's The Night* album to the previously released *Roxy,* but the performances here are definitely more interesting and with a mellower vibe - the spookily atmospheric take on the title track being a particular highlight. Likewise, *Citizen Kane Jr Blues 1974* has an intriguing, infrequently heard set list including rare acoustic versions of some of *On The Beach*'s finest moments and a version of the traditional English folk song 'Greensleeves'. Finally, *High Flyin',* a compilation of live recordings by The Ducks, the Santa Cruz bar band Young joined in the summer of 1977, is a likeable document of the great man playing purely for fun alongside less heralded fellow musicians, with his familiar classics sharing equal billing with the compositions of the other group members. 2023 also saw a vinyl-only release of *Odeon Budokan.*

Compilations and Archives box sets

For an artist as prolific as Young, genuine compilation albums offering whole or partial career retrospectives are thin on the ground, probably in part because he has only had two record labels during his entire 50 year plus solo career - Reprise and Geffen.

The first and by far the most essential is *Decade* (1977), a three-album (and later two CD) retrospective covering the whole of Young's recording career up until that point, including the pick of his songwriting contributions to Buffalo Springfield and Crosby, Stills, Nash & Young as well as his solo albums up to *American Stars n'Bars*. With the addition of several unreleased tracks, alternate versions of well-loved songs and handwritten sleeve notes by Young himself, it's the best introduction one could wish for to his daunting back catalogue, but also with enough new inclusions to interest diehard fans. It's brilliantly curated, with no obvious omissions in the outstanding running order, and the soulful, elegant 'Deep Forbidden Lake', with its gorgeous fiddle and pedal steel textures, is the pick of the unreleased tracks.

Perhaps unsurprisingly given the paucity of the material, 1993's *Lucky Thirteen,* a compilation of tracks from Young's unhappy five album tenure with Geffen during the 1980s, is an altogether less impressive collection. A haphazard mix of Young's choices from the Geffen albums and unexceptional unreleased tracks: the plodding 'Depression Blues', from the original, rejected version of the *Old Ways* album, two live tracks from the *Everybody's Rockin'* tour ('Don't Take Your Love Away From Me' and 'Get Gone')and another from a Bluenotes gig shortly before Young returned to Reprise, 'Ain't It The Truth'. A live version of the *This Note's For You* album title track is also included. While there are slim pickings of high-quality Young songs from this period, it's disappointing that the excellent 'Misfits' isn't included, but overall, *Lucky Thirteen*'s uneven blend of synthesisers, country, blues and bland stadium rock is an accurate if often unappealing document of Young's Geffen years.

In 2004, Young finally released a one disc *Greatest Hits* compilation, with 16 tracks featuring a straightforward chronological selection of his best loved songs from *Everybody Knows This Is Nowhere* to *Harvest Moon,* including 'Ohio' and 'Helpless' from CSN&Y's *Deja Vu.* It's hard to knock the quality of the choices, which are universally superb, but *Greatest Hits* lacks the depth and attention to detail of the more expansive *Decade.*

That the *Neil Young Archives* are one of the most extraordinary undertakings in the history of popular music is hard to dispute. Long in the making – work began in the late 1980s - so far two multimedia box set volumes have been released of a planned five spanning Young's entire musical career, as well as a host of individual album releases in the *Live Performance, Official Bootleg* and *Special Release* series, already covered elsewhere in these pages, and remastered versions of many of his classic studio albums. The project has also spawned a comprehensive website featuring almost the whole of Young's recording output throughout his career, available for streaming in high resolution audio format, which can be visited and subscribed to at https://neilyoungarchives.com/.

The first volume, *The Archives Vol. I 1963–1972*, was released in June 2009. Encompassing Young's early years with The Squires and Buffalo Springfield, it also includes demos, outtakes and alternate versions of songs from *Neil Young, Everybody Knows This Is Nowhere, After the Gold Rush* and *Harvest*, as well as tracks he recorded with both Crazy Horse and Crosby, Stills, Nash & Young during this time. Also included in the set are several live discs, as well as (on the Blu-Ray/

DVD versions) a copy of the film *Journey Through the Past*, directed by Young in the early 1970s and previously unavailable for decades. Volume I was released as a set of 10 Blu-ray discs in order to present high resolution audio as well as accompanying visual documentation. It is also available as a 10-disc DVD set and an 8 disc CD set.

Neil Young Archives Volume II: 1972–1976 was released as a deluxe CD box set and for streaming on the Neil Young Archives website in November 2020. It covers Young's work with The Stray Gators, Santa Monica Flyers, CSN&Y, Crazy Horse, and The Stills-Young Band during this period, including album cuts, demos, outtakes and alternate versions of songs from his albums *Time Fades Away*, *Tonight's the Night, On the Beach, Zuma*, and Stephen Stills collaboration *Long May You Run*, the whole of *Homegrown* (recently released on its own as part of the Special Release series), tracks from CSN&Y's sessions for the shelved *Human Highway* album and several live discs. Volume II was released as a set of 10 CDs (with a deluxe edition containing a hardbound book), and unlike Volume I, did not have accompanying Blu-ray or DVD editions.

A detailed review of the vast contents of *Neil Young Archives Volumes I* and *II* would take up far more time and space than is available here, but suffice to say the entire box sets are for Young completists only. Most of the standout content has also been made available under the various associated series mentioned previously - in particular, the *Special Release Series* studio albums and strongest live albums such as *Live At Massey Hall* and *Songs For Judy* can be enjoyed individually without investing in the multi-disc behemoths. What the box sets do undeniably achieve is to provide the key phases of Young's formidable career with a breadth of context and artistic insight that can only be reached through an exercise of this scale, with the evolution of many of his key works rigorously explored.

The remaining three volumes of the Archives series are expected to cover the late 1970s and 1980s, the 1990s and the 21st century respectively. Young continues to work on them with his usual passion and rigour, but it remains unclear when, if ever, the project will finally be completed.

PART 7

Ranking Young's albums

Neil Young - the albums ranked!

🎧　🎧　🎧

S o, as promised at the beginning of my book, I'm now going to take on the daunting but hugely enjoyable task of ranking the records I've covered in Neil Young: Album by Album, from 50-1! As mentioned earlier, this is purely the humble view of one listener, and I've no doubt many of you reading this will have your own thoughts you'd like to share. To get involved, please visit this book's Facebook page (also accessible through my publisher White Owl's website) or email me directly at thebigneilyoungalbumdebate@gmail.com.

I've split the albums into four categories - **Below Par**, **Worth Exploring**, **Very Good** and **Greatest Works** - before confirming my final rankings at the end.

Below par

Perhaps unsurprisingly, this category features many of the records from Young's much-maligned 80s era, with the remaining choices spanning from the mid-1990s to his most recent work. After a decade where he could do little wrong, with great album after great album released back to back from 1969 to 1979, his stratospherically high artistic bar dropped several notches with 1980's *Hawks and Doves*, a slight, throwaway collection that, bar a couple of strong tracks culled from the aborted *Homegrown* album, was the flimsiest work of his career to date. The following year's *Re.ac.tor*, a furious, hard rock assault on the senses written and recorded while Young's life was dominated by son Ben's intensive therapy programme, is largely bereft of melody, repetitive and gruelling.

1983's *Everybody's Rockin'*, Young's infamous musical riposte to record label boss David Geffen request for a "more rock and roll album", is as bad as its reputation suggests, a perfunctory (if enthusiastically performed) mishmash of 1950s covers and substandard originals that few will want to listen to more than once. Even worse was to come with 1986's *Landing On Water*, a frequently excruciating synth-rock folly blighted by unsympathetic production and vapid song writing, which has aged horribly.

Young's creative and commercial rebirth in the first half of the 1990s saw another strong run of albums, ended by 1996's *Broken Arrow,* a sloppy, undercooked melange of mostly forgettable songs with Crazy Horse which, some decent guitar work in places aside, has to go down as one of their least memorable collaborations together. The decision to shelve 2001's Young and Crazy Horse's *Toast* recordings in favour of an incongruous hook up with Booker T. & the M.G.'s on 2002's *Are You Passionate?* proved to be ill-advised, with the latter record's slick but dull R&B pastiches only enlivened by the one Crazy Horse performance - 'Goin' Home' - that survived a very Young-like change of direction.

The past decade has seen Young's output mostly fluctuate between decent and mediocre, with few very good or particularly bad records. However, 2012's *Fork In The Road*, a loose concept album inspired by the 1959 Mark IV Lincoln Continental he converted to run on eco-friendly fuels, is one for diehard fans only; an uninspiring, ramshackle group of songs that feel like they could have been dashed off by Young while queuing at a gas station. In contrast, 2017's *The Visitor* opens with one of his finest compositions of the century to date, the fabulous 'Already Great' but then gradually unravels into a sprawling, frustrating mess of different styles.

Worth exploring

Neil Young's eponymous 1968 debut album, while featuring a few excellent songs, was an uncertain start to his solo career, negatively impacted by production issues and best viewed as a stepping stone between his Buffalo Springfield years and his future work. However, it would be almost a decade before he made another average record, which - with the honourable exceptions of the gorgeous 'Star of Bethlehem' and the incendiary brilliance of 'Like A Hurricane' - 1977's cut and paste exercise *American Stars 'n Bars* undoubtedly is.

1982's *Trans*, Young's often derided flirtation with electronic music, is brave but predictably flawed. While hardly likely to have Kraftwerk quaking in their boots, there are nevertheless some intriguing songs here, in particular a deft reworking of Buffalo Springfield's 'Mr Soul' and the ambitious synthesiser textures and robotic voices of 'Computer Age'. Similarly, 1985's syrupy, twee *Old Ways*, Young's attempt to reinvent himself as a bona fide country artist, has some good moments - notably the surreal, hypnotic 'Misfits '- amid what's a genre shift of limited success overall.

After the career low of *Landing On Water*, 1987's *Life*, Young's first record with Crazy Horse since *Re.ac.tor*, is somewhat underrated. While still suffering from an unflattering veneer of 80s production and the singer's questionable political views, it has some of his strongest songs of the decade so far, arguably starting to pave the way for his fully fledged second coming on *Freedom* a couple of years later. In between came the last and perhaps most successful of his unconventional style shifts during this period, the mostly assured if occasionally self-indulgent blues, big band and soul influences of 1988's *This Note's For You*.

Of all Young's mid-career purple patch albums, 1995's *Mirror Ball*, his collaboration with grunge stars Pearl Jam, is the weakest, with patchy song writing and a sound that, while impressively vast and layered, can get a little monotonous. That said, its best moments - 'Song X' and 'I'm The Ocean' - are fabulous. After the disappointment of *Broken Arrow*, 2001's aborted *Toast* project would have been a creditable comeback for Young and Crazy Horse, and its belated release in 2022 as part of the Archives series was a welcome move. The next official Young and Crazy Horse album - 2003's *Greendale* - is ambitious but messy, with an interesting overarching narrative let down by scruffy songs that lack focus and melody, meaning it's one of Young's least accessible records. The gentle, autumnal *Prairie Wind* (2005), on which a now 60-year-old Young contemplates his own mortality, is pleasant if unexceptional record in the *Harvest* vein, while 2007's *Chrome Dreams II* is another example of the artist cobbling together a ragbag selection of old and new songs with mixed results.

Young went through another of his freewheeling musical phases during the early 2010s, throwing up an intriguing trio of albums that are all worthy of investigation. 2012's *Americana*, his garage rock trawl through the Great American Songbook with Crazy Horse, ranges from scintillating to appalling; the following year's *A Letter Home*, recorded in Jack White's 1947 Voice-O-Graph recording booth, is an atmospheric if sometimes fuzzy acoustic tribute to peers including Dylan, Springsteen and Willie Nelson. Perhaps the best of the three is 2014's *Storytone*, ten orchestral and big band songs which, while sometimes overblown and a little mawkish, feature some of Young's loveliest melodies in years.

Most of Young's recent albums are enjoyable enough without ever threatening to hit the heights of his 70s and 90s work, and are more notable for their themes and mood than the enduring quality of their songs. 2015's *The Monsanto Years*, with new backing band Promise of the Real, has passion and energy, although the tubthumping environmental activism does eventually wear a little thin. *Peace Trail (2016)* is charming in a ramshackle way, if largely unmemorable, while the 2017 soundtrack to Daryl Hannah's film *Paradox* ambles along amiably but inconsequentially.

Both the bruised, world-weary *Colorado* (2019) and the more mellow *Barn* (2021) are very solid latter day outings with Crazy Horse, with the return of Nils

Lofgren instilling new fluidity into the veteran septuagenarians. 2022's *World Record*, featuring the same line-up as *Colorado* and *Barn*, is arguably stronger than both, combining their best elements around a more consistent, climate change-focused theme. Finally, 2023's *Before and After* is a thoughtfully constructed acoustic revisiting of some of Young's less well known tracks spanning his whole near 60-year career, with his weathered but still beautiful voice compelling throughout.

Very good

If these rankings were based purely on sales and public recognition, 1972's *Harvest* would be number one. While it's undoubtedly a Young classic, arguably featuring four of his all-time greatest, most recognisable songs (the title track, 'Heart of Gold', 'Old Man' and 'The Needle and the Damage Done') the remainder of the album is quite uneven in quality and tone, with the two orchestral tracks - 'A Man Needs A Maid' and 'There's A World' definite missteps. *Harvest* therefore falls just short of being one of Young's greatest works.

Its controversial follow-up, 1973's raw, occasionally chaotic *Time Fades Away*, is a pivotal moment in Young's discography, demonstrating for the first time his willingness to take his music in unexpected, sometimes unpopular directions rather than simply repeating a proven, commercially successful formula. However, with the exception of the stunning 'Don't Be Denied', the songs are good rather than great. The same could be said of 1975's *Homegrown*, finally released in 2020 after over four decades gathering mystique in Young's vaults. The album chronicles a deeply turbulent period in its creator's life, and marks a return to a more accessible, country-folk influenced sound after the 'ditch trilogy'. But it doesn't have the consistent excellence his finest records offer, with its best tracks long since having seen the light of day elsewhere in Young's canon. *Chrome Dreams*, meanwhile, is one of the most difficult albums of all to rank. Had it been released as planned in 1977 and we'd heard songs like 'Pocahontas', 'Like A Hurricane' and 'Powderfinger' for the first time, it would have to be placed higher, but experienced in its 2023 context, the impact of the record is unfortunately reduced by the familiarity of the material.

1978's *Comes A Time*'s warm, effortlessly melodic country rock is perhaps Young's most accessible album but doesn't quite have the depth to be ranked in his pantheon. After the largely barren 1980s, Young closed an otherwise undistinguished decade with the barnstorming *Freedom* (1989). Its status as a long-awaited return to form and the beginning of a second stellar run of albums has perhaps led to it becoming slightly overrated, but there's still some great songs here, notably the anthemic 'Rockin' In The Free World' and the epic 'Crime in the City (Sixty to

Zero Part I).' Another standout album from this period is 1992's *Harvest Moon,* the long-awaited follow up to *Harvest* 20 years earlier. While maybe a bit too gentle and unadventurous for some, its best songs - the title track, 'Unknown Legend' and 'From Hank to Hendrix' have a timeless grace, and the reassembled Stray Gators play beautifully throughout.

By the mid-1990s, Young's reputation was close to its 1970s peak, with the new bands of the grunge scene heralding him as a major influence. *Sleeps with Angels* (1994) is a moody, murky alternative rock record inspired by the death of Kurt Cobain, perhaps a little lacking in memorable songs but with a strange, unsettling sound unlike anything else Young had ever released. Likewise, his atmospheric 1996 soundtrack to Jim Jarmusch's *Dead Man* is another example of Young branching out into new territory, with its evocative instrumental textures showcasing his awesome abilities as a guitarist in a completely different setting to his more conventional rock records.

Young's 21st century work, while lacking any masterpieces, still has a sprinkling of records that unquestionably belong in the higher echelons of these rankings. Dismissed by some critics as Young putting his feet up in his cosy slippers, 2000's *Silver and Gold*, while admittedly hardly cutting-edge fare, is nevertheless a consistently good, very enjoyable collection of nostalgia-tinged acoustic songs. Young still had plenty of fire in his belly though, as the vociferous *Living With War*, released in 2005 in response to the War on Terror, showed. Recorded in just nine days and brimming with indignation and purpose, it's the most successful of the increasing number of issues-focused, activist records he has released over the past two decades.

Perhaps Young's most artistically important album so far this century is 2010's *Le Noise*, an already promising collection of solo songs given another dimension by producer Daniel Lanois' extraordinary sonic manipulations of the artist's guitar. Less ground-breaking but equally recommended is 2012's *Psychedelic Pill*, a sprawling Young and Crazy Horse double album that in 'Ramada Inn' and 'Walk Like A Giant' boasts their two best songs together since *Ragged Glory* over 20 years before.

Greatest works

In the writer's view, there are eight Neil Young albums that stand apart from the rest of his output as truly outstanding examples of his unique talent. While I've approached my analysis of the previous three categories chronologically and saved the rankings of each until the end of this chapter, for the greatest works, I'm going to use a slightly different approach and directly discuss the process of selecting the final order.

Neil Young - the albums ranked!

The contenders I have selected for the title of Neil Young's greatest album, listed here in order of release, are: *Everybody Knows This Is Nowhere (1969)*, *After The Goldrush (1970)*, *On The Beach (1974)*, *Tonight's The Night (1975)*, *Zuma (1975)*, *Rust Never Sleeps* (1979), *Ragged Glory (1990)*, and *Hitchhiker (2017)*.

Some fans may question the inclusion of *Hitchhiker* in this rarefied company, quite reasonably pointing out that it's a special release from the Archives series and sharing the view of Young's record label Reprise that it's ultimately a selection of demos rather than a 'real' album. Like *Homegrown*, most of its tracks went on to appear on other records. Yet as a pure distillation of Young's song writing brilliance, unadorned by other musicians and studio wizardry, I feel it is an important, hugely impressive work in its own right. The calibre of the songs - 'Pocahontas', 'Powderfinger' and 'Campaigner' among them - is exceptionally high, so although *Hitchhiker* lacks the completeness and depth to be in the very highest reaches of this list, eighth place feels justified.

I have *Rust Never Sleeps* in seventh place. Typically seen as the final flourish of Young's classic era and revered for its peerless dichotomy between his acoustic and electric styles, for me it falls short of being a top five album due to the inclusion of a few average tracks, particularly the comparatively pedestrian garage rock of 'Welfare Mothers' and 'Sedan Delivery'. However, in 'Thrasher', 'Pocahontas', 'Powderfinger' and both versions of 'Hey Hey, My My' its peaks are very high indeed.

Despite the undoubted moments of genius on *Harvest Moon* and *Freedom*, the only album outside Young's 1969-79 vintage period that I consider truly great is *Ragged Glory*, which belongs alongside *Everybody Knows This Is Nowhere and Zuma* as one of his three great records with Crazy Horse. The guitar sound here, which proved such an influence on the emerging grunge scene, is thrillingly raw, muscular and expressive, giving songs like 'Country Home', 'Mansion on the Hill' and 'Over and Over' an almighty heft. Only the excellence of the albums above it, which arguably all have a little more variety in their locker, prevent it from making the top five.

From here on in, the standard is uniformly superlative, making the final rankings more about personal preference than anything else. After much deliberation, I have *Zuma* in fifth place. It's occasionally overlooked, in part due to the towering reputations of the two albums released immediately before it, *On The Beach* and *Tonight's The Night*. Yet in terms of sheer enjoyment factor, it bears comparison with any record Young ever made. Lighter and more immediately accessible than the records that preceded it and featuring a revamped Crazy Horse with Poncho Sampedro on board for the first time, *Zuma* has something for everyone, with highlights ranging from the momentous guitar epics 'Danger Bird' and 'Cortez the Killer' to the joyous jangle of 'Lookin' for a Love.'

As the record that established Young as a solo artist to reckon with and gave birth to his iconic recording relationship with Crazy Horse, *Everybody Knows This Is Nowhere* is an absolutely key album in his musical history. But not only that, it's also a work of exceptional quality when held up against anything he has released during the half century and more since. The smouldering, meandering guitars of Young and original Crazy Horse guitarist Danny Whitten and simple yet strangely hypnotic rhythm section combine to make *Down By The River* and *Cowgirl In The Sand* instant classics, while *Cinnamon Girl* is a near-perfect combination of joyous melody and rock edge. I have ranked it fourth, as I feel the top three are all very slightly stronger in terms of overall quality of song writing throughout an entire album.

Tonight's The Night, Young's harrowing tribute to Whitten and CSN&Y roadie Bruce Berry, is in third place. In terms of consistent flow and mood from start to finish, it's an astonishingly cohesive, impactful work, with some of the most memorable moments in Young's entire catalogue (think the Nils Lofgren guitar solo on 'Speakin' Out', or Young's anguished vocals on 'Mellow My Mind' and 'Tired Eyes'). It could easily be ranked even higher, but the sheer relentlessness of its stark, bruised garage rock means it can occasionally feel a little overwhelming, so I would narrowly favour the two albums above it.

So, that leaves us with *After The Goldrush* and *On The Beach*. The singer songwriter masterclass versus the frazzled beauty of the 'ditch trilogy's closing act. After a first half that is merely very good, the second side of *On The Beach*, featuring the majestic title track, 'Motion Pictures (For Carrie)' and 'Ambulance Blues', has a meditative, almost transcendental quality that in this writer's opinion represents the pinnacle of Young's achievements as an artist. The blend of evocative instrumental textures and startlingly vivid lyrics questioning the impact of fame work in perfect tandem to create a suite of three songs he would never better.

Yet the claims of *After The Goldrush* are also hard to ignore. Using a musical backdrop that compellingly mined America's traditional country and folk influences, the songs Young was writing at this time - the gorgeous title track, the wistful 'Only Love Can Break Your Heart' and the hymnal 'I Believe In You' to name but three, possess a seemingly effortless melodic grace that perhaps only the two Pauls - McCartney and Simon - can rival among popular musicians. Throw in the incandescent rock of 'Southern Man', some impeccably crafted briefer delights ('Till The Morning Comes'; 'Cripple Creek Ferry') and lyrics covering everything from relationships and racism to climate change and extraterrestrials, and the result is a record that feels pretty much perfect from beginning to end. Choosing my favourite Neil Young album has been incredibly hard, but if I could only play one for the rest of my life, it would have to be *After The Goldrush*.

The final rankings (50-1)

50) Landing On Water
49) Everybody's Rockin'
48) Re.ac.tor
47) Fork In The Road
46) Broken Arrow
45) Hawks and Doves
44) The Visitor
43) Are You Passionate?
42) Chrome Dreams II
41) Paradox OST
40) Life
39) Americana
38) Greendale
37) The Monsanto Years
36) Peace Trail
35) Old Ways
34) Prairie Wind
33) Toast
32) This Note's For You
31) Barn
30) Colorado
29) Trans
28) World Record
27) Mirror Ball
26) A Letter Home
25) Before and After
24) Neil Young
23) Storytone
22) American Stars 'n Bars
21) Dead Man OST
20) Living with War
19) Sleeps with Angels
18) Silver and Gold
17) Homegrown
16) Chrome Dreams
15) Psychedelic Pill
14) Le Noise
13) Freedom
12) Time Fades Away

11) Comes A Time
10) Harvest
 9) Harvest Moon
 8) Hitchhiker
 7) Rust Never Sleeps
 6) Ragged Glory
 5) Zuma
 4) Everybody Knows This Is Nowhere
 3) Tonight's The Night
 2) On The Beach
 1) After The Goldrush

Bibliography and Resources

🎧   🎧   🎧

Books

Kubernik, Harvey - *Neil Young: Heart of Gold*, Omnibus Press, *2015*

McDonough, Jimmy - *Shaky: Neil Young's Biography*, Vintage, *2003*

Rogan, Johnny - *Neil Young: Zero to Sixty*, Rogan House, *2000*

Williams, Paul - *Love to Burn: 30 Years of Speaking Out 1966-1996*, Omnibus Press, *1997*

Young, Neil - *Waging Heavy Peace,* Blue Rider Press, *2012*.

Young, Neil - *Special Deluxe: A Memoir of Life and Cars*, Blue Rider Press, *2014*

Young, Scott - *Neil and Me: 25th Anniversary Edition*, McClelland & Stewart, *2009* (first edition published 1984).

Zollo, Paul - *Songwriters on Song writing*, Da Capo Press, *1991*

Various authors - *Neil Young Uncut Ultimate Guide,* Future Publishing Limited, *2017*

Magazines and websites

The Neil Young Archives
Thrashers Wheat.org
The Guardian
The Observer
Uncut magazine
Melody Maker
Pitchfork.com
New Musical Express (NME)

Radio appearances

BBC2 FM Radio interview with Dave Ferrin, 05/06/1987